Storying Ourselves

Cathy,

One of my students shared with me a quote from F. Buechner who said *all* of our stories are essentially part of *one* story... the Jesus story. Hope you enjoy some of these stories.

Thanks for being a part of our story, John

4/95

Christian Explorations in Psychology
Edited by David G. Benner and Hendrika Vande Kemp

Wisdom and Humanness in Psychology: Prospects for a Christian Approach C. Stephen Evans

Family Therapy: Christian Perspectives Hendrika Vande Kemp, editor

Death in the Midst of Life: Perspectives on Death from Christianity and Depth Psychology Lucy Bregman

Storying Ourselves: A Narrative Perspective on Christians in Psychology D. John Lee, editor

Storying Ourselves

A Narrative Perspective on Christians in Psychology

Edited by

D. John Lee

Published by Baker Books
a division of Baker Book House Company
PO Box 6287, Grand Rapids, Michigan 49516-6287

Printed in the United States of America

Library of Congress Cataloging-in-Publication Data

Storying ourselves: a narrative perspective on Christians in psychology / edited by D. John Lee.
p. cm. — (Christian explorations in psychology)
Includes bibliographical references and index.
ISBN 0-8010-5683-7
1. Psychology and religion. 2. Psychology—Methodology—Religious aspects—Christianity. 3. Christianity—Psychology. I. Lee, D. John. II. Series.
BF51.S76 1993
261.5′15—dc20 93-1889

Dedication

To my mother and father,
Dorothy and Danny Lee.

Contents

Introduction to the Series

Christian Explorations in Psychology is a series of books designed to explore the interface of contemporary psychology and Christianity. All the volumes in the series are intended for those in the field of psychology (either the upper-level undergraduate, graduate student, or professional) as well as those thoughtful Christians who have interest in issues in psychology and a desire to examine those from a Christian perspective. Each volume presents a scholarly treatment of the issues in one field of psychology; future volumes in the series will address such matters as epistemological and methodological aspects of psychological research and practice, cognitive psychology, psychotherapy and culture, and personality theory. It is hoped that these volumes may make a significant contribution to the ongoing dialogue between psychology and Christian theology, a dialogue which has often been better developed at the level of popular and journal article-length works and is somewhat deficient in book-length treatments of a more scholarly sort.

David G. Benner
Hendrika Vande Kemp
Series Editors

Introduction

D. John Lee

Once upon a time . . .

About ten years ago I was in graduate school trying desperately to find out who I was. Much of my search involved an analysis of North American culture, and in particular my own ethnic group, Chinese-Canadians.

I did my Masters thesis with Chinese-Canadians[1] and concluded that the "identity crisis" I was experiencing was, in part, a language problem. (Racism was also contributing to this crisis, but that is another story.) Since I could only speak English (and some French), most of my self-expression had to be in a language foreign to my experience.[2] The conceptual categories available for me to understand myself were bound to a culture that did its best to either destroy other cultures or make them over into its own image (a part of that racism

1. Half of this thesis was published in *Canadian Ethnic Studies* (Lee and Trimble, 1982). The other half, which is much more interesting, remains unpublished, but explores Chinese-Canadian identity through the use of a survey that asked open-ended questions like, What are the characteristics of a person you identify as being "Chinese-Canadian"? (Lee, 1981).

2. Ronald Tanaka revealed this linguistic prison to me in his analysis of Sansei (third generation) Japanese-American poetics and the "circle of ethnicity" (cf. 1979; 1980; 1981). He has continued to develop this line of representation, most recently in his "Bizen Sonata" (1992).

story). As I tried to make sense out of my experience I usually felt inferior and inadequate. The adjectives used to describe the Chinese culture made us appear immature, weak, and boring. To become a person meant denying my familial culture and trying to look like someone I was not. And the only comfort social scientists could offer me was that I was a victim of a natural scientific process they called "assimilation" (i.e. more racism).

I felt as if I was trapped in a prison. But the prison I was in had bars much stronger than iron. In jail there is an expectation that someday the door will open and you will walk through, leaving the bars behind. The prison cell I was in would go wherever I did.

Popular Culture

One of my hopes for escape was to study the psychology of language. I began a doctoral program in psycholinguistics at Kansas State. During that time, I received a small grant to attend a week-long seminar sponsored by the Christian College Coalition on "Christianity and Linguistics." William Smalley and Donald Larson, both linguist-anthropologists, led the seminar, which outlined the puzzles of how language, semantics, thought, and Christianity interact. One of the arguments they made was that the meaning of a word cannot be divorced from the context in which it is used. And since most words are used to tell stories, the study of a language cannot be divorced from the study of its literature and culture. One of the books we were asked to read was John Wiley Nelson's *Your God Is Alive and Well and Living in Popular Culture.* Although this probably was one of the simplest books on their reading list, it was, for me, the most profound.

"Popular culture" is what most North Americans involve themselves in for entertainment and recreation. It does not include "high culture," or what is normally referred to as the "fine arts": classical art, literature, music, and dance. The study of "popular culture" includes the analysis of television, film, radio, genre fiction (romance novels, westerns, detective or spy mysteries), and professional sports.

Professor Nelson, a systematic theologian by training, studied popular culture for several years and in his book presented the following thesis: popular culture is the framework for a secular religion in North America. Contained in popular culture are all the elements of an institutionalized religion: creeds, rites, rituals, and worship services.[3] At the heart of a religion is an epic story or a master myth that is reenacted through various rites and rituals and is propositionalized in creedal or doctrinal statements.

The creed of this religion, Nelson argued, is based on a master myth that underlies much of popular culture. This story has been referred to as "The Western" since its predominant expression has been through cowboy films like "Shane," "High Noon," and so on. The Western can take place in a variety of settings (from outer space to the inner city), but the plot is basically the same. A community on the frontier is threatened by some bad guys who come from outside the group. Just at the right moment, when all else has failed and it appears that the bad guys have won, a white male with some extraordinary ability rescues the people through an act of violence. The hero does not stay in the community, but he does plant his seed and passes the torch onto some person who will follow the "way" established by him. The Western is mythical in its form, presenting answers to all of life's questions, offering a framework for understanding our past, making sense of the present, and providing hope for the future. I think one of the reasons why the North American public devours movies and television is because they are hungry for story. Moving and talking celluloid has become this culture's preferred form of storytelling. The storytellers of North American culture are the writers and producers of "popular culture."

I was raised in a family that gathered around the television on Sunday evenings to watch "The Wonderful World of Color" (Walt Disney), "Gunsmoke," and "Bonanza." It was a ritual for our family. My brother and I were responsible for setting up the card table in the living room so we could eat supper together while watching our favorite programs. According to Nelson, my family was involved in a worship service. In a ritualistic fashion our corporate attention was given over to the passive participation in a story. There was even the partaking of food together, our stomachs *and* souls were being fed! Each time we watched a program we were being persuaded that the Western is and should be our story. This family event on Sunday evening was more meaningful to me than the morning at church. Our electronic storyteller presented its story in a language I could understand, and

3. The metaphor of popular culture being a religion certainly has its problems. The producers of popular culture are not organized like most religious communities. However, members of the entertainment industry do share a common mission of maximizing their profit. They also closely monitor each other's activities since a successful market for one medium might be successful for another (for example, TV shows based on movies and vice versa).

it was certainly more entertaining. Even though there were several Chinese and Christian traditions in my family, the story that guided my life was the North American "Western."

A Conversion to Narrative

Reading Nelson's book was a conversion experience for me. A conversion is like the sudden rearrangement of glass pieces in a kaleidoscope. The elements are the same but they now reveal new designs *and* possibilities. By analyzing my own popular culture Nelson invited me to see my life through story. The people and events in my life had not changed, but I was able to see them from a different perspective. My life was not a puzzle which would make sense when all the pieces were in place. My life was not a machine that had to be disassembled and would only operate properly once all the mechanisms were understood. My life is a story. It has a beginning, a middle, and it will have an end. There are primary and secondary characters in my life; there is a plot with several subplots; and there is a "way" that I believe should be followed. More than any other, this metaphor for life resonated with my own experience of life.[4]

My conversion to narrative thinking brought with it some new faces for some old problems. My sense of inferiority was due, in part, to popular culture's presentation of Chinese males as either the "bad guys" or the servants who provided comic relief (for example, Hop Sing on Bonanza—more racism). And even those movies that did present Chinese men positively had their problems. The fact that *Chinese* men were not cast for the "Charlie Chan" or "Kung Fu" roles sent the message that I could only be a real man if I were an imposter, white underneath the yellow mask. And although Bruce Lee made several Chinese "Westerns," my talents were playing the piano and basketball, not the martial arts.

I also now see my search for identity as a search for community. My individuality emerges from the network of relationships in which I participate. The flip side of the question "Who am I?" is another

4. Stephen Crites (1971) has argued that experience itself has a narrative quality. It is impossible to talk meaningfully about one's experience today without implying that there was a yesterday and there will hopefully be a tomorrow. Experience exists in a context and the metaphor used to describe that context is *experience is a story*. Stories have a beginning, middle, and an ending; experience has a past, present, and future. This metaphor for understanding experience grasps the tension created by the past and future simultaneously existing in the present. Stories also contain intentional beings who create and participate in a purposeful life; I experience myself as a character in a story.

question: "Who are my people?" Or, narratively speaking, my character cannot be understood apart from the other characters in my story. Also, the ambivalence I experience over community is probably an extension of the plot my grandparents began over one hundred years ago. All my grandparents were immigrants: they left their land, their home, and their people. Both of my parents moved away from their family farms to the big city. The tradition into which I was born was one of "leaving home." My story is one of a stranger in the "new world" in search of a home.

If my identity emerges from community, then a common-unity is defined by its mission or direction. In other words, my questions about the purpose and meaning of life are questions of *author*ity. Growing up in the city I heard many voices claiming authority, wanting to be the author of my life. The most compelling story I heard was the Western in its various forms—including professional and collegiate sports. During high school my daily devotions consisted of reading *Sports Illustrated* (SI) while eating lunch. My brother and I were filled with anticipation before a new issue of *SI* arrived in the mail. It saddens me that I don't remember ever going to church with anticipation. Despite this idolatry, by the grace of God we both responded to the Christian gospel as teenagers.

In summary, my quest for understanding myself through studying language and culture arrived at story. To understand who I was, I reviewed the stories that defined my life; to understand a culture, I listened to the stories of its people; to communicate the Christian gospel, I *thought* I should learn how to tell stories.

Storytelling and the Christian Message

Two years after my narrative conversion I was fortunate enough to participate in another Coalition-sponsored seminar on "The Christian Message and Storytelling." Robert Detweiler, a Professor of Comparative Literature at Emory University, led the seminar and introduced me to myth studies, narrative philosophy and theology, and the art of storytelling.[5]

5. The literature in these areas is far too vast to list. Here are some examples of authors who appeared on our reading list or within our discussions: Joseph Campbell, Mircea Eliade, Clifford Geertz, and Northrop Frye on myth studies; Paul Ricoeur and Alasdair MacIntyre on narrative philosophy; Robert Alter, Hans Frei, Gabriel Fackre, Amos Wilder, George Stroup, Michael Goldberg, Stanley Hauerwas, John Dominic Crossan, and Sallie McFague TeSelle on narrative theology; and Ruth Sawyer and Marie Shedlock on storytelling.

One of the requirements of the seminar was to tell a story. Detweiler did not specify what kind of story we had to tell so we heard a variety of folk tales, Bible stories, and stories from our own lives. The time we devoted to storytelling was, for me, the high point of the seminar. As we storied I believe something miraculous happened. A group of people who were essentially strangers become "one." Storying ourselves allowed the mysteries of life to speak freely without abstraction. The story of creation, separation, suffering, death, reconciliation, and renewal became flesh. I believe Jesus Christ entered our midst through our presence to one another in story. Christ's presence caught me by surprise. My expectation for this seminar was to learn how to more effectively communicate the Christian message through storytelling. What I experienced was Christ's presence as we shared our stories with one another. That is, storytelling became a vehicle for God's incarnation. We "gathered together in Christ's name" by telling our stories.

During Detweiler's seminar we discussed propositions about narrative, but also through narrative we entered relationship. We talked about story, we told stories, and we lived out our stories. I came to the seminar expecting to learn how to better communicate the Christian message through storytelling. I left the seminar convinced that sharing the Christian message is more incarnational than propositional. In narrative terms, "sharing Christ" is an invitation to participate in a "storying relationship": a relationship where people deliberately participate in one another's stories and respect the *author*ity of Jesus Christ.[6]

The distinction I am making here is represented as a debate among Christians over the nature and purpose of narrative.[7] On the one side are the theologians who affirm the importance of story in communicating propositional truths about God, Jesus, and the Holy Spirit. For them, the narrative form of the majority of Scripture is because of the communicative value. For example, preachers will often use stories to illustrate the message they wish to deliver to their congregations. The proposition, "God is merciful,"

6. This storying relationship is similar to what Newton Malony (1983) has described as the dialogical model for how the Christian faith can be communicated in psychotherapy. Also, Kirk Kilpatrick (1986) and Paul Vitz (1992a; 1992b) have explored the transformative or therapeutic power of narrative. This is not the place to critique their theories, but I believe the therapeutic power of narrative is because stories can be a vehicle for God.

7. George Stroup (1991) described this debate and distinction in his review of Hauerwas and Jones's book *Why narrative: Readings in narrative theology* (1989).

can be illustrated by the story of the prodigal son (cf. Luke 15:11–32). An abstract statement is made concrete through story. On the other side of the debate are those who argue that God, the Truth, and the Comforter are actually manifested by story. From this perspective, the Christian message is not a set of propositions illustrated through story. The Christian "message" is Jesus Christ whose presence can be revealed by story. A person who shares his or her own story of rebellion and reconciliation may invoke the presence of God, full of mercy and grace. The Word can become flesh through story. Narrative can be a vehicle of God's incarnation.

"Jesus spoke all these things to the crowd in parables; he did not say anything to them without using a parable" (Matt. 13:34 NIV). But Jesus was not simply a storyteller. Jesus is the "Author and Finisher of our faith" (Heb. 12:2 KJV). The parabler became a parable; the storyteller became a story. At the heart of the Christian faith is Jesus Christ whose presence is made known through story. Story is certainly an effective way to illustrate a proposition, but story can also be used to embody God. Narrative can be used for illustration *and* incarnation.

Narrative Psychology

Having been converted to narrative and having experienced the power of story, I found it exciting to discover that several psychologists were already articulating narrative approaches to psychological topics.[8] A narrative perspective in psychology represents a shift in what Stephen Pepper has called one's "root metaphor."[9] Much of psychology is rooted in metaphors that treat people as if they were machines. The most common example comes from cognitive psychol-

8. The beginnings of narrative psychology in North America can be found in the early writings of Theodore Sarbin and Erving Goffman. In 1943, Sarbin used a drama metaphor to propose that social behavior could be more meaningfully explained as role enactment. Erving Goffman (1959) took Shakespeare's "All the world is a stage" literally and developed a social psychology around the metaphor that people are actors. Roy Schafer (1980) and Donald Spence (1982) introduced narrative concepts into the interpretation of what occurred during psychoanalysis. Carol Gilligan (1982) relied heavily on narrative in her interpretation of women's development. The first book titled *Narrative Psychology* was edited by Theodore Sarbin in 1986. Contained in Sarbin's anthology were some of the leading "narrativists" in psychology: for example, Kenneth Gergen and Mary Gergen (1983; 1986), Karl Scheibe (1978; 1986), and Brian Sutton-Smith (1981; 1986). Recently, George Howard (1989; 1991) has entered the scene with his articulation of what a narrative approach might look like in psychology. Several of these psychologists have written autobiographical essays in a book that I am currently editing (Lee, in press).

ogy, where computer terminology has dominated the discourse (for example, short-term and long-term memory). Thinking of the world and people as machines is useful for some purposes, but the limitations and dangers of this metaphor also need to be recognized.[10] To the narrative psychologist the root metaphors are LIFE IS STORY and PEOPLE ARE ACTORS. Instead of thinking of human beings as machines in a machinelike universe the narrativist thinks of people as actors or storytellers participating in a story.

I now do psychology from a narrative perspective. This means I make use of narrative concepts in my attempts to understand human experience and behavior. For example, I interpret people and the events in their lives in the same way I would interpret a story. I consider the "setting," the time and place in which their behavior occurs. I pay attention to the "plot" within people's lives, or the value and meaning they place upon their experience. I try to discern the significant "characters" or relationships in a person's drama to identify his or her community. In my own research on what and how people remember events from their own lives, I think of memory as a creative and constructive "storying" process.[11] Narrative approaches in psychology are only beginning to mature but they are already proving to be interesting and useful.

One of the common threads among the narrative approaches is the recognition that psychology cannot be divorced from psychologists. Psychological theories have been written by human beings: persons who lived within some time and place or some historical and cultural context. This proposition is obvious when one thinks of psychological theory as a type of narrative. Stories are not without authors and

9. Stephen Pepper's root metaphor theory (1942) has become a useful metaphilosophy for psychology and other disciplines as well.

10. Lakoff and Johnson (1980) revealed the prevalence of machine metaphors in psychology and cautioned against the reliance on a single metaphor for understanding anything. Weizenbaum (1976) carefully outlined the power and limitations of computers and encouraged people to carefully consider what the costs and benefits were of computer applications. Of course, the narrative metaphor also has its limitations and dangers. It is easy to fall into an extreme form of relativism or even solipsism when thinking of life as a story. I do not believe that individuals are "authors of their own lives." *Co-authoring* is a more accurate metaphor for me. Who I have been, who I am, and who I will be is within a context or a story which is bound by a time, a space, a set of relationships, and God.

11. A reconstructive view of memory is certainly not new, but cognitive psychologists have been so stuck on computer metaphors that any alternative seemed radical. Neisser (1988) described what he saw to be the "new vistas" in the study of memory. My own narrative perspective is described in a chapter, "Memories and Assessments of a Christian College: A Longitudinal Study" (Lee and Smalligan, in press).

theories are written by theorists. Interpreting theories and stories, then, involves reviewing the context of their theorists and authors. For example, psychoanalytic theory cannot be fully understood without considering who Sigmund Freud was, and the historical cultural context in which he developed his ideas. The same can be said for behaviorism and B. F. Skinner, or Carl Rogers and his version of humanistic psychology.

The relationship between theory and theorist, story and author is important to point out because it challenges the popular view of scientific inquiry. To most lay persons, a scientist is someone who uncovers the facts of reality in an objective, detached manner. But, as many historians and philosophers of science now argue, there is a creative and imaginative side to scientific inquiry.[12] In fact, hermeneutical principles derived from literary criticism are sometimes applied to the interpretation of scientific data. When scientists are framed as authors, it suggests that there is a two-way relationship between the observer and the observed, the theory and the data, the story and the storyer. Science is a human activity that occurs within a human context, and interpreting science involves discerning the context of the scientist. One way to discern and appreciate the context of scientists is to listen to their stories . . . which brings me back to the story behind this book.

In the fall of 1990 I invited several Christian psychologists[13] to write their autobiographies. One of the reasons I decided to compile a collection of autobiographies was to provide an opportunity for some very influential Christian psychologists to describe the context from which their academic and professional lives have emerged. The personal lives of these people are just as important as their ideas or work. I believe that these essays should and will play a crucial role in interpreting the contributors' scholarship.

12. Rabinow and Sullivan's reader (1979) is an excellent introduction to interpretive social science. Essays by Thomas Kuhn, Paul Ricoeur, and Hans-Georg Gadamer are included in this collection. More recently, Polkinghorne (1988) explicity used narrative concepts to lay out an epistemology for the human sciences. When talking about scientific theory as being narrative, I think it is important to qualify this metaphor by saying that science produces *non-fiction* literature. Authors of fictitious stories do not have to deal with the limitations that reality imposes on scientists. Interestingly, science fiction has sometimes provided the imagination for science (for example, Jules Verne's novels still inspire scientists).

13. One of the contributors, C. Stephen Evans, is a philosopher and not a psychologist. I decided to invite Stephen to participate in this book since he has written some important books on the philosophy of psychology from a Christian perspective (Evans, 1977; 1989).

I gave three guidelines to the participants as they embarked on their autobiographies. My first guideline, from my letter of invitation, regarded style and content and is worth quoting:

> You may adopt any form or style that you desire but please tell your story. Please do not treat this as a forum to make arguments or to propose theories. You may certainly find yourself arguing a position or making a recommendation, but this kind of discourse should not dominate your story . . . unless, that is *your* story.

I wanted to give the contributors the freedom to decide how they would tell their stories. Given ten people with their Ph.D.s, however, I suspected there would be a strong temptation to tell only the "academic" version of their lives. And I wanted to minimize the possibility that their autobiographies would become intellectual histories.

My second guideline limited the length of their essays to somewhere between thirty-five and forty pages. As expected, most of the contributors felt constrained by this limit. As difficult as it is to write your autobiography, there always seems to be something or someone more you sense should be included. This compulsion, I believe, is a result of the narrative quality of our experience and our lives in general. Every event and person we recall can be connected in some fashion to who we are and who we are becoming: autobiography is a process of remembering ourselves. The third guideline I gave the contributors was a request that they respond to the following question at the end of their story: "How has writing your autobiography affected you." As interesting as this question is, I think it would be inappropriate to summarize their responses at this point. I will say more about the autobiographical process and its effects in the Epilogue.

My Story and "The Story"

An introductory chapter usually provides the background for a book. I hope the story of how I arrived at editing this anthology has provided a context for this collection. I must confess that I broke the first parameter I gave to my contributors. As stated above, when I outlined my expectations for their essays I asked the contributors not to use their story as a platform to make academic arguments. I wanted to hear about the events in their lives that shaped who they are as academics. Ironically, I used part of my story to present some propositions about psychology and about life in general. I have three excuses for breaking my own rule. First, I am the editor. Second, my story explicitly reveals how academic interests can be an expression of a person's journey of healing. And third, a story told with the purpose to propositionalize does not imply that its arguments are or should be applicable to everyone. Excuses aside, I apologize to my contributors for being a hypocrite.

The opening chapter of an edited book is also supposed to give a short preview of each chapter. However, I do not think it is appropriate for me to review each essay since such a process would demand a hermeneutic. I would rather let readers bring their own interpretive lenses to these stories. Unfortunately, by telling a portion of my own story I have suggested that autobiography is a healing journey. But healing is only one of many purposes or effects of autobiography. It is my hope that each of these essays will be read on its own terms, without a lot of predetermined expectations or conclusions. One characteristic of a good story is that it can have different meanings at different times for different people.

Finally, as the editor, I feel compelled to offer some insight into the collection as a whole. The following stories certainly share some common themes, but I think it would be a mistake to try and draw conclusions from these commonalities. There is a temptation to propose that these stories, when taken together, are a collective testimony of *the* Christian Story. A more accurate proposal, in my opinion, is that these stories simply represent *my* story as a Christian practicing psychology in North America. The basis on which I make this bold proposal is simple: I selected the contributors.

I invited people from within my own limited sphere of contact to participate in this book. It is no accident that half of the contributors are friends of mine. When I made my selections I had two basic criteria in mind: (1) gender and ethnic diversity, and (2) the contributor had in some way influenced my own story. Thus, most of the commonality among the stories is probably due to my own biases or preferences. And at the risk of sounding arrogant, the points at which these stories connect are probably best seen as points in my own life. I have had to confront and deal with the "idols of our times" or the various "isms" within modern life (sexism, racism, ethnocentrism, religious and scientific dogmatism, professionalism, materialism). I have had to negotiate my way through graduate school and other institutional bureaucracies. I have had to walk the fence between mainstream secularized psychology and Christian psychology. I have suffered, offered forgiveness, accepted death, and experienced renewal. In a sense, my story can be found in these stories.

Please do not misinterpret me. I never intended to represent my story through the stories of others. In fact, my intent was to uncover more of my story through the storying of others. As I have participated in the storying of the contributors' lives, I have been storying myself. I too have been recalling the events of my own journey, reframing my own memories, remembering who I consider myself to be, and revisioning who I want to become. Some day I may write my own autobiography, and, if so, these autobiographies will be part of it.

I think I can speak for all the contributors when I say that we were privileged to be involved in this somewhat self-indulgent exercise. But I think it is also accurate to say that we hope the effects of this project will go beyond ourselves. Perhaps God will use this collection of autobiographical essays to illustrate and incarnate. I certainly have heard God's voice as I reviewed these stories. Personally, I hope that this book will remind me to think and act more justly, more compassionately, more with Jesus Christ. My hope for the contributors and all those who read this anthology is that . . . we all will live joyfully ever after.

References

Crites, S. 1971. The narrative quality of experience. *Journal of the American Academy of Religion* 39:291–311.

Evans, C. S. 1977. *Preserving the person: A look at the human sciences.* Downers Grove: InterVarsity Press.

______. 1989. *Wisdom and humanness in psychology: Prospects for a Christian approach.* Grand Rapids: Baker Book House.

Gergen, K. J., and M. M. Gergen. 1983. Narratives of the self. In *Studies in social identity,* eds. T. R. Sarbin and K. E. Scheibe. New York: Praeger.

______. 1986. Narrative form and the construction of psychological science. In *Narrative psychology,* ed. T. R. Sarbin, 22–44. New York: Praeger.

Gilligan, C. 1982. *In a different voice.* Cambridge, Mass.: Cambridge University Press.

Goffman, E. 1959. *The presentation of self in everyday life.* New York: Doubleday/Anchor.

Hauerwas, S., and L. G. Jones, eds. 1989. *Why narrative? Readings in narrative theology.* Grand Rapids: Eerdmans.

Howard, G. S. 1989. *A tale of two stories: Excursions into a narrative approach to psychology.* Notre Dame: Academic Publications.

______. 1991. Culture tales: A narrative approach to thinking, cross-cultural psychology, and psychotherapy. *American Psychologist* 46 (3): 187–97.

Kilpatrick, W. K. 1986. The use of literature in character formation. In *Content, character and choice in schooling: Public policy and research implications,* 85–92. Washington, D.C.: National Council of Educational Research.

Lakoff, G., and M. Johnson. 1980. *The metaphors we live by.* Chicago: University of Chicago Press.

Lee, D. J. 1981. Psychosocial differences and perceptions of identity among Chinese-Canadian and non-Chinese students. Master of Science Thesis, Western Washington University.

______. in press. *Life and Story: Autobiographies for a narrative psychology.* Westport: Praeger.

Lee, D. J., and P. Smalligan. in press. Memories and assessments of a Christian college: A longitudinal study. In *Assessment in Christian higher education,* eds. D. J. Lee and G. G. Stronks.

Lee, D. J., and J. Trimble. 1982. Psychosocial differences among Chinese-Canadian and non-Chinese students. *Canadian Ethnic Studies* 14 (3): 43–56.

Malony, H. N. 1983. God talk in psychotherapy. In *Wholeness and holiness: The psychology / theology of mental health,* ed. H. N. Malony, 269–80. Grand Rapids: Baker Book House.

Neisser, U. 1988. New vistas in the study of memory. In *Remembering reconsidered: Ecological and traditional approaches to the study of memory,* eds. U. Neisser and E. Winograd, 1–10. Cambridge, Mass.: Cambridge University Press.

Nelson, J. W. 1976. *Your god is alive and well and living in popular culture.* Philadelphia: The Westminster Press.

Pepper, S. C. 1942. *World hypotheses.* Berkeley: University of California Press.

Polkinghorne, D. P. 1988. *Narrative knowing and the human sciences.* Albany: State University of New York Press.

Rabinow, P., and W. M. Sullivan, eds. 1979. *Interpretive social sciences: A reader.* Berkeley: University of California Press.

Sarbin, T. R. 1943. The concept of role-taking. *Sociometry* 6:273–84.

______. ed. 1986. *Narrative psychology: The storied nature of human conduct.* New York: Praeger.

Schafer, R. 1980. Narrative in the psychoanalytic dialogue. *Critical Inquiry* 7:29–53.

Scheibe, K. E. 1978. The psychologist's advantage and its nullification: Limits of human predictability. *American Psychologist* 33 (10): 869–81.

______. 1986. Self-narratives and adventure. In *Narrative psychology,* ed. T. R. Sarbin, 129–51. New York: Praeger.

Spence, D. P. 1982. *Narrative truth and historical truth: Meaning and interpretation in psychoanalysis.* New York: Norton.

Stroup, G. 1991. Theology of narrative or narrative theology? A response to "Why narrative?" *Theology Today* 47 (4): 424–32.

Sutton-Smith, B. 1981. *The folkstories of children.* Philadelphia: University of Pennsylvania Press.

______. 1986. Children's fiction making. In *Narrative psychology,* ed. T. R. Sarbin, 67–90. New York: Praeger.

Tanaka, R. 1979. On the metaphysical foundations of a Sansei Poetics: Ethnicity and social science. *Journal of Ethnic Studies* 7 (2): 1–35.

______. 1981. The circle of ethnicity, Part 2. *Journal of Ethnic Studies* 8 (4): 37–94.

______. 1992. The Bizen sonata: The bayfront gallery-Fort Mason project. *Journal of Ethnic Studies* 19 (4): 15–112.

Vitz, P. C. 1992a. Narratives and counseling, Part 1: From analysis of the past to stories about it. *Journal of Psychology and Theology* 20 (1): 11–19.

______. 1992b. Narratives and counseling, Part 2: From stories of the past to stories for the future. *Journal of Psychology and Theology* 20 (1): 20–27.

Weizenbaum, J. 1976. *Computer power and human reason: From judgment to calculation.* San Francisco: Freeman.

1

God's Child

Vivian Nix-Early

I and my sister, who was eighteen months older, were excited and giggly that morning. The weather was just right for our annual outing to the Ice Capades to see Ronnie Robertson, the fastest spinning human ever, and to see the "Old Smoothies"; it was cold and rainy, with snow predicted.

Gramps was busy bundling us up to weather the outside as well as to keep us warm during the show: three hours sitting on the ice.

"You kids run on down to Sunday school now," she would say when we were finished buttoning our coats. "And as soon as class is over, you come out to the corner. I'll be there to meet you and we'll rush down to the show."

It was one of those special Sundays that my sister, Phenoris, and I looked forward to—NO CHURCH! We knew, of course, that such a happening was not to be taken lightly or expected often. Big Mom, Gramps's older sister, our great aunt whose house we lived in, and who for all intents and purposes was our "mother," did not care at all for this Sunday matinee idea that caused us to miss morning worship. But as eight- and nine-year-olds, we were thankful that our grandmother took a slightly more "liberal" view of the "one rests on the Sabbath" rule. Somehow, Big Mom allowed the exception to be made for the Ice Capades, while never relenting on the movies (Gramps loved the movies), the Uptown (Philly's rock and roll showplace where all the kids were going), or card playing. My observation of, and occasional participation in, these debates between Gramps and Big Mom about what good Baptists do caused me to wonder where such obviously unquestionable and sacred rules came from. (Yes, I know, the Bible. But where in the Bible and why? What harm had been done so early in history as to cause these things not to be considered "rest"?) It was good to have Gramps fighting for us to have fun.

Phe (short for Phenoris) and I came to live with Big Mom when I was still in kindergarten, in what served as the "family house." It was the second house the family had after migrating from Farmville, Virginia in 1916. (Men were needed to work in the factories along the Delaware River, and so my great grandfather, Samuel, came with other African-American men to find a living in the North.) Gramps was the youngest of twelve children, most of whom lived in that house at one time or another. It was where Big Mom and Gramps raised my mother, whom we called Little Mom. And so it seemed only right that circumstance (God's divine hand?) should have us also end up here for nurturing, attention, and encouragement.

Little Mom married Dad in 1947 when she was eighteen, less than two years after he returned (in November, 1945) from fighting in World War II. As a part of the Twelfth Armored Infantry Division attached to troops under General Patton's command, Dad participated in the Normandy Beach invasion (D-Day plus two), and then fought on through Austria and Germany to the end of the war in June, 1945. Dad was ambitiously and single-mindedly focused on building his new business as a mortician and becoming the number one black undertaker in the state. This endeavor left little time for attention to new wife and kids, although it led to wonderful financial security for my sister and me, and would have for my mother, had she lived. Mom was bright and beautiful in her own right and started out on a career of her own—nursing school—then a switch to the executive secretarial world that seemed to please her a lot more. That meant two working parents and the need for day-care. A wonderful woman in our predominantly black North Philadelphia neighborhood, whom we called Aunt Marceline, cared for us and other pre-schoolers in the community. But Big Mom, of the opinion that no one cares for little ones better than one's own family, came one day to whisk us off to the "family home" in Tacony, a small black and Italian neighborhood in the greater northeastern section of Philadelphia.

The concept of "family homes" was, and for many still is, a familiar tradition in the African-American community. It was usually the home where the oldest members—the patriarchs and matriarchs of the family—resided. The home extended the concept of family beyond any "nuclear" situation, and was most often a multigenerational hub or anchor out of and into which various family members moved. It was the source of the family's history, identity, values, religious education, and love. It was important that all the family be connected through "the source." And so it was that while both nuclear parents worked, we were introduced to "the source" (the family home) by the reigning matriarch, Big Mom, who was our great aunt (Gramps's older sister) and the "keeper" of the family home following the deaths of her parents, Samuel and Belle. We were brought to this house to be raised in the Vaughan tradition, to become members of the Star of Hope Baptist Church, of which the Vaughan twelve were some of the first members. (Great-Grandpop Vaughan was a Founder.) The move, in retrospect, was the prologue of God's dream for my life.

Holmesburg was the small community neighboring Tacony. The Nixes, my father's people, were living there as the most recent (and the last) stop in a long series of family relocations resulting from Grandpop Nix's church assignments. A Baptist preacher from Texas, he arrived in Philadelphia by way of Chicago, Cleveland, Massachusetts, New York, Pittsburgh, and New Jersey. Grandpop Nix became the minister of Mount Zion Baptist Church of Holmesburg. As is the case for many in the black Baptist Church tradition, Star of Hope and Mount Zion also served as an extension of the "family home"; it served as central control for cultural, personal, social, and spiritual education. More important, it surrounded me with people who generously and genuinely gave constant praise, encouragement, love, and recognition.

God made me smart (along with quiet, shy, insecure, and lonely). My Sunday school superintendent recognized this fact and appointed me secretary of the Sunday school. My Sunday school teacher also recognized the talent and started giving me the longest poems to recite at Christmas. Likewise, my Pastor began asking me to speak at our annual youth day services, and church auxiliaries would ask Little Mom, my dad, Phe and me to play for their garden teas, which were held to raise money for the church. (Phe and Dad played violin,

Mom played piano, and I played flute.) My peers elected me president of our Baptist Youth Fellowship, and my piano teacher, who taught most of the kids in the two communities, gave me the most challenging pieces to play for the annual recitals held at Mount Zion. I was always last on the program. It was exhilarating: the applause, the bows, the encores, the gifts, and the receptions that followed. It began my appreciation for classical music and prepared me to sit as second chair flautist in the All City (the best of Philadelphia youth musicians) Band. It nurtured my natural interest in performing, being out in front, although at the time I was not confident enough to enjoy it as much as I could have. Clearly, the experience was the forerunner of my feeling quite comfortable and at home as teacher, consultant, trainer, keynote speaker, administrator and choir soloist. While these experiences were affirming enough, I in many ways still felt in the shadow of my sister, who was a star in her own right.

Phe was who I wanted to be like. I remember feeling quite jealous of her, always feeling that she was prettier, more sensible and more talented than I; and she was much more social. All the girls—and boys—her age seemed to like her and to invite her to their parties. She also served as secretary of the Sunday school, and assisted in the church's general office. I also envied Phe's musical talent. She was taking voice lessons in addition to piano and violin, was singing in All City Choir, and was selected for a young people's group that sang with Duke Ellington! It was only lately that I realized it has been Phe whose footsteps I have been following. Was it any wonder that one of our favorite childhood scenario games cast me in the role of lost child in the park, and she a caring person who finds me? Most recently, it is Phe's spiritual fervor and dedication that encourage my own growth.

Lessons from School

Big Mom had tried many times to warn me. "Vivian, those white children are not coming to your house. Their parents aren't going to let them. You can't depend on white people to be your friends." The concept was foreign to me. As an elementary school student I was still naive enough to believe in people's inherent goodness. I was a member of a self-formed group of five girls from my class. We all liked science and math and would once a week after school go to each others' houses to do little science activities and eat little goodies that a parent would prepare for us. It was my turn and there was nothing in the girls' behavior to suggest that they weren't coming. We were enthusiastically planning the project to be done at my house. We were meeting this particular week on a school holiday, so we agreed that I would meet them at the school and we would walk to my house. Big Mom was a trained caterer and at my insistence went ahead and made fancy sandwiches and baked goodies for us. I waited at the school yard for two hours and then returned home . . . alone. I tried to forget about racism as a personal concern, but I found myself often wishing that being black in a white school didn't have to mean you had few real friends. God (and Big Mom) were right. People (most likely their parents) are inherently hurtful.

1967. We had survived the assassination of President Kennedy and had felt a part of history, having "been there" for Dr. Martin Luther King, Jr.'s "I Have a Dream" speech in Washington, D.C. My dad, Andrew W. Nix, Jr., now a prominent Philadelphia mortician and political activist in the North Philadelphia black community, made sure that Phe and I were part of "the movement." He had put himself on the line in many small ways to fight for the rights of the folk in his neighborhood. He was assertive and unafraid of the white man. He knew that being Christian meant fighting oppression. So into the fight he brought us, not to miss a single moment of the liberation that would have so much to do with me being a member of the largest black student contingent admitted into the University of Pennsylvania up to that point; not to miss a single moment of the struggle that would result in the Ford Foundation encouraging "minorities" to pursue graduate psychology degrees. All the churches were running buses to the March on Washington. Obviously, God and my dad were insisting that we be on one of them.

High school graduation was nearing. I had, with great anxiety, run for Jamboree Queen as only the second black girl to do so. As expected, I lost, and "missed being in the Queen's court by two votes," according to Virginia Fricke, one of my white friends on the committee to count the votes. For being so young she had a keen consciousness about racism and equality. She campaigned for me, believing that "it" needed to happen. That "it" didn't happen brought great disappointment and hurt to both of us.

My church family healed the wounds. Big Mom was a member of the Willing Workers auxiliary. (They did just what their name indicates.) Unknown to me, the Willing Workers had been collecting money from individuals and groups in the church for a scholarship for me to attend college. All the checks and cash were placed in a leather album and presented to me as part of a surprise ceremony held during the middle of the Sunday morning worship service. At a certain point in the service I was asked to leave the choir loft (our junior choir was singing that Sunday) and to take a seat in a chair that had been placed in front of the pulpit. I had wondered why Big Mom and Gramps had wanted me to wear one of my nicest dresses to church that day. Usually when we sing we don't worry about what we wear under our robes. I also thought it unusual that my dad and Grandmom Nix were worshipping at our (Little Mom's, Gramps's, and Big Mom's) church. They belonged to Mount Zion. The answer to my wondering was shortly to be revealed.

My choir sang a rousing anthem version of The Battle Hymn of the Republic, whose crescendoing "Amens" at the end were met with excited and generous applause. Startled at the special high spirit that seemed to have invaded the building, I got nervous about what might be coming. Not to worry. I sat and listened to testimonies of my accomplishments and excerpts from local newspaper articles about my academic achievements: I was graduating as the number two student in my high school class, local and regional essay contest winner, and National Achievement Scholar. Others offered more personal remarks, and then they presented "the book." Now to worry. I was expected to make a "speech." I had no words. I could hear Gramps's admonitions that she had given me a thousand times about proper grammar when speaking in public, and how I should never lean on the lectern when speaking. In the anxiety of the moment I felt myself raise my elbow so as to lean on the lectern.

My early church experiences seemed so much to be God's angels keeping me afloat. Events like the one last described were able to dim the rejection from the secular high school. Two years earlier the sharp edge of racism had cut deeper than the Queen episode when my then new and progressive predominantly white high school was starting an experiment in learning. The top students were to have the opportunity to be placed, for their last two years, in an "ungraded" class situation, where they would work at their own pace in math, science, and English. The obvious planned outcome was that, by the end of the twelfth grade, these "honor" students would have probably covered first year college level material in some if not all of the major subject areas, thus giving them advanced standing for college. I was clearly among the top ten (really, the top three), and was excited about the chance to move into college level calculus. My math teacher had for two years been particularly praiseful of my brilliance (his word) in math (he often said he used me as the answer book), and he wanted to see me major in mathematics in college.

But when the ungraded roll was called, my name was not. Funny. The entire student body immediately questioned and puzzled over my absence from the ungraded list, but mature, adult educators couldn't figure out how they "overlooked" me. Of course, this excuse came months after persistent challenges from my dad, Little Mom, Big Mom, and Gramps. In the period between the challenge and the "finding" that, yes, a mistake had been made, and that I did indeed belong in the group, I was placed in solitary confinement. Oh, they didn't call it that; but I was removed from my regular classes and told that I could sit and study in the professors' offices (those that were assigned to the ungraded class), and that they would "school" me alone until a decision was made. Neither the teachers nor I knew what to do with that kind of situation, so we handled their embarrassment and my pain by leaving me quietly to educate myself.

Friends and Enemies

For the most part, I was pleased with the way God was handling my life; but there were some small puzzling disappointments. I had been taught that God answers prayer, and had uttered these words convincingly myself. For six years, I prayed unceasingly and expectantly for the reuniting of my mother and father (they were divorced when I was ten). When it didn't happen I wasn't sure how to square this with the absolute regarding God and prayer. My dad kept my hope alive with what I took to be a nonverbal message that he clearly still loved mom and always would. This message, I thought, was further corroborated when I visited my mother's grave the first year after her death. (Both my parents had remarried, but my dad didn't until after my mom. He had promised not to unless she did.) My father handled the funeral, of course, and selected a beautiful grave site for her. My first visit was around Christmas time, and I found her grave covered with a stunning, full length blanket of flowers. Obviously, that episode of my dream for my life (my parents' reconciliation) had a different ending than God's. The real rift between God and me happened at the University of Pennsylvania.

There was never any question but that I was going to college right after high school—all the Nixes did; it would become tradition. Dad and Grandmom Nix had spoken of nothing else for my and Phe's life but college, and Grandmom had me considering my "Junior Year Abroad" before I ever got admitted for the first year! The path, then, was pretty well lit. As it was, I loved school and learning and was therefore pretty agreeable to "their plan." Besides, unlike Phe, I wasn't having much luck socially with boys. I had turned down admission four years ago to the premier high school in Philadelphia because it was an all-girls school. Instead, I chose coed Lincoln High in hopes of remedying my unfamiliarity with the opposite sex. But by graduation, still nothing doing! I looked forward to going to college in hopes again of meeting a larger circle of friends, particularly black friends, and more specifically, black men.

It was a wonderful time to be in college. As Nina Simone would sing, it was the time to be "Young, Gifted, and Black." I was finally feeling proud and glad that God made me who I was and the color I was. The civil rights movement was now at its height and the wonderful, talented young black women and men on Penn's campus were active and outspoken. We all felt the mostly welcomed pressure (from each other) to be "real" Afro-Americans, studying our history and our roots; washing our hair back into its natural state. I wore a wild afro for the first time since infancy. Those of us who could sew were making dashikis: long for women, short for men. (I had been designing and sewing my own clothes since elementary school, a skill learned early under Grandmom Nix's influence and tutelage.) We were writing to the campus newspapers, imploring the President to improve "conditions," and we were organizing nonviolent protests and sit-ins.

Penn housed a number of its research projects and departments in The Bank Building as it was unofficially called. The building, located in the center of campus, which itself was situated in the predominantly black West Philadelphia community, was owned by a corporation whose head was Penn's assistant to the President for Athletic Affairs.

A "test case" conducted in February of 1968 by a professor and three students led to charges of racial discrimination in the building's hiring policies. This was a fitting and obvious target for our desegregation efforts; Penn money could not be allowed to support such a corporation. It was this symbol of local oppression that triggered what I remember as our most unified sit-in effort.

In April, following Martin Luther King's death, the Society of Afro-American Students (SAAS) denounced the University Administration for its mishandling of the incident, this after having worked privately for two months with them to try and resolve the problem. Now we were demanding the firing of the Assistant to the President and that the University cancel all the leases it held for space in the building.

We arrived early to bar the entrance to The Bank Building. The event, of course, attracted the attention of the local media, and the attention of our parents. Little Mom, like my fellow students' folks, wasn't so hot on us taking this kind of action. It had brought arrest and imprisonment to students on other campuses in America, and our families were all eager to keep us in school and out of jail. But we were fearless and absolutely committed to the cause. (My dad's influence!) It was as much, if not more, a part of our education as going to classes, and we were aware of being a part of the American History that had been sweeping everyone along since the early 1960s.

Little Mom, unable to come herself because of the morbidly progressive rheumatoid arthritis that now had her firmly in its crippling grip, sent loyal friend Bob down to the protest to watch over us, as well as to assure that Rizzo's Men (the notorious Philadelphia Police Chief) did not get out of line at the expense of our heads. But, alas, martyrdom was not ours that year. Before we could offer ultimate sacrifice, the protest ended; the Penn officials responded, and no one went to jail.

Many of us attending Penn had been raised in the church. We believed in God, in Jesus as our Savior, and we sometimes shared the words to the familiar hymns and gospel songs we learned in our respective "junior" choirs. My own choir history was unremarkable at the time but was to prove a necessary preparation for what was to come. My sister, on the other hand, was the mainstay of our young adult choir (the next step after "junior" choir), doing much of the solo work. I had not yet established my voice, but being a "musician" with a good ear, I was content to make harmony in the choir's alto section. When we were yet teenagers, Big Mom decided it was time for Phe and me to sing with the Women's Day Choir. That was the choir we were all waiting to get big enough to sing in. It was made up of women from the four or five black churches in our area. They were, many of them, the church "pillars," riding God's chariot to sing at the annual Women's Day services at each of the churches. This choir was as good as any of those making records, and the community looked forward to the fourth Sunday of each September at Star of Hope when the women did everything: preached, prayed, sang, took up collection, ushered. (Needless to say, Star of Hope gave women every opportunity to know and live out the fact that God calls them as readily as He does men. As a woman, I felt empowered by my church, not oppressed.) As Big Mom marched us up with her onto the choir loft for the first Women's Day Choir rehearsal, we were aware of the tension. You see, there were some who believed we were too young to sing, that this "was a women's choir, not a children's choir!" But Big Mom, undaunted by this attitude, was determined to introduce us to a tradition that would become a major vehicle for my present witness and testimony. Big Mom became a pioneer again, opening the door for other "younger" women to feel more fully included in the day also set aside for them, to follow closely in the footsteps of their female relatives, and to eventually rejuvenate and provide for the continuation of a legend begun by a legion of faithful but aging soldiers.

It was rare that I missed a Women's Day while attending Penn, this despite what was now a growing uneasiness with religion. I hadn't yet distinguished "religion" from abiding faith, so I was easy prey for the brand of (black) political activism that brandished religion as part of the white man's vehicle of oppression:

> You can't really fight for freedom and equality down here and still believe in that pie-in-the-sky, heaven-is-my-reward stuff. Religion breeds passive acceptance of our plight. What are we doing bowing down to and worshipping some white Jesus? It is the Christian religion that has justified slavery and kept us in our place too long. It's time to throw it all off!

I weakened under the argument; under the need to be fully "black." "But how," my mind asked, "could Jesus, whose picture hung for years on the wall directly in front of my and Phe's twin beds, how could he suddenly turn out to be the enemy?" I struggled to fix it, angry that Sunday School and Star of Hope, which pushed me out of the nest with such confidence, had not prepared me for this challenge; angry that my peers were talking about their childhood church teachings now as child*ish;* saddened that the group of us no longer found occasion to visit the Sunday services of the many historic black churches in the West Philly neighborhoods, in the midst of which sat our white Ivy League Institution. It didn't seem to matter that Martin was being fully empowered by this white Jesus enemy to do what he was courageously and successfully doing. People like those who spoke the speech above were trying (unbeknown to them) to separate Martin from his power source.

Martin's death in the second semester of my freshman year sent waves of overwhelming emotion through the black (and, I imagine, the entire) student body. Among other things, it sent us marching in the night up to the "strip"—52nd Street, the main commercial drag of the West Philly black community—to join the community. The men in our group quickly realized the potential danger in our walking into the singing, shouting atmosphere of the strip, where like so many other urban cities in our country, African-Americans were in shock and rage at the latest demonstration of racist hate that had just slain the world's most recent hope. Our men protectively pushed the women into the doorway of a building just off the main street, out of the way of molotov cocktails and clubs that were beginning to destroy the community. We listened to the sound of breaking glass; to the internal cries of a powerless, hurting mass until the guys—wishing to be a part of the whole, but not wishing to be a part of the violence—returned to escort us home.

The sorrow and tears of that night and the next days over Martin matched the pain and tears of my own growing loneliness and distance from people and from God, who was still being stoned by my peers.

Our nonviolent militancy was only strengthened by Martin's death. SAAS was staging a motivational rally, and some of us were asked or volunteered (I don't remember which in my case) to participate on the program.

"Okay, I'll sing."

Despite the peer pressure to see God and religion as impediments to our progress, and despite the inner dissonance it was creating for me, I chose a gospel song to render as my contribution to the rally. It seemed the only way I could respond in (acceptable) protest to the attack on a faith and a church that had done pretty well by me all these years. I was too ignorant as yet about God and theology to be confident in the knowledge that Jesus was squarely on the side of social justice, that he was himself a militant liberator, pushing to overturn oppression. Martin, of course, had known this.

So I played the piano and sang: "I am weak and I need Thy strength and power to help me over my weakest hour." (I was nervous and scared. I wanted to play the right notes. I was a classical pianist, not a gospel musician. I worried how my fellow students were receiving this message. I continued.) "Help me through this darkness Thy face to see. Lead me, Oh Lord, lead me." (The melody was familiar enough. There were signs that the audience recognized something that might have been meaningful to them at one time. I was encouraged. I sang the chorus.) "Lead me, guide me along the way. For if You lead me I cannot stray. Lord, let me walk each day with Thee. Lead me, Oh Lord, lead me."

Applause. (Sigh!) Thank God. I started to speak what had been the result thus far of my own confusion.

"My Bible tells me that Jesus had hair like lambs wool and skin the color of bronze. That doesn't sound Anglo to me . . ."

I don't know where it ended, but I knew I was arguing for the privilege to be faithful and black at the same time; for a time when misuse of the Bible, by those who would use it to justify oppression, would be distinguished from its truth. I think it came out okay that night.

As Penn responded to the times, as I approached the end of my sophomore year, and as new students entered, my focus turned more fully to my studies: getting through Calc II, Sociology of the Family, and Music Theory; to finding an answer to the great career question, "Do I really want to be a math major so I can proceed to MIT and become the astronaut I always said I would be?" (When I was a little girl, this, and conducting an orchestra, were the clearest dreams I had about my future.) I loved the computer science courses at Penn. We were solving real life problems with our creative programming projects, like retiming traffic lights for better traffic flow on our major city streets. But the "higher level" post-Calc math was kicking my you-know-what.

But the close college friendships I looked forward to hadn't developed past superficiality and false caring. I dated several guys and quickly discovered that they had more interest in sex than in communicating and relating. Steve from high school turned up on campus one day during the height of the "black power" era. I had had a crush on him in twelfth grade. (He was in the ungraded class with us.) I had spent days dreaming about him and had wanted to go to my senior prom with him. I told him how I felt after he and Sally had broken up. Admitting this was a big accomplishment given how very shy I was and given that he was white. He was one of the first students to speak up when I was excluded from ungraded. He wasn't intimidated by the subject of race. He was Italian, as was half my neighborhood, and our ethnicity gave us some things in common. So I told him how I felt and he wasn't shocked. He in fact said he would like to go to the prom with me, but would have to think about it. In the end, he couldn't. He would take Sally as a proper end to a long high school romance before she went off to Sarah Lawrence.

So a year later Steve had come to Penn in the midst of the civil rights revolution to find me to tell me he'd like to date. It was too late. Regrettably, it was now *I* who couldn't. Steve understood. Martin, Malcolm, and Nina had caused too much "awareness." Black solidarity, unity, the black family—they were all now of prime importance. Also, my feelings for Steve had mellowed in the wake of opportunities to attend school with more African-American "brothers." Steve and I pal'd around for a short while and then he was gone.

By the end of my sophomore year, the focus of my affections was firmly fixed on Forrest, the handsome hometown boy-next-door. He was returning (in uniform!) from his last tour of duty in the army when Thelma, visiting me and my folks at the end of the semester, saw him standing outside his grandmother's house.

"Who is THAT?" she asked in excited whisper.

I introduced them. He invited us in to catch up on each others' lives. Had we not been good friends Thelma and I might have struggled for who would date him. She was gracious.

His was the first serious relationship I would have. Finally! I was still not as pretty and successful as Phe. (She had married by now and was into her career.) But someone was valuing *my* talents. Confidence soared because of the Boyfriend; and there my affections would stay for the next seven years.

Save Thelma, I had few genuine female friends. I was annoyed by roommates: one stole my A+ philosophy paper, another locked me out of the room when her boyfriend was over. So when it came time to move out of Hill Hall, I opted to go to one of Penn's off-campus apartment dorms, to live in a rare commodity: "the studio single." I had the opportunity to room in the upper-class residence hall with Thelma, the woman who was then and is now my best friend and confidant. (She was more worldly and aware than I was and had a tremendous influence on my "social coming out." She was, as I recall, the first black female since elementary school who was a *real* friend.) I may have angered (hurt?) her by saying no to her offer to room together. We were then recognized as an inseparable duo around campus, and it was expected that we would be roommates. But I had the feeling we would stay friends longer if we didn't live together. I knew that, unlike me, Thelma had several established friendships; she seemed comfortably universal in her ability to care about others. She would find someone to room with. Plus, I felt an overwhelming need for isolation and quiet; a need to get the splintered guideposts of my life back together. I *wanted* to live alone.

Thelma and I had decided to leave the math major and become psychology majors. We had much ground to make up regarding our credits. But we also discovered that because of a change in requirements, if we hustled, if we went to summer school, we could graduate from Penn in three years instead of four. We buckled down.

The capstone course to my major turned out to be a seminar in experimental psychology. I sat there with ten to twelve other students—most of them graduate students—and Dr. Solomon. I enjoyed my one-on-one meetings with Dr. Solomon. He made me feel privileged and special. He seemed interested in what I wanted to do with my life, and he encouraged me in that direction.

"If it's clinical psychology you want, don't come to Penn," he would say. "The best graduate programs are at University of Chicago and New York University."

I had settled into a pretty nice routine, walking the six long blocks from my apartment to my classes, and to Dr. Solomon's seminar; but one particular day the walk was different. Nothing dramatic; it's just a vague memory now, but it happened. I wasn't more than two blocks from my apartment. I felt agitated but joyous; tears started down my cheek; should I continue walking to class? No, turn back. No . . . I don't remember which I decided to do. I don't even know if this is an accurate recollection of the moment. But the moment happened. It was the moment in which I felt the God conflict melt away. The awareness took place in an instant. God reclaimed me. We were friends again.

Another Level

Bill had decided to go to Princeton after being heavily recruited by West Point, Dartmouth, the Naval Academy, Brown, and University of Pennsylvania. He was a true scholar athlete, winning top academic honors and becoming the all-city, all-star running back for the Lincoln Railsplitters (our high school football team). He had followed me through Disston Elementary School and Lincoln High, being two years younger than me. I didn't take too much notice of him and wasn't impressed with his popularity, but I knew him around our neighborhood. His grandmother lived two doors down from the Vaughan Family Home on Hegerman Street, and I would see him when they came over to visit. He lived "on the other side of the tracks"; that is, literally across the railroad tracks near the river where many of the black families migrating from the South had settled. The Vaughan family had lived along the river too, and the first Star of Hope Baptist Church was over on that (eastern) side of the tracks near the homes of its founding members. But after a time some families moved to homes three blocks the other side of the tracks. When highway I-95 came through, the city bought out some more of the families and tore down their houses . . . and the Church. Funny how quickly the building of the highway razed our little community. That was in 1961. The Philadelphia part of I-95 was not completed until the 1980s. The holdup? The rich white folk living on Society Hill didn't want the highway coming through their neighborhood. They held things up in court for years! And although it was finally built, the city "had to" build high stone barrier walls along the highway so that traffic noise wouldn't "pollute" their gentrified streets. Anyway, Bill's nuclear family was still on the eastern side of the railroad tracks, and he and his brothers and sister would come over to play with Phe and me when they visited their grandmother. My seven-year boyfriend, Forrest, also lived (at the time we started dating) in the grandmother's house, and later on, with Bill's family. He and Bill were cousins. And it would be through him (the boyfriend) that I would coincidentally keep track of Bill's life.

Like Bill, the boyfriend had played football for Lincoln some years earlier, and the boyfriend had become Bill's "idol." Very few of the black youngsters in Tacony were getting the opportunity to go to college as yet. Bill was one of the next to go after me.

Penn and Princeton were Ivy League sports rivals, and in my third year, it was fun to have someone on their team to root against! It was fun having a guy from my hometown come to visit Penn, and it was great fun taking Thelma and others up to Princeton to see Bill and to party. Bill and I were on the way to becoming good buddies; he came down to watch me graduate in May, 1970.

Going to graduate school was almost as much a given as undergrad. It was the next step on Dad's and Grandmom's "well lit path." Following Dr. Solomon's advice, I applied to Michigan, Chicago, and NYU. Rejection and negative outcomes had never been my experience in the academic arena, and so I had no reason to suspect it here. But none of the schools I chose, chose me. This would never do, I resolved, and I called NYU. I reached the grad student who was on the clinical psychology admissions committee. He was one of the two black students in the clinical Ph.D. program. But like many American colleges and universities in the late 1960s and 1970s, NYU was making special efforts to give unbiased consideration to the competitive applications of African-American and other women and students of color. The field of clinical psychology on the east coast was, up to then, heavily Jewish and male.

"Can you tell me why I wasn't accepted?" I asked the student committee member.

He conveyed that they simply ran out of room and financial aid funding. It was well known that NYU ran a small, quality clinical program, accepting no more than twenty students each year from the hundreds of applications received.

"I'd like to come up for an interview." (My paper credentials were good, but I knew my face-to-face impression would be even better.) "I think it will make a difference."

It did. I went up to be interviewed the next weekend. At the end of the interview, I heard the words I'd hoped for.

"We'd like to offer you a spot in the program, but we just don't have any more scholarship money." (It was assumed that if you were African-American you'd need money to go to school.)

"No problem," I said, glad to be able to blast the stereotype and glad that Dad's business was flourishing! "I'll pay my way. I'll accept your offer."

Another one of God's miracles. No, I don't mean the getting in. I mean the positive aggressiveness of my response to the initial rejection letter. Calling NYU and gently insisting on being seen was probably my most assertive act to date. I wasn't familiar with this part of myself: assertive, confident, directed. A few years later I would hear Dr. Bernie Kalinkowitz, the Director of our clinical program, recognize and confirm the growth of this part of my person.

I was good at many of the aspects of the field I had chosen. My coursework, my ideas, my clinical reports, and my supervised therapy practica showed as much. My math background made me unafraid of the statistics courses dreaded by many of the other students and I felt good being able to tutor them to success. I took pride in the fact that I was the baby of the program; I was just about the youngest person there. I found out that the kinds of students being accepted to NYU in the 1970s were those who were returning to school after having worked in another career or field; few were undergraduate psych majors; many were thirty- or forty-something, with spouses, children, and lots of "life" experience. It occurred to me that I was a real anomaly, and that that might have had something to do with me not getting accepted initially. I would soon be asked to serve on the Program's admissions committee (Dr. Kalinkowitz believed in heavy student input in all aspects of the program). That experience would make me even more aware of the wonderfully diverse and nontraditional group of people deciding to move into a relatively new and open field: clinical and community psychology. It was one of the areas being "encouraged" by the National Institute of Mental Health and the Ford

Foundation, two of the organizations providing major funding for graduate/doctoral education in this discipline. The civil rights movement was of course instrumental in forcing open the door to this and other gender/race imbalanced professions. With racial and community politics still occupying a significant part of the American agenda, psychology was beginning to do its part to address the relevant social and health issues. The five of us, who now made up the largest group of African-Americans ever admitted at one time to NYU's Ph.D. program, joined with the two who helped admit us to keep before the department the relevant issues for our discipline. Students needed to see and read the works of black psychologists and sociologists. What was the relevance and validity of Freud's Victorian theories to blacks growing up in rural, racist America? Why was there a disproportionate diagnosing of young black males as paranoid schizophrenic by a largely white male health-care system? Was there such a thing as black psychology? When was paranoia in blacks a healthy and realistic reaction to the American racist experience? What could be the new models of therapy and community psychology that would respect the values and structure of the black family?

I had had a rest from the undergraduate college sit-ins and protests of the 1960s. We were no longer concerned with whether athletes could keep their afros and moustaches. The cause had jumped to another level. This was real life where the ugliness of unequal and biased thinking meant systematic disenfranchisement, mental demoralization, and at times physical death. It was obvious to me in my admissions interview that being a "politically aware" black person was important. The student's questions were clearly aimed at discerning the level of my political and militant position vis-a-vis race and the role of psychology. I had resented that aspect of the interview, thinking that it would again mean dealing with the whole "there's only one way to be black" thing! As it turned out, I would have to deal in a big way with this in the first two years. But that interview with a very wise student readied me for the level of protest now required of me as a budding "professional" beginning to work in a field that, like many others, had not included any but whites as central to its teaching, research, theory, or practice.

Confirmations

Opal, Ted, Madelyn, Art, and me. There was no need for us to say it aloud. We simply knew we would do all we could to get each other through; we must all finish the degree. Needlessly or not, we were still carrying the weight of representing "our race." If we didn't do well, maybe they would not let others of us in. We were still burdened by being "firsts." The first phase of our vow was characterized by our moving, speaking, and acting as one. We had many of our classes together, probably more because we were first year grad students, but we also chose to spend a lot of our study and free time together. We ate lunch together, socialized together, and attended ABPsy (Association of Black Psychologists) meetings where we "spoke" politically together. For an advanced-year seminar we were all supervised by Dr. Adelbert Jenkins (Del), the only African-American psychologist on the tenured faculty. While the oneness served its purpose the first year, it was, by year two, becoming stifling and destructive to our own development and progress as students. I began speaking quietly to Art about how I was starting to feel "confined." We needed to be a part of the total department and to let go of the limiting safety found in the blurred boundaries between us. It all came to a head in the middle of one of Del's sessions.

"I have something to say," I blurted out nervously. I described how I was feeling, how I didn't want to continue eating all my lunches together, or voicing the same opinion when perhaps mine was a variation, or needing or wanting the same kinds of graduate experiences. I found support from Del who seemed to understand and appreciate that my "rebellion" against the group was not personal toward any of them. He encouraged what he knew to be an expression of growth for me as an individual and for us as a group. He guided us through the growing process, allowing the expression of anger and interpreting the love beneath it. It turned out that others in the group had "yearnings" similar to mine and offered their own "directional'" needs. It was tough on us; we broke up as a whole, but formed more natural clusters, making sure to keep tabs on the others we had less contact with. We were all able now to take full advantage of the program and the university and all it had to offer to nourish our individual talents and interests. Some were called to community psychology; others to family and group emphases; still others continued to maintain the political activism necessary to push the field of clinical/community psychology (considered then still to be a young discipline) toward addressing the social issues of racism, sexism, poverty, and unequal health care. As well, we all in our own way advanced the need for more students of color to obtain doctoral degrees in the mental health disciplines. It wasn't hard. The enlightened leadership of the clinical program listened.

I hadn't noticed the internal changes that were occurring. It had been so gradual. I hadn't noticed it until Bernie Kalinkowitz confirmed the outward manifestations of the change. (Bernie's gentle, humble, and wise nature gave him the aura of a teacher-prophet. His silver hair worn long, and his philosophy of never charging a client more than twenty dollars an hour for therapy—he valued people over money—helped the image.) I had decided to attend one of the receptions held by the clinical program. What the occasion was I cannot remember. I may have been off doing an externship or something since it seemed a while since Bernie "K" and I had seen each other. I was mingling and chatting more easily than before, the painful shyness all but disappeared. My handshake had gotten stronger, and I had opinions, something to say. Alice, my wonderful therapist, had helped me see that I didn't need to be able to talk about "the Arts" and "Painting" like my white colleagues. The things I knew about were as cultured and worthy, and I could introduce them into a conversation. I didn't need to be able to comment on everything, nor did I need to make excuses (unconsciously) for being black through a heretofore somewhat obsessive drive for exactness and perfection. I had integrated well enough the wine and cheese "thing" into my internal culture. My ethnic upbringing didn't include this "thing." Yes, we knew of tea parties and such, but it was more like cold fried chicken, potato salad, and punch; and the only time I endured the strange taste of wine was on Holy Communion Sunday, and this only when the usual grape juice substitute ran out. Of course, Big Mom's catering of rich white dinner parties enabled her to answer my questions regarding the wine and cheese phenomenon encountered in New York.

Confirmation was close at hand. Walking over to greet me, Bernie Kalinkowitz remarked something like, "Vivian, I hardly recognized you, you've changed so. You're carrying yourself so confidently. You've matured."

I had turned the corner. It showed. While he offered little detail about why, I could feel what he meant. I rejoiced internally for this validation of a metamorphosis that began with an assertive phone call in May, 1970. I now looked more like a woman than a girl (New York hairstyle and dress had helped). I felt myself circulating among the faculty and students, holding my own in intellectual conversation. I was worthy of having been chosen as student number twenty-one of the entering class of 1970, and being there had nothing to do with being black. Those issues had been there, but I had made them invisible. I sighed at my awareness that once again, I was okay; better than okay: I was *good*!

I followed my interest in neuropsychology, music therapy, and religion. I wanted to focus my dissertation research on the interface between psychology and religion. My leaning was toward the practice of psychology, and I wanted what I would spend a considerable amount of time and effort on to be directly applicable to the knowledge base of how we as clinical psychologists do what we do. What from our lives (faith?) do we bring to bear on the therapy process in order to lend strength and healing to others? The NYU clinical program was heavily psychoanalytic, and I of course had read all that Freud had written about the role of religion in the lives of the masses. His notions, many of which I eventually rejected, spurred me to read other scholars' thoughts on the subject, including those who recognized the healing concepts that psychology has borrowed from religion. The first notions of wanting to study at seminary were stirred around this time, notions that I have not yet fully followed and have relegated to what I will do when I "retire"!

I was warned that the kind of research I was thinking of doing was not conventional, that I might have trouble "getting it thru." Not to discourage me, but to insure degree completion, it was suggested that I do something more straightforward and focused—you know, the control group, two or three experimental groups, apply the treatment and analyze the variance. Certainly worthwhile, but my heart (and soul) were elsewhere. I heeded a second bit of advice: get a strong, well-respected member of the department to chair my committee. Such a person, I supposed, would be experienced in the "subjective" research I wanted to do, would assure that I took a rigorous approach, and would supply the necessary amounts of "credibility." I found support from Paul Vitz, a faculty member I'd just come to know about. Whether he was or not, I assumed him to be a Christian by the work he was doing in the faith area. He gave me some books to read including one written by him. I expressed my desire to have him on my committee. He accepted. My committee was chaired by Dr. Isidor Chein, a master thinker regarding life, a spiritual and religious man himself, and one of the most respected of the senior graduate faculty. At the end of three years, he had guided me through the successful conception and defense of a national survey study of "The Religious Values of Psychotherapists and their Implications for Treatment."[1]

1. Unpublished dissertation.

I had immersed myself in classes, practica, clinical internships, and my own personal psychotherapy for the first four years of graduate school. (In those days, we got our courses out of the way and then started thinking about the dissertation!) In 1974 I began my research, and at the same time I started working full time at Montefiore Hospital in the Bronx where I had done my "APA approved" internship the year before. Both the inpatient and outpatient psychiatric rotations afforded me plenty of opportunity to work with clients for whom religion was a part of their health as well as their illness; a wonderful context for formulating questions and beginning to examine my own integration of faith and psychotherapy. Several clients' dynamics and symptoms would serve as clear case illustrations of healthy vs. unhealthy religious development. I would, over the next several years, present these cases at instructional workshops and grand rounds seminars for seminary students, social workers, psychiatrists, and psychology colleagues who were working with severely disturbed clients (claiming to be Jesus Christ and relating holy visions), or who were working with the laity of church congregations.

Upon the heels of the Bernie Kalinkowitz "wine and cheese confirmation" came another *professionally* confirming statement from my clinical therapy supervisor. It was my turn to present to my supervision group the therapeutic work I was doing, including the presentation of audio tapes of actual therapy segments to illustrate my conclusions. The "exposure" of one's work was always the most anxiety provoking aspect of supervision, but it tended to evoke feedback of immense value in improving one's insight. I presented the case of a young African-American woman with whom I had worked for several years and who presented a complicated symptomatic picture, of which maladaptive religious beliefs and practices were a part. Three-quarters of the way through my presentation, my supervisor—Dr. Helen Gediman—stopped me, a puzzled look on her face. I steeled myself for some statement of the "you have no idea what you're doing" sort. But I had misinterpreted the expression.

"It's remarkable! How have you so accurately tuned in to what this woman is feeling, is going through? You know much more than she has told you verbally."

Dr. Gediman was observing what I have now come to call my "intuitive wisdom and judgment." It is what I now recognize as *the* most cherished of God's gifts to me. Dr. Gediman described the gift to me over our year of work together. I have since consciously tried to understand how I "feel" (know) another's affective experience; how I anticipate it and can speak to subconscious aspects of it in my therapeutic strategy. It is more than a familiarity with the person and her life. It is like a familiarity with and exposure to the vulnerable soul and spirit of the human yearning, my own included. I have tried to respect and nourish the gift in both the therapeutic and administrative work I do, not diminishing its value in the face of those whose gift it is to work more successfully with the tangible, factual domain.

Personal and professional confirmations were followed by yet a third, and by far the most significant and profound, confirmation: a confirmation of faith.

Following my job at Montefiore, but still while I was completing the dissertation, I worked at a drug and alcohol clinic and then moved to Flatlands-Flatbush, a more comprehensive outpatient mental health clinic that served primarily those who had been discharged from inpatient settings. Our work was delivering long-term care to help people reestablish and maintain their lives in the community. During the first four or five years of graduate school, the habit of regular worship waned. I hadn't found any particular church in the West Village where I lived for most of my nine years in New York, and after a while I stopped looking. I would, however, on occasional Sundays travel to the Harlem or Brooklyn communities to attend service at some of their historic and famous black churches. It was not until I began work at Flatlands and met Wayne, another struggling Christian mental health social work colleague working in our unit, that church attendance grew. I had lapsed into the Greenwich Village yuppie habit of spending late-rising, lazy Sunday mornings with the New York Times crossword puzzle and bagels 'n lox; this would be followed by work on the dissertation and runs to the computer lab for more analysis of my data. Wayne also lived in the village and had a car, making it possible for us to ride to Flatbush together. The clinic staff was at that time a close knit group, and when our particular circle worked the evening shift, we would all leave at nine p.m. in Wayne's car headed for a Chinese banquet feast at one of Chinatown's best. We had lots of opportunity then to get to know each other. A piece of this "knowledge" led Wayne and I to try and support each other's spiritual growth. We trusted each other enough to share the things we needed to "correct" in our lives, and we made a pact to travel to church together on at least two Sundays a month. We began to be semiregular fixtures at Riverside on the upper west side.

Wayne became a "rock in a weary land" for me, rushing over in the late night to drive me and my cat-child to the hospital after she swallowed a needle. (He had cats too and understood how important pets were in our lives. We of course knew the therapeutic value pets had for our clients and for the older citizens we saw.) Wayne helped me put things into compassionate perspective after I experienced my first "suicide" (anyone working for long periods of time with chronically ill people will have this experience); and he celebrated my accomplishments. (He threw me the only Ph.D. party I had and managed to surprise me with getting my father and Bill to come up from Philly. Wayne had travelled to Philly with me one weekend to attend a Star of Hope service. He met members of my family and endeared himself to them in quick fashion.) Of course, it was Wayne who covered my caseload when I had to go home after receiving the call in November 1977, announcing that Little Mom had died.

Throughout my stay in New York, I made frequent trips home to see Little Mom. She had for many years been struggling with degenerative rheumatoid arthritis. She was experiencing severe handicaps when I was in high school and she proved to be the inspiration for the many local and statewide essay contests I won. She was often the subject of my writing about courageous people. I still cannot comprehend the degree of pain she lived with constantly, never giving up her job as executive secretary to the 33rd Degree Masonic Order. She got up every day, even if she was so weary after getting dressed that she couldn't make it out to the car. She would return to bed and try again the next day. She was a subject for arthritis research at the time, progressing from aspirin to cortisone to gold injections to innumerable surgeries on various bones and joints. I became her main psychological support (while Phe, Gramps, and my brother—all of whom lived locally—carried the burden of her day-to-day needs). She was following every step of my dissertation and was keeping up with the advances in the field. She was receiving the Ph.D. right along with me. It had always been our plan for her to type my dissertation, but her fingers and hands had become too knurled for her to do so. Intellectually, she was remaining alive as a counter to the death of her physical body that was intensifying. I witnessed her own struggle of faith, her anger at God, her mystification at his allowance of her suffering, our discussions of her affliction and its (non) connection with past "sins." I saw her tiring finally of the struggle. We often spoke now of her feelings about being ready to die; how she wanted me to make sure the pillow was just right under her head so that she could be comfortable during any long comatose state. I often teased her about not visiting her at the cemetery, sloshing thru the mud on (always rainy) Memorial Days. In fact, we said we could have her cremated and that way I could keep her (ashes) with me. I was visiting her in Philly much more frequently now—almost weekly—as she was in and out of the hospital so often.

It was Sunday. We were at Gramps's apartment having dinner. It was time for me to return to New York to begin another week. I turned to hug and kiss Little Mom goodbye as I always did. She was crying and spoke thru the tears.

"I'm afraid. I think this is the last time I'll see you."

Despite a rising apprehension of my own that I didn't acknowledge then, I confidently disagreed.

"Of course you'll see me. I'll be down next Sunday."

But to reassure her, I announced that I would come home again on Wednesday rather than wait for the weekend.

On Wednesday morning I rushed to the beauty parlor early to get my hair done. This took longer than usual and I thought for a moment to call home to say I'd be delayed, but didn't. I would wait to call when I knew what train I'd be on. Now, just a quick stop at the computer center to pick up my last data run and then I'd be off to Penn Station. I ran home from the center to call home, but the phone was ringing as I entered the door. I caught it. It was Brian.

Brian was the Jewish psychologist I met while working at Montefiore. We had dated seriously for a couple of years and had talked of marriage. In addition to our profession, Brian and I had a lot in common. Both of us working and having an income allowed us to enjoy all the wonderful culture that New York offered. My dissertation didn't leave me much time for leisure reading, but Brian's enthusiasm for Dorothy Sayers mystery novels and New York Times crossword puzzles rubbed off on me, as did his pursuit of gourmet cooking. (Sundays always promised one of Brian's romantic three- to five-course delights!) He was not Orthodox, but was intelligent about his faith. He, I, and a few other Montefiore colleagues had started a group study of Isaac Asimov's *Guide to the Bible* to strengthen our biblical understanding. My relationship with Brian immersed me in the experience of the Jewish tradition, which, coupled with my earlier student travel to Israel, deepened the historical context of Christian traditions and holy days. He had come to Philly to meet my family and join in some of my Baptist traditions. He had already met my Dad on one of his (Dad's) visits to New York. Everyone liked Brian. My mom, to whom he was extremely compassionate and kind, perhaps because of the illness and death of his own mother, was quite fond of Brian and could see that I loved him. Her most unselfish act of love came during my return home at Christmas time. It was mainly she, my brother, and I at the Vaughan Family Home (left to me and Phe when Big Mom died), and holidays had become depressing to her. But she "read" my sadness at not being able to be with Brian and gave me "emotional" permission to go back to New York. "Young people in love," she would say, "should be together. I'll be fine."

We talked, Little Mom and I, about my possible marriage to Brian and what it would mean to her. She said honestly that she would be disappointed that I didn't marry someone of my own race, but that it was my choice and Brian was a wonderful person.

Brian and I spent a good bit of time with his sister and her family out in Long Island. She had married an Italian and had gone through the trauma of an "interreligious" marriage. While she was at first uncomfortable with our dating, her attitude ("If it's what Brian wants, it's okay with me, and you're both welcome in my home") offered much-needed support. It was in stark contrast to the sentiments of Brian's father, who had up to now refused to meet me. I never did meet him, and Brian stopped communicating with his dad for a year after his father made it known that I would not be welcome at a family wedding. Brian's pain was, I imagine, eventually unbearable. He and I were having dinner at the home of Yoni, one of our psychiatrist friends, and his wife, Lisa. They were just married and inquired about when we would do the same. Brian's quiet announcement that we would not be getting married was jolting. It was unfamiliar to how the relationship was going, unfamiliar to what we were saying, and, I thought, feeling. Had I missed something? He must have been ruminating for a time about how he would convey the internal resolution he had obviously reached. We broke up. However, forgiveness on both sides would be possible after a year, and Brian and I still continue the mutual respect and caring characteristic of most of our time spent together.

I had given Gramps and Little Mom Brian's phone number, since he was the most likely person to know my whereabouts if I was not at home. I didn't figure they'd need to use it, but that Wednesday they did.

"Vivian, call your grandmother. She's been trying to reach you." Brian's voice was quiet but had a tone to it that I couldn't recognize.

"Oh. What did she want?"

"Just call her," he repeated.

I remember Gramps's voice; clear and calm it was. I would always gratefully remember that tone of voice that conveyed her ability to get us both through whatever.

"SissyBabe," she answered, using her pet name for me. "We had to rush Little Mommy to the hospital this morning. She tried to hold on 'till you got here. But a few hours after that, Little Mommy passed."

I was surprised to hear myself gasp. "Little Mommy's dead?" I asked, not quite able to believe that the moment had come. "Okay. I'll be down tomorrow." I called Wayne, who answered the phone with his usual cheer. I had to break into his long greeting. "Wayne, my mom just died and I'll have to go home tomorrow." He caught the need quickly and simply conveyed that he would take care of things at work.

I was anxious to get home. The train ride down was full of thought. If only I had called from the beauty parlor, I might have gotten there in time to see her. (My dad quite correctly reminded me that I wouldn't have.) I hope her pillow was positioned correctly, but I really always thought that when it got to this point, the pillow wouldn't much matter. My brother had been with her when she died. I was worried more about how this would affect him: he was still young.

Grandison, or "Sputnik" as we nicknamed him, since he was born in the same year that the first Russian Sputnik was launched, was technically our half-brother. However, in every other way, he was and is a full-fledged sibling. Little Mom had remarried around the time I was eleven or twelve. The marriage never really worked out and, as Mom's physical condition was worsening, the decision was made that he too should come and be reared with his sisters in the Vaughan Family Home.

He grew up under Big Mom and Gramps until Big Mom died. Little Mom then came to live in the Vaughan Home with Sputnik (and me on my trips home from New York) until God beckoned her. My brother, more sensitive to the "loss" than any of us, decided it was time for him to relocate to Denver with two of his long-time school buddies, there to "find" themselves and make their own way in the world.

I marvelled at how Little Mom "knew" that last Sunday. I'm glad I didn't know. Funny how one is never really prepared for the death of those you love no matter how long the illness that anticipates it. But I was thankful we had talked about it. I was, too, grateful that her pain was over and that peace and rest were hers.

Nix Funeral Home had her body and Daddy was of course tending personally to the funeral. I wondered how he felt, preparing and arranging for the funeral of someone he had been so close to. Separation and divorce notwithstanding, death is always difficult when it is someone you were close to, someone you cared deeply about, someone who was the mother of your children. Daddy had the "perspective," though, and I didn't have to ask. He had said to me times before that the "person" was no longer residing in the body. It was just a body.

I couldn't wait to see her. Daddy knew the right time for this: after he had dressed and cosmetically restored her to health. We would go down to "the inspection," as it is termed in mortician's language, the day before the funeral. I was so looking forward to it. It was as if we would be greeting each other after a long hiatus. Of course, I knew she would not be responding, but it would be our final connection, especially since I wasn't there when she died. And until I saw her, her death wasn't real. I also knew that any disappointment I felt at not getting there on Wednesday would be gone as soon as I could see her.

Dad and my stepmother walked with me into the chapel where mom was lying. I was smiling in anticipation of seeing her. My smile turned to a frown when I reached her. I heard my father ask, "Doesn't she look good?"

"No!" I said urgently. "It *doesn't* look like her!" My upset subsided the next day as everyone else seemed to agree with my Dad. All of her friends who grew up with her remarked how Daddy had made her look like herself, like he and they had known her. My stepmother had tried to explain that to me; that I had really only known Little Mom after the illness started. I had never really seen her well. Of course, my favorite picture of her was as a young healthy person. And in fact, she looked just like that picture.

By the end of the funeral day, all was well and Mom was in heaven. That's when the confirmation dawned on me. Without a single doubt, I knew where Mom was, and it was comforting. It was true. Jesus had in fact died to allow us eternal rest with him. And Mom was the recipient. I hadn't ever felt so resolute about "the end." But now I was certain. Mom's death confirmed it; erased the last shadow of skepticism. I felt joyous that heaven exists.

Mom's death opened the door to another blessing: my husband. I hadn't heard from Bill since his first year in law school. (My Ph.D. party was after he'd graduated.) He'd left for University of Toledo in

Ohio in 1974 and our friendship went on hold for three years. Suddenly, in the Spring of 1977, my phone rang.

"Hey, Nix," the familiar cadence sounded. "What's up? I'm coming to New York for an interview with the public defender's office, and I need a place to stay. Can you put me up for a night?"

It would be good to see Bill again, but as it turned out, I didn't see very much of him that trip. I handed him some keys when he arrived, and then I whisked immediately off to a dinner date with Brian.

As I always did, I returned to Star of Hope for Women's Day the fourth Sunday in September. I missed being in the choir but enjoyed listening from the audience. Everyone walked around to the collection plate at "tithes and offerings" time. Church was packed, and this was always a good way to see who was there. A familiar looking young man was returning to his seat by way of the aisle where I was sitting. He was wearing a striking cream-colored three-piece suit with a mauve shirt and print tie. "Stunning," I thought to myself. "Heart be still. Who *is* that!" As the cream suit neared my row, the details of the face were clearer. It was Bill! I'd never seen him look so good! I'd never realized his handsomeness. I managed to wade through the crowd after church to say a quick hello and to get a closer look before both of us were swallowed up by old friends and family greeting the college returnees. He did have time to tell me that the public defender thing in New York didn't work out. Bill had graduated a Juris Doctor in May and returned to Tacony to study for the Pennsylvania Bar to become one of those Philadelphia lawyers.

The next time I saw Bill was that fall at Little Mom's funeral. My sister and I stood at each end of Mom's casket to greet and thank those who came to the viewing. I found myself hoping that he would come. A few minutes later I watched him come down the aisle toward me. His words were soft.

"Let me know if I can help you with anything. I'm home on National Street."

The time after the funeral is the loneliest. Bill came over to sit with me for a couple of hours one evening. I and my brother were the only ones staying in the big family house on Hegerman Street. We had to start cleaning out Mom's things. There were several items I wanted to keep and take back to New York. I'd need help getting them there. I called Bill.

The drive back to New York was quiet but comforting. He reached out with another act of kindness.

"The O'Jays are gonna be at Valley Forge in a couple of weeks. Why don't you come down and go with me. It'll be good for you."

I really didn't feel like a rock concert, and I couldn't think that far ahead. My lease was up, and before the news of Mom's death, I had scheduled to sign a new lease at the Old Fifth Avenue Hotel, a grand old building at the corner of 8th and Fifth Avenue that had been converted to apartments. I had to summon all my energy to focus on packing for the move. I had hoped Bill could stay to help with that chore but he had other business to tend to and so returned to Philly. But two weeks later he insisted again.

"Hey, Nix. I got the tickets. You're going with me. Come down Saturday. I'll pick you up at the train."

I had a great time. I'd forgotten how much fun it was to be around him at Princeton.

The first Christmas without Little Mom was difficult. I couldn't stay in Philly. I called Thelma, my best buddy from Penn. She was living in Cincinnati. I would spend the holidays with her and Hogue, her husband, also a Penn alumnus. I took my gifts for the family down to Philly on the twenty-second of December. With the assistance of Bill and his green Cougar, I made the rounds: Gramps, Dad, Phe, and Sputnik. Bill drove me back to New York on the night of the twenty-third and got me to the airport very early on the morning of the twenty-fourth. I wasn't paying attention; there was disappointment in his eyes. He was sorry I was leaving.

Bill invited me down to Philly on several more occasions in the New Year: dinner with some old friends of his, men's day service at his church, another concert. He was taking very good care of my spirit and asking nothing in return.

We started talking on the phone more and visiting each other's cities. (By that time, I considered myself a New Yorker, rooting for the Mets and the Knicks instead of the Phillies and the Sixers. Besides, Frank Rizzo was Mayor of Philadelphia and I'd vowed not to return until he was gone.) We were slipping into something beyond friendship. He spoke it out loud in one of our marathon long-distance calls.

"Hey, Nix. Are we, uh, becoming 'involved'?"

During the Spring of 1978, the relationship progressed as well as it could, between my making the last push to successfully defend my dissertation and write final revisions, and Bill studying again for the Bar exam. It had been my turn that past winter to lighten his spirits. He learned just a few days before the exam, and after weeks of grueling study in the Bar Review Course, that "they" had lost his application. He would not be allowed to sit for the exam and would have to wait until Spring. He was *r-e-a-l* bummed out about that. But he geared up again. And he passed.

Things happened in rapid succession after that.

I graduated in May, 1978. Bill came up along with Grandmom Nix, Gramps, Dad, and Cousin Alfred, who lived in New York. Certainly this was a proud day: the first Nix with a Ph.D. Little Mom had missed the celebration by a few months, but she was there. (The acknowledgements page of my dissertation dedicates the entire work to her memory.)

Bill and I were both in need of celebration. We were at the end of our student careers and were about to take on adult-type lives. Poor, but inspired, we decided to drive cross-country. It would be the marriage test. Could we plan, organize, cooperate, share, budget for, and live through a sustained (three-week) experience that would require us to do things unfamiliar to both. We bought the tent, the camp stove, the lantern, the sleeping bags; I was working and so funded the trip. He tuned up the Cougar; he mapped out the route. In July, 1978, we set out, driving across the North, down the Pacific coast, back across the South. I was no girl scout; the test was an awesome one.

- pitching the tent in mud and pouring rain. (Oh, my hair and nails!)
- meeting grizzly bears and snakes. (Not just tall tales. Write for details to Davy "Bill Early" Crocket! He knew to put his hand over my mouth to stifle my scream so as not to incite the bear.)
- scaling the mountainous steps of Yosemite's Mist Trail in order to drink from the Emerald Pool.
- rafting the white water of the Snake River. (I can't swim and I hate water!)
- driving through thunder, lightning, and torrential downpours on winding mountain roads. (I was no driver then. Bill says I almost killed us!)
- arguing the philosophy and validity of Black English and other weighty issues of the day. We had to test the compatibility of our politics: we didn't agree. "I don't think I can marry you," I pronounced. My dad made sure before leaving that I had a plane ticket home in case things didn't work out. I was remembering every father's classic words of safety to his daughter: "Always have cab fare home!" I patted the ticket in my pocket. Escape was there if I needed it. Alice's words were also helpful. "Don't

> blame him (meaning Bill) for being black." Okay, our racial politics were different. But his views were as okay as mine. We'll continue the trip.

I didn't need the plane ticket.

Bill landed a job in November (and paid me back for the trip!). We set "The Date" for August 25, 1979.

Little Mom didn't like Bill. She didn't trust him. She said he cheated at cards. (He doesn't.) I'm not sure what she sensed, but it was very different from Big Mom's opinion. Big Mom adored Bill's father—Shinamite, they called him. "He was an example of what men should be," Big Mom always said, "always loyal, taking care of his family, kind." Bill inherited some of his traits. "He's such a nice boy," Big Mom was fond of saying. "He always speaks when he sees you. So polite." Were Little Mom alive, maybe I wouldn't have married him. (Of course, Dad says that if she knew that I really loved Bill, she would have "come around.") At any rate, it occurred to me that God was answering another prayer of mine: the gift of a Christian husband.

Epilogue

Bill and I continue to work on what is now a thirteen-year marriage. All of the years have not been easy, but they have all been in the right direction. We continue to share a blessed life. We have been able to have everything we need and much of what we want. We have excelled in our careers, advancing steadily, me in higher education administration, he in environmental law. We continue to try to return our blessings through work with the young people of both our churches, hoping to do half the good that our folk and neighbors did for us. Abundant blessings can sometimes be burdensome. The Bible reminds us that much is expected of those to whom much is given.

Memories are often inaccurate, but does that really matter when what continues to influence us is the "experience"? I'm not sure if the events and quotes I have related happened just exactly as I stated them; but they are true to the message being conveyed and true to the way I experienced them then.

It takes many good people and lots of care to influence a life. The process of writing this story has caused me to remember with humility and gratitude all the people God used to lift me to where I am; people who weren't family and who didn't have to be encouraging. How easy it is to keep moving and to forget how important others were and are to your development.

I took the invitation to write this chapter as but another opportunity for outreach; to witness to what the Lord will do with a life for no other reason than *Love*. It has stirred a desire to return to my dissertation research; to again involve myself in thinking about how and whether things have changed in the interface of psychology and religion. It has raised again for consideration studying at seminary when I retire. I have looked at my husband many times during this writing with greater fondness and appreciation. I have felt renewed gratitude for my sister Phe who, as do many older, first-born siblings, paved the way, took the heat from, and broke in the new parents; so that by the time I came along, our folks weren't spanking as much and weren't nearly as strict about dating and other such things.

I have remembered with particular gratitude the soft words of Connie Chalick, a psychologist colleague. I shared with him a growing concern and preoccupation with premature death, a dread that seemed to accompany my midthirties. He remarked quite matter-of-factly that obviously God still had work for me to do and would not take me until that work was complete. Since then I have had peace. My life has been rich and full and I often feel content and ready to die, assured that whenever I am called it will be the absolute right time.

I have mourned Little Mom's absence again, but also, I have remembered the joy and lightness I felt the morning I awoke having seen and visited with her for the first time since her death months before.

"Alice!" (I couldn't wait to report the news to my therapist.) "I dreamt about her last night! I embraced her. She was well and looking wonderful and happy."

God's dream for my life is not yet ended. It feels much like the reunion dream with Little Mom: bright, shining, and full of hope. None of it has been coincidence. I continue to carry Mom's love as reassurance; Dad has always "fixed things" so that I would never have to worry; and Gramps dotes on me as if there's no one better on earth. Recounting the story has sharpened the blurred image of my guardian angel. It has confirmed my parentage and my role in the Family. It has made me know even more that I am God's child.

2

As I Recall

Mary Vander Goot

How can I tell the story of my life? It is not a single strand that I can trace from the beginning to now. Rather, it is a complex mingling of things that rearrange as time changes me, and the complete story is not yet clear. The best I can do to tell my story is to set out the categories within which I myself try to assemble the memories and experiences that now, at this time of my life, I can identify as mine.

These are some of the ways I think of myself. 1) I am an ethnic child. 2) I was born a girl-child; I am a woman. 3) I am a psychologist. 4) I am a post-ecclesiastical Christian.

I Am an Ethnic Child

I am a Dutch American. My parents were one of the many Americans who, as children, were put into the melting pot at Ellis Island. Although they moved their home from coast to coast, New Jersey to California and many places between, they were always part of the Dutch ghetto and huddled "with their own kind." The first generation of immigrants needed to huddle for safety. Outside of the Dutch ghetto they were always somewhat out of balance and, therefore, at a disadvantage.

My parents were optimistic immigrant Americans. They did not criticize their adopted country as if they were not responsible for it. Neither did they sentimentally idealize their country of origin as if it were better. They had strong views of social justice and public obligation, were socially conscious, stayed informed about current events, and at times fretted about current social problems. They never expected anything for which they did not work; they avoided either waste or extravagance; and they accepted without question that discipline and hard work are among the basic virtues of the good citizen.

In spite of their deep loyalty to the United States, my parents were also the type of immigrants who never felt truly American in quite the same sense that they believed other Americans were. It was always clear that for them, being an American was a privilege, while for "real Americans" it is a fact of birth. Even after they had spent half a century in the United States, and even though they had left the Netherlands at such a young age they could barely remember it, were you to ask them where they were from, they would not have named a state or a city, but would have told you that the Netherlands was their country of origin. It will always be where they are from, and they will never escape the sense that they are unlike other Americans because they are Dutch.

In witnessing the lives of my parents and persons like them, I have come to believe that first generation immigrants, born in one nation and raised in another, become confused about where home is. They always feel somewhat marginal, and just under the surface of their well-assimilated exteriors there is the soul of an orphan. The sense of being displaced and homeless lasts long after daily thoughts of the old country have passed and long after the last traces of an accent have been erased. It lasts long after the oath of allegiance is sworn and the new citizenship papers have been carefully tucked in the safe drawer beside the other official documents of birth, baptism, education, marriage, and military service. In the soul of the first generation immigrant there is a homesickness that never goes away, because it is for an ideal of home that exists neither in the new world nor the old.

An intricate mixture of feeling rises up out of the immigrant experience. Many immigrants suffer from insecurity because they have repeatedly experienced rejection and humiliation. They remember too well how they were ridiculed and patronized because their clothes were different, their speech was strange and hard to understand, their social habits were odd, and their surnames were awkward to say and spell. On more than one occasion when I was a girl a non-Dutch person thought to comfort me by reminding me that someday, if I married right, I would have an American name with which to face the world.

Many immigrants are also proud. They know that they have stood the test of courage and have proven that they can endure hardship. They harbor a set of memories that are not everyone's, and by which they feel set apart. The courage it takes to meet the challenge of immigration often goes unrecognized by anyone other than immigrants themselves. Ethnic persons share a common story. It is a story of courage and survival. Some of the chapters of the immigrant story are very tender and precious, other chapters are quite bitter and ugly.

When you are one of the bridging generation that still knows the story of the struggle but does not have to live that struggle, you are caught in two worlds. You are the witness of a past that you cherish but that you hope will not interfere with the present. You are the bearer of the story that does not deserve to be forgotten because, if it were, a small bit of human nature would go unacknowledged, and that would be the worst dishonor to your ancestors. You feel the obligation.

There is another subtle and continuous stress with which immigrants live. It is the challenge of preserving dignity in the face of perpetual messages about your inferiority. This struggle against inferiority does not only last for years; it lasts for generations. Just often enough, ethnic persons are reminded that they and people like them are misunderstood and judged inferior.

Here is a simple example. I have often been amazed at the liberty with which some nonDutch persons will say insulting things about Dutch Americans to me, even though my surname obviously identifies my ethnicity. Sometimes the comments strike close to home and there is an element of truth in them. But it is still odd to hear them because in most social situations people are not blunt about their criticisms of others. Things that might be said behind the back normally are not said face to face. The liberty to criticize or patronize goes with rank, status, and privilege. Whether it is fair or not, more important persons have more license to criticize. Less important people must keep criticism to themselves because it is too costly to reveal it.

When as an ethnic person you are confronted with one of the unflattering stereotypes about your group, you are insulted on two levels.

First, it is insulting to be saddled with a whole group's reputation. But second, and equally important, you are reminded that you and your group are perceived as inferior, because if it were not so, your critic would have exercised the social tact of an equal.

Often group stereotypes are based on misunderstanding, and the group's virtues are perceived as vices because they are unfamiliar. There is an ethnic habit among Dutch Americans that reminds me of this. The Dutch are group oriented in their social manner and there is a little familiarizing ritual that the Dutch engage in when getting acquainted. They ask questions about family, town, or church; they are not as likely to ask personal questions of a strictly individual nature. Parading one's own accomplishments or engaging in anything even vaguely resembling bragging is strictly taboo. Flattery is also rare and viewed with disapproval. They may tell a little story about someone not present, but whom they all know; they will almost never promote themselves.

The familiarizing ritual serves to establish that, even if we do not know each other personally, we all know the same set of rules for fair exchange and proper treatment of others. There is nothing unusual about the need to establish good will in social exchange. The same thing motivates a handshake when two business persons meet, or the gifts that Asians bring to social exchange. The need to establish good will is universal; the way it is done varies from group to group.

Dutch Americans carry out the familiarizing ritual in a way that recognizes an important social norm, the priority of group loyalty over the promotion of individual interests. NonDutch persons sometimes accuse Dutch Americans of carrying out this ritual to exclude outsiders. Actually it is quite the opposite. It is an attempt to establish belonging and get the social interaction started on an equal footing. In this sense it is a friendly gesture of inclusion, not one intended for exclusion at all, and quite democratic in its intent.

The familiarizing ritual is just one example; there are myriad ways in which ethnic persons are misunderstood. Persons who have not experienced geographical displacement have difficulty imagining the extent of the disorientation that occurs. The process of immigration is a trauma. It involves stress, grief, uncertainty, and the loss of identity. For many it is a wrenching experience. Disorientation is a stimulus to group loyalty among immigrants. They hold onto the most admirable qualities of their ethnic group because they believe that these qualities are a resource with which they will survive.

It is in part because ethnic children feel the pathos and admire the struggle that they also feel obligated to remember. But the assimilating immigrant also discovers those ethnic characteristics that stand in the way of success. For the ethnic child the tradition is something both to be preserved and escaped. It is both a treasure and a burden, a source of pride and shame. Often when I have been asked if I am Dutch, I have not known what to say. If I say that I am, I feel bound in by assumptions. If I say that I am not, I feel terribly disloyal. Sometimes I just wish I could ignore the question.

There was an event that vividly captured for me something quite good in the ethnic experience, but also brought to life again the strange pattern of double loyalty and lack of a real home. It happened a few years ago when Queen Beatrix of the Netherlands made a tour of the United States and stopped off at the campus of Calvin College. I was on the faculty of Calvin College at the time. It was not really a momentous event, but it was a very "immigrant" one.

Grand Rapids, Michigan is one of the huddling places of Dutch Americans. They are Calvinists and believe in the virtues of discipline, hard work, and an orderly life. Because of this mindset, education is one of the primary ways in which Dutch Americans assimilate, and Calvin College is living proof that they can educate, work, and prosper as well as anyone else in mainstream America. The ethnic supporters of Calvin College were eager to have the queen visit their campus and admire what they have accomplished.

Normally I am not much interested in queens, kings, and royal families. The Queen of England visited Toronto on a few occasions when I lived there. I never bothered to see her. Once when her motorcade passed within a block of the building where I was working, I politely excused myself when the others walked down the street to see her. Devoted as I am to the work ethic, I took the opportunity to get a little extra done without interruptions while nearly everyone else was out. I am not much impressed by honor that is not earned. I have been known in arrogant moments to say that unearned honor tends to bloat the ego: as if all of us do not have some degree of that bloating.

In any case, when Queen Beatrix visited Calvin College I cleaned up my children on a lovely sunny day and took them to the campus to watch her plant a tree. I also took my camera, so apparently I was trying to collect some memories, if not for myself then at least for my children. As it turned out, the event meant much more to me than it did to my children. They were disappointed that the queen did not have a crown and royal robes. I knew the minute I saw her that she was a queen.

As the motorcade approached I could see necks stretch and eyes search for the first sight of her. The Dutch are a somewhat taciturn lot when it comes to showing emotion. When their feelings are strong they tend to get quiet and let the feeling run deep. The crowd was quiet.

When the queen spoke in perfect English with a perfect Dutch accent, faces softened. Dutch is a language that is spoken closer to the vocal cords than English. To the sentimental it sounds as if it is spoken closer to the heart. When this good Dutch woman spoke our immigrant language (careful English with a Dutch accent), it called forth from the deep sea of memory the feelings of the familiar huddle. She spoke it just the way our ears wait to hear it, and like an old tune, it stirred deep nostalgia.

Queen Beatrix has an image that appeals to the Dutch American's longing for home. She does not look like a jet-setter; she looks like a mother. The Dutch are strong on mothers and home. There is a word that Dutch immigrants hang onto and still use in English among themselves because they do not believe there is an English word that even comes close. It is the word "gezellig," and it refers to all those qualities that exemplify home: coziness, congeniality, lightheartedness, contentment, and a well-tended hearth. The mark of a good Dutch woman is that she can make anything gezellig (a meal at a roadside table, a tent in a campground, or a cup of coffee on the front porch). Dutch homes are kept clean, Dutch mothers take the favorite family tea pot on vacations to make the lodgings homelike, and Dutch meals are hearty and served so regularly that no one ever really gets hungry. Obviously this is more a dream than a reality, but the ideal is a strong one.

There is more. Queen Beatrix is a tall and powerful woman, like many Dutch women. And when it was time to plant the tree she did not let the assistant turn the soil. She reached over with royal hands, but also hands like ours that are large and able to work, and she took the spade herself. Queen Beatrix bore the image and dignity of a solid, industrious, and plain woman. She had none of the marks of Hollywood: showy clothes that make anyone look rich and royal, long nails that make hands unfit to industry, bold makeup or glamorous hair that hide the character in a face and turn it into a mask. Traditional Dutch Americans associate these things with artificiality and an untrustworthy American ideal; they are not inclined to admire them in their women. Beatrix was our type of good Dutch woman, and she was a queen. What's more, that day she was being honored among us and as a celebrity in America.

Some of the significance of Queen Beatrix's visit was that this time she came to our home. Many Dutch Americans visit the Netherlands. Even some Dutch Americans who can not speak Dutch anymore and were not born there go "home" to find their roots. They visit beautiful Dutch towns and villages from which their ancestors hail and meet some distant relatives, many of whom speak English far better than Dutch Americans can speak Dutch after a generation or so.

Visiting the Netherlands is an odd experience for an assimilated Dutch American. There are things about it that are hauntingly familiar. The faces and body types make ordinary folks on the street look like distant relatives. And there are many social mannerisms that do not feel strange at all.

There is also a sense of strangeness. Although somewhere back in the collective unconscious of a family this little country is home, in the eyes of its inhabitants today, the Dutch American tourist is just another foreigner. They cannot recognize the Dutch American searching for roots as one of theirs, although we harbor the secret nostalgia that we are part of them in some distant way and that their lovely little country is our long lost home.

This is all tied into the significance of the queen's visit. It was an occasion for having a representative of our past recognize our new home. The queen had come to put a blessing on our new home and confirm for us that we had honored our origins by making a place for ourselves in the new world.

As with each year I gain greater distance from my childhood and the Dutch American ghetto as it was in my youth, it is no longer quite clear to me how I feel about my own ethnicity. I do know that I no longer need to, nor in fact feel comfortable, confining my life to the safe huddle. There are too many wonderful things outside of that protected world that I am not willing to forego. Today I feel more natural and authentic when I am operating outside of it.

Although I am no longer dependent on the ethnic tradition, I also know that it has placed its stamp on me. It is one of the factors that shaped my life and made me what I am. I remember with both awe and protectiveness the colorful characters who made up that world. I recall as one might recall a flavor or a fragrance the mood of that ethnic world: in the streets of its neighborhoods, its shops and businesses, its schools and churches. I would not want to go back to live in it the way I did as a child, but sometimes I wish I could go back in time and stay for just an hour to feel it all once again. That is when I understand most clearly that the tradition lives on in me.

As I look at my contemporaries, the offspring of the same ethnicity, I see the institutions and communities built by Dutch Americans. There has now been a significant shift toward becoming multicultural. While this trend is a reflection of a much broader phenomenon in American culture, it takes on a particular twist in the Dutch-American ethnic community. I think many of the persons who still participate actively in those communities believe that the shift is a matter of principle. Personally, I believe it is a matter of time. Once they defended their ethnic separation with the same principles that now they use to dissolve it. In both cases the rationales are expressions of an ethnic community trying to find its way in a new world.

I see with the shift toward multiculturalism a tendency to treat Dutch pride as a prejudice. Sometimes I wonder if this is really a sign of greater confidence, or whether it is just another expression of the same old ethnic shame. Is the same inferiority that once showed itself in the defense of the tradition and a fight for dignity now manifest in the denial of that same tradition?

Perhaps the burden of ethnic insecurity and the fight for dignity took too much effort, and now it is just easier to blend in with the mainstream. Our parents and grandparents could not do it. They did not know how to talk and to act like other Americans; their foreignness was too obvious. But we can blend in. Unless we make an issue of our ethnicity, no one really notices much anymore, especially if we "Americanize" our names and drop our ethnic rituals.

I do not exempt myself from some confusion about ethnic identity. It is not easy to sustain both an ethnic and a nonethnic sense of identity at the same time. I suppose if I had to choose, I would prefer the more inclusive nonethnic identity over the smaller ethnic one. But best of all would be not to have to choose at all, and in this respect I still am, and probably always will be, an ethnic child.

I Was Born a Girl-Child; I Am a Woman

I was born in the era before feminism found its voice in the twentieth century. Before feminist issues achieved broad exposure I had been raised as a girl and had become a young woman. I have always had a certain natural pride about being female. In the matriarchal family in which I was raised, women were taken seriously. I think it was easier to be a daughter than a son in my family. It always seemed to me that being a woman had advantages because the things that interested me most (children, relationships, feelings) were more present in the world of women than they seemed to be in the world of men.

I do not really know which came first, my inclusion in the world of women or my appreciation for it. I can remember the first conscious wishes to someday be a mother. It happened during a summer vacation when the toddler son of some friends stayed with us. I took him for long walks in his stroller and doted over him. To be trusted with him and to discover that he was content in my care was a wonderful, tender feeling. I missed him terribly when he went home again.

This strong longing to be a nurturer was repeated often and long before I ever became a mother. With children I felt natural and free. I babysat often. The freedom of imagination, the energy for play, the self-forgetfulness of children's activities were also parts of me that sought avenues of expression.

When combined with caring for younger children, the childlike in me seemed to flow easily. Even as an adult, when I played, read, or went on outings with my children, I was sometimes aware that the activity was also a form of self-nurture. Although I know it would not work to be that way all the time, I respect the fresh and immediate ways of children: no yesterday and no tomorrow.

As a young person I discovered "nest building." Making a homey space out of whatever space and resources I have has always been, and still can be, a great enjoyment for me. Sometimes in my childhood it was making a tea party in a tent built with a blanket over the clothes line, or building a homey space for my dolls in the corner of the basement. Later in my student years it involved making a home of one simple room or a humble student apartment. Even today, decorating, whether a home or an office, appeals to me not as an opportunity to make a fashion statement, but rather as a way of making a harmonious and comforting environment. I believe that at the root of it is my longing to make a *Home*.

Of course these same interests that I associate with being a woman can be developed by men. But in my case I know that they are an expression of feminine energy, and I like it. When I engage in these ventures I feel well integrated; I am confident that the impulse from which these motives rise is vital and good; I feel pride and contentment in being a woman.

I did not become conscious that being female would have an impact on my life choices until I was faced with the challenge of identifying career goals. It was, in fact, the era in which women were still being told that it is good to have a college education and some work potential in reserve: in the unfortunate event that you need to support yourself someday if your husband should die, become disabled, or if you never find a husband at all. But the assumption was that a career for a woman was a luxury rather than an economic necessity.

As a young college student I did not want to see it that way. I was and had always been quite attentive to women who had vocations beyond the family. I was intrigued by women writers, women academics, and women in public life. There were not many of them, and among those there were not many who had succeeded in combining a family life of husband and children with a vocational life of productivity.

Think for a moment of Emily Dickinson, Margaret Mead, Golda Meir, Helene Deutsche, and Emily Bronte. They were not a college woman's most encouraging role models. As important as the prospect of a career was to me, marriage and motherhood were most important. I do not believe that my priorities aligned this way only because someone told me that it should be so. To want these things was deep in my constitution: a feature of my personality.

Without meaning to make a judgment about what women in general should do or feel, I can say with great certainty for myself that if it had not been possible for me to combine marriage and motherhood with a career, I would have given up the career. This is something that I would have been shy about saying in 1970, and disclosed only to a few people who knew me very well. I was younger and more timid then, and feminism was a newer and more dogmatic movement. But as I have grown older it is more important to me to tell the truth about myself than it is to be politically correct.

As a young student, and in particular a woman, I wanted it all. In particular I knew that I would not be willing to give up being the primary parent to my children; deep in my heart I wanted to be their first and most important; the person to whom they attached and was their firm base of security. Professionally I wanted much more than employment. I was determined to have a vocation that put me to the test and that I knew was worthwhile.

In having a profession I was trying to do something that women do not routinely do. In maintaining the role of primary parent I was doing something that is seldom done by men who are strongly invested in their careers. But that did not change my wanting it all.

Several personal circumstances shored me up in the pursuit of my vocation. I was raised in a family in which the life of the mind was valued highly. No member of my family, neither my parents nor my siblings, ever discouraged me in the pursuit of education or a career. Never was I told that it was not fitting for me as a woman to pursue a career, or that it would detract from the quality of my life with my husband or children if I were to do so. Both my parents and my sister have cheered me on and helped me out, when juggling the various responsibilities of my life seemed to require more than one person and more than twenty-four hours a day.

In addition, my husband has always supported my pursuit of intellectual interests. We have shared great enthusiasm for the exchange of ideas and the challenges of work. When we went to graduate school he was willing to enter a program less well-suited for him, so that I could enter a program better suited for me. As young graduate students we learned a lot from each other because we found a ready audience in each other. His own energy, and the determination with which he can head toward a goal, was an inspiration to me.

Over the years of our marriage it has been clear that each of us had a significant impact on the thinking of the other. Sometimes this was because we agreed with each other, and sometimes because we did not. There has always been a certain existential honesty in our relationship. It shows itself from time to time when we drop the guard of social expectations and speak the truth to each other about God, the world, and our own individual place in it. In this sense I think ours is a relationship without pretense, and I know that quality is one not easy to find.

Because my husband understood the place of my career and commitments in my life, he never stood in the way of either. I am not aware that it ever occurred to him to question whether I should have a career. I am quite sure that if I had ever thought to give up graduate school or to not continue in a profession, he would have challenged me strongly; I believe he knew that it would have been relinquishing part of my identity.

Some discouragements in the pursuit of my career did occur outside of the context of my immediate family. When I first began to apply to graduate programs, I wrote away for materials, much as any student does. In the packet that I received from Princeton University there was a letter informing me that it was still a men's school on the undergraduate level and that very few women were admitted to the graduate departments.

In the graduate department to which I was applying one woman per year was admitted. That was 1968. It was before the era of women's liberation and the changed consciousness about the rights of women that occurred in the 1970s. Though disappointed, I simply accepted the letter as a statement of fact. I applied anyway, and added to my application a strong statement to the effect that, were Princeton's psychology department to admit me it would be making a good decision, because I was a hard working, responsible, and dedicated student. They did admit me.

Oddly enough, I was not insulted by being a token woman in a graduate department of all male professors and all male students. Neither was I insulted, but rather a bit humored, by the venerable professor who began every lecture with, "Gentlemen . . . ," and stared straight at me.

That was not the end of the story. I was a woman alone in a program of men. I felt as if I were an oddity, and I also missed the familiar company of women. Sometimes I was very anxious because I felt as if not only my own honor, but the honor of women in general, rested on my shoulders. I was fearful of making mistakes, or not performing well enough, and of drawing the ultimate criticism that women never quite live up to the expectations set for men.

In the years that followed my admission to Princeton, policies did change and there were other women in the program. But I think we were somewhat paralyzed in supporting each other. We did not hang together. Rather, each of us seemed to draw back into our own small world of work. I tried to keep the company of men and pretended that our gender differences did not matter.

There were a few instances when I was the object of insults and aggression because I was a woman; one time I did encounter what today would be considered sexual harassment. My reaction was to draw back and detour the threat. There were some stone age men who had no idea about how to deal respectfully with a woman as a peer, but there were also some very enlightened, gracious, enjoyable men. I sought out the collegial company in which I was safe and avoided the other.

Over time I have come to see that in denying that I was different professionally, because I was a woman, I did a certain injustice to myself. I think I was not inclined to admit differences for fear that it would be used to disadvantage me. I preferred to assimilate. I no longer feel that way.

As my place in my profession became more secure, I also felt freer to recognize in myself that there are certain tendencies in my style of thinking, my manner of communication, and my investment in ideas that are closely tied to my sense of myself as a woman. Men also have certain patterns and styles, but when they are the majority, they have less occasion to notice it in themselves. In any case, I celebrate variety because I am convinced that the resources are richest when the greatest variety is encouraged.

I like the company of men just as for other reasons I like the company of women. I have learned, though, that I do not do well if I let myself be caught up in an ideological battle on either side. I do not wish to be adversarial with men, to compete with them about our differences, or to demand of them that they be like me. Neither do I want to be a queen bee or neglect the support of other women as they find their way in the world. I refuse to take sides because when that has happened it has not been good for either side. It is very important to me to get along well with men and women, because most of all I want to be the woman I am in the company of men and women alike.

There are events in a lifetime that solidify a sense of identity. In the course of my development as a woman there have been many of these, but in the course of my identity as a professional woman, one of them stands out in particular. It was a simple event during the time that I was writing my doctoral dissertation, and it represented some sort of turning point for me.

I was sitting in a study carrel in the Psychology Department library at Princeton University and was reading the biography of Mary Whiton Calkins. She was a student of William James and was an active participant in that circle of New England intellectuals who saw the discipline of psychology forming its own destiny, separate from the other sciences and philosophy. These were the founders of American psychology.

Calkins, like the others, mastered the materials and wrote a significant scholarly work of the sort that usually led to the granting of the doctor of philosophy degree. But her degree was not granted because the university was not granting degrees to women. As a supposed courtesy to her, efforts were made to arrange an honorary degree for her from a women's school. But Calkins preferred no degree at all to having one that was given for any other reason than that she had earned it.

When I read the story of Mary Whiton Calkins I cried in my carrel. I felt a powerful identification with all my sisters who had experienced that gender casts doubt on the quality of their minds and the value of their achievements. It also made me stubborn. It was the point at which I decided that I myself would always be the first judge of my work: that I would try to be honest with myself about limitations, but that I would never give in to believing that thinking like a woman, or that a woman's thinking, was second class.

Eighteen years after sitting in my carrel and weeping over the thwarting of Mary Whiton Calkins, I went back to Princeton on a visit. One evening as I walked the campus to review old landmarks I also strolled to Green Hall where the psychology library is. Although the door to the library was locked, there was a graduate student who had a key and let me in. In the back room where the many rows of journals are shelved it was easy to locate the place where my habitual study carrel had been.

As I remembered my first encounter with the story of Mary Whiton Calkins, I could also remember so well the young woman I was at twenty-four, with my armor of bravery and paper-thin confidence. But now with the passing of time I could also see that some things had changed for women in the few years since I have been a student. In many ways the professional world is more hospitable today than it once was, even if it is not perfect. It fortified my belief that hope lives somewhere in the middle between indifference and idealism. We live each day in our own place and time, and it is only out of that place and time, with its best and its worst, that we can hope to live most fully.

As I look back on my adult life I realize how much I have prized the company of women. My mother was a confident and competent woman. She was also sociable and extroverted. Her life was a fine model of the quality relationships that women form for support, cooperation, and companionship.

A strong pillar in my life has been the presence of my older sister, who is by anyone's estimation a gifted and extraordinary woman. Together we have shared our poems and our gossip, household hints and lofty thoughts; we have loved each other's children and spoken the truth. She is most truly a sister and a friend. I have also known the joy of rich and fine friendships. I have luxuriated in small groups of women who were able to spend high quality time together. The smooth, kind, and honest company of happy women is a very beautiful thing.

As much as I value being a woman and the company of other women, I have always resisted being identified as a feminist. I am a woman, not a feminist. I have supported and prized the progress of women, but I have not felt comfortable with efforts to make men the enemy. They are, after all, our fathers, sons, husbands, and brothers.

Although I like men, and some of them impress or intrigue me, they are something of a puzzle to me and probably always will be. Sometimes I can get close enough to appreciate the puzzle, although it remains a mystery to me nonetheless.

When I watch men play football I sense there is something important going on, and I know it has something to do with a way that they are different from me. If I dare to be naively honest, I must admit that if I were a football player I would try to change the rules. I would want to walk out on the field and suggest that with some minor changes we could play the game without getting so dirty and without getting hurt.

There is also something in me that knows that, even if I could, it would be better that I not change the rules of football. I would be tampering with something that I could not understand. Sometimes I do wish that men would let me in on those hidden male meanings. Not because I want to be in their world with them, but because there is some kind of harmony that comes from appreciating difference. After all, we are not enemies, but rather two mysteries living side by side.

Men have their own ways. I was aware of it this past winter as I observed three silent fishermen bent over the lake, and again passed them still silent and fishing an hour later. That is not the way women make company. But I could sense that this small band of men—out in the harsh elements with their lines in the water, waiting quietly but also challenging that hidden form of life under water—did have the company of men. It was peaceful, and it was good.

I do not know how men carry out the process of self-validation in themselves, but I hope they do. I am quite sure that the more each of us, men and women alike, treasure what we are, the better we will be at appreciating each other. If we do, then perhaps we can also live well in the balanced and textured harmony for which our nature intends us.

It has happened to me more often, as it did that day when I returned to Princeton, that I think about events that have had an effect of deepening my own sense of being a woman. It stirs in me a feeling that resonates with what I also have felt at times when looking at my sleeping children. I feel then as if I am looking on at something that I do not want to disturb or change. I treasure it and feel protective. It is a very tender experience, and where there have been events in my life that have hurt the girl or woman in me, these deepening moments are very healing. Perhaps it is the mother in me that does this, because in those moments I have intimations of what it is to be my own mother, and I am thankful to be a woman.

I Am a Psychologist

Why did I become a psychologist? There are any number of reasons. But these are just a few.

I was raised in an era in which attention to human nature was considered far less important than fulfillment of public duty. By the time I reached adulthood that had changed. Psychology was an important ingredient in the transition, and I was choosing my vocation just as the transition was happening.

I was a child in the 1950s. It was not the era of the child; it was the era of the citizen. The focus of child-rearing, education, and family values was to form the good citizen. Parents were not encouraged first and above all to monitor the happiness of their children. Instead parents were impressed by their duty to form an industrious, law-abiding, and well-behaved person.

I do not mean to suggest that parents did not care at all about the happiness of their children or that they did not love them. Many parents seemed to work on the assumption that the well-adjusted and well-behaved child would be happy, and that the acceptable child would feel loved. The model for the happy child was the Girl scout and Boy scout.

Toward the end of the 1960s and into the 1970s the image of childhood changed, as did the image of adulthood. It was the era of the unencumbered, free spirit. The sons and daughters raised in the era of the good citizen were taught that it was their duty above all to raise happy children. The happy child was one who felt loved and admired without condition and was free to express whatever he or she thought, felt, or wanted.

I took my first psychology courses just at the time of this transition. Being a psychologist was a very inviting prospect. The discipline was in the forefront of the new cultural trend. It was the era for embracing nature.

I don't know that I consciously understood all of this when, as a seventeen-year-old college student, I chose to major in psychology. I did sense as I read and studied psychology that it had a certain spirit of adventure. In some other disciplines I had to push myself to keep reading, and going to class was a chore. Now and then in psychology I could hardly put the book down, and I was often eager for the next class. It seemed lively and current. And it seemed real because what we talked about in class I could see all around me.

There were other disciplines that appealed to me: literature, the visual arts, drama, and music. But I never thought of these as careers. I did not believe that I had the natural talent to be able to produce something beautiful in these fields. I do think that if I had pursued any one of them I could have become a skilled enough observer to be a good teacher. But the pull of that was not strong enough.

The other career that tugged at me was medicine. I liked the idea of a science uncovering hidden levels of vital events. Why do humans live if they can absorb oxygen and die if they cannot? Why can an organism so tiny that it evades the human eye topple the human body? Why do bodies grow? Why do they heal when injured? Why do they eventually die?

Along with this natural curiosity about vital science I was drawn to the healer's art. Life and death, pain and ease, function and dysfunction seemed so basically human. One only needs to be ill, in pain, or facing death to know how profoundly embodied we are in life. Both medicine and psychology seemed to me to be closely in touch with where vitality and earthboundedness are most vivid.

As I look back now on my choice I see that there may have been another personal reason that I elected to study psychology. I grew up in a subculture that is quite squeamish about human nature. Little credit is given to feeling, impulse, and human motives. If they are acknowledged at all they are seen as something to harness and control. In my ethnic subculture people had deep feelings, basic human needs, and powerful motivations, but they rarely admitted them to themselves and certainly did not speak about them to others. The Dutch Americans among whom I was raised were passionate people; it is a well-kept secret.

Of course, just because the psyche is repressed and denied does not mean that it can be gotten rid of and forgotten. Instead, what happens is that the basic expressions of human nature get called by different names and described in nonpsychological terms. In some instances they are sublimated quite exquisitely.

For example, I think back to prominent public persons whose angry and hostile personalities were probably expressions in part of deep personal frustration and confusion. They were persons in distress and causing damage to others. But in the context of repression they were powerful in intimidating and controlling people. So, while their human nature came to expression, no one else's could with the same freedom or force. Where these dynamics were acted out in the religious arena, these persons were called soldiers of the cross and defenders of the faith. Things might have gone better were a spade called a spade.

I have always had a fascination with human nature. The boldly human. The things that people do because they can not keep themselves from them, and human nature is not easily diverted. Perhaps it is not strange that a discipline that uncovers human nature should be so interesting to a little girl raised in a strict and repressive subculture. I think I always knew that behind the quiet exteriors of the Dutch Americans there was another world. In the therapy room where now I do my work as a psychologist I have witnessed over and over that indeed it is so.

There is a deep sadness that I feel about these cautious and hidden lives. Just often enough I saw, although rarely in excessive ways, that they too are ambitious, resentful, anxious, and needy. I saw the frightened preach courage, the prophets of sacrifice act greedy, and the guardians of rationality engage in their own rationalizations. Even as a child I could see that things are not always as they appear to be. I know, because I know it in myself. How often and how easily this can be the case. So what does it prove? Not much about the goodness or badness of people. It is only more evidence to the fact that we are inescapably human.

As a child I saw it. I felt it. And I wanted to find a way to speak about it, to acknowledge it. I think that in my childhood the silence about human nature caused me deep loneliness. A feeling that I could not be together with others the way they were inside. I could only be together with others the way we wanted to appear.

My first escape from the silence was through literature. I have always felt delighted when words can be put to events. When the not yet spoken gets said or when the often spoken sings in a new way; it is such a relief. When I taught in a Christian college and circulated among faculty from similar schools, I was always impressed by how well-developed departments of literature were in these institutions. I think living in the world of literature was for many Christians an attempt to have it both ways. Their piety excluded them from a certain rawly human world, but their escape into literature let them wander in it mentally nonetheless.

Traditions of excessive religiosity that demand caution and restraint not only withhold permission to talk, but they also harness experience. Righteousness demands that you think before you act. In these traditions persons really do become convinced that we act as we do because we thought about it first. Their fascination with the justification of action is in part tied to their sensitivity to guilt.

Repressed persons are afraid of the unjustified action because they are afraid of divine disapproval. How can you avoid mistakes? By justifying your action in advance. And how can you justify your actions? By having ideas about them that explain and judge them before they are allowed to be. Sometimes the justifications only echo what has been determined by impulse, instinct, or will in the first place, but that is seldom recognized.

Frankly, I have never felt right in that framework. There is too much human nature that is prior to thought. There is too much that can not be understood until it happens. I do not believe that the way of wisdom requires that we never make a mistake. Instead I believe that the way of wisdom recommends the lively and spirited life. If along the way there are mistakes, then the way of wisdom recommends that we see them really and in the interests of life and happiness do what we can to not make them again.

I am convinced that genuine reflection is a very progressive process. It can empower change in the most wholesome directions. If we really know ourselves, if we live with our sense of the meaning of things wide open, the better choices are more often than not the happier and more inviting ones. Repression is not necessary. Human nature thrives on the good; it does not desire its own destruction.

I am convinced that there is far more vital power, far more potential for knowing mercy, grace, forgiveness, and growth in the expressive and daring life than there ever can be in the life intercepted by caution and thought. The sense of this is what drew me to psychology.

I Am a Post-Ecclesiastical Christian

In my childhood the church was our world. In adulthood the world is my church. I was raised in a family whose highest priorities involved correct faith and the preservation of a pure theological tradition. Today I see more clearly that the gospel has meaning in the world outside of the church, and I am often confused by what goes on in the church. For me the process of coming to spiritual consciousness has been a hard and ambivalent one. It still is not clear, nor is it easy. But I do know that it is more precious to me with the passing of time.

I was raised in the 1950s and 1960s, the fourth and youngest child in a minister's family. Life in our household was busy, and at the center of its concerns was the church. When our family focused on things together it focused on ideas. When we socialized it was with people who shared those ideas and could discuss them as if life and death depended on them.

Social occasions had a certain tone. The adults sat in the living room gathered around in a large circle and they talked about very serious things. These were not meetings; they were social occasions. There was always a steady supply of good food, sometimes a cigar or two, and on special occasions a round of dessert wine was served. But overlaying this hospitality there was serious discussion about theology and church politics.

The participants in the discussions were not all formally educated persons, but when it came to theology they were all experts because they read theological books and magazines, spent large blocks of time each week listening to heavy theological sermons, and discussed these same matters in church societies, consistory, and other church meetings.

If one were to count up the accumulated hours that the average adult had spent being taught and studying theology, I have no doubt that the total would be far more than the average minister spends in college and seminary during the course of training. I guess in this sense they were well-educated, although somewhat narrowly. Nonetheless the level of eloquence was remarkable. And the intensity and commitment was enough to leave a vivid impression on a child.

As a child I knew many other families like my own, but I also knew a few children in the neighborhood whose families went to church only on Christmas and Easter. The ways in which these families seemed different from mine went far beyond the matter of church participation. Our whole way of life was separatist, and it engendered a daily awareness of those who were like us and those who were different.

As a child I felt set apart by the things that I was allowed to do as well as the things that were required of me. For example, on Sunday when the other children in the neighborhood played, I spent the day in Sabbath quietness. We did not ride our bicycles, swim, go to stores, play ball, picnic, or do other leisure activities on Sunday. We went to church twice, had a large Sunday dinner, visited with other persons like ourselves, or rested and read. Overall, the Sabbath was a depressing day for me as a child, and even as an adult it took me a long while to shed a blanket of heaviness that always seemed to weigh me down on Sunday.

There were other customs too that set us apart. In our household, meals began with prayer and ended with scripture reading and prayer. My school days began and ended with prayer, and my day ended with bedtime prayers. There were not many arenas of my life that were not marked with religious custom, and for most important activities there was a well-developed religious justification. For example, education was viewed as a means of developing personal abilities so that one day those skills could be returned to the work of the Kingdom of God.

At one stage of my childhood we lived in a neighborhood that was not part of the Dutch ghetto. In spite of this the activities of our lives such as school, church, and family socializing were all done with fellow church members. But on my own in the neighborhood I became acquainted with playmates outside of this familiar circle. Among the ethnic Dutch they would have been referred to as Americans, even though we ourselves were all American citizens. I suppose they were Americans because the United States was their country of origin—at least as far as we knew. And among the members of my church these families were considered unchurched, even though they were all church members somewhere.

There were things about the lives of "American" families that fascinated me very much, although I knew that they did not fit into the ways of my family. For example, many of the neighborhood families started getting televisions in the 1950s, and in these households the set was on much of the time. At the neighbors I watched Saturday morning television and after school the Mickey Mouse Club. These were things never mentioned in my family. We did not have a television for a long time because it was considered unimportant as entertainment. As far as any information or education that television might offer, books and newspapers were considered better sources.

It also impressed me that my friends went to the movies on Saturdays. I recall one of my playmate's birthday parties that included games and party food at her house and a movie after. Although I can not recall today which film it was, I do recall that it was a Disney animation. I was not allowed to go, so when the other children left for the movies, I went home. It was not a struggle. I don't recall that I even discussed it with my parents. It was clear as crystal to me that we did not do that. I accepted that I was different.

I also recall that the father of one of my playmates was a baseball fan. The Detroit Tigers were an important matter in their household. I wondered sometimes what it was like to live in a house where the Tigers were important. In our household that was considered an unimportant preoccupation. To give too much energy to baseball would have been considered "worldly," and thus not a good thing to do.

The strict religious practices of my childhood reflected in the very fabric of our daily lives what was reinforced over and over again by the church: that we were in the world but not of the world. Our way of life was intended to keep us uncorrupted by events around us. If we were concerned at all with the world it was not to enjoy it but rather to reform it. There was no doubt about the fact that this world was not our home.

The experiences of my childhood have left me bewildered. I can see that there were some habits of living I learned as a child that served me well. I learned to be studious, to think through a body of ideas, to build a coherent argument, to comprehend a passage of writing, to articulate a statement clearly, and to use vocabulary with care and precision. Translated to a liberal arts setting these would all be considered valuable educational skills.

Beyond mere education I learned to take life seriously, to consider that choices have consequences, and to believe that the effects of my actions go beyond me. A clear sense of obligation to look at the meaning of things, to examine motives for action, to weigh the consequences of deeds was part of both the pietism and the theological systems that were everyday fare in my childhood.

I do believe that I was raised by parents who did their best to care for me. They worked hard to feed, clothe, and shelter their children. Given the circumstances of their lives and ours they did all that they knew to do to bring us up well. Particularly in the case of my mother, devotion to her children and her family was apparent. She wanted very much for everything to go well.

There was a deep personal pietism that underlay our family life. When life was difficult, when well-assembled intentions came apart at the seams, or when tragedy struck there was genuine comfort in this piety. It rested in the firm belief that the future and the past are in God's hands.

Woven through my memories of childhood and church there is also a deep sense of pathos. I have come to realize that as much as life was made orderly and secure by the theology that bound it, that same theology weighed down the spirit. Preoccupation with religious practice and religious ideas took us out of the world and detached us from so much that was meant for us and is good. In some sense it even robbed us of ourselves, because we lived with a practiced sense of indifference to ourselves.

Today I believe there is good reason that persons who are excessively religious also tend toward anxiety and depression. They only live part time, and their spirits are rarely present in the here and now where their bodies are wearily waiting. Because they only half live, they only feel half-alive. Their lives are a delightful gift that they never get around to opening. I think that if God witnesses our loss, then there is sadness in heaven.

Calvinism has grown out of a long and strong scholastic tradition. Many Calvinists believe that God holds them accountable for having their theology straight. To believe an error—or even worse, to defend it to others—is a grave sin. As a result, conservative Calvinists work their ideas over endlessly to give them the appearance of coherence with the teachings of the Bible and the church. Unfortunately, when applied to the events of everyday life, these same teachings seem overwhelming. And injected into the consciousness of a child they create an insecurity that is difficult ever to overcome.

These are some of the assumptions that get planted in the consciousness of children long before a child would have the skills to question or doubt them: God is angry a lot because people (no exceptions) have misbehaved a lot. Although these people do not deserve it and there is no way to earn it, God has given some of them a second chance. Proof of the second chance is the good life. If you can not live the good life it may be because you are not included among those to whom the second chance has been given. There is always the risk that you could offend again and cause God to lose patience with you forever. If pious people more powerful than you lose patience with you, they may speak for God and tell you that God has lost patience with you too. On the one hand, you are told that the risk is not very great that God will give up on you; on the other hand, the list of ways to try God's patience is very long. Therefore you should live in fear of your own mistakes. The mistakes included are all those that issue from weakness of character or a break of conscience.

While I know in theory that a good Calvinist theologian would shoot holes in this formulation faster than you can say "sin," this mindset is nonetheless very pervasive in the naive views of Calvinism that are absorbed by children. While a more reasonable and encouraging formulation of theological doctrine may appear on the books, there is a quite frightening one that is in the air. It crushes the spirit; it drives the fumbling believer to the edge of hopelessness.

Never far from the awareness of the earnest Calvinist is a premonition of a very impatient and angry God. The possibility that you are able to make the eternal error is somehow more convincing than the security that God will hold on no matter what. While there is a certain conviction that God will hold on through tragedy, the terror is great that God will not hold on through sin.

The intense fear of God's anger has some rather debilitating effects. It tends to make one more afraid of mistakes and limits than aware and honest about them. It is too easy to choose a rigid and ultracareful life in order to be convinced that whatever sins one does commit are minor enough to keep it simple and safe. And because the denial of mistakes is rampant, learning from them is rare.

If one does not have the discipline of spirit to live the ultracareful life, there is another set of consequences. I think this was my way. I do recall as a child believing that I had not sinned very much, because I knew that to be saved I needed to keep my record clear. I was not very good at it, and I also came quite soon to the realization that the belief in my own innocence was an arrogant assumption. At that point I began to worry about the sins I had committed and chosen to forget. I felt trapped because, if I could not remember them, I could not repent of them and be forgiven either.

It did not take long in my life for me to realize that my early concerns were purely academic. The standard was high. I was not a particularly rebellious child. However, I was not comfortable with what I thought was expected of me. The sacrifices were too great, and life was too inviting. For instance, I was burdened with guilt because I envied my secular friends their simpler and more exciting lives. But the very fact that I was envious was evidence to me that I was not a good person. It seemed that in my childhood there were infinite ways to sin and only a few ways to be righteous. Unfortunately, the most righteous ways were not very interesting to a child.

It was hard to deny myself an interest in human nature. I liked things that were human and lively. It was terribly disappointing to me that so many of these things were deemed worldly. When I was twelve years old I went with a friend to see a movie. I did not have my parents' permission, and I knew that if I had asked for it I would not have received it. Acting in defiance of them was a double jeopardy. Not only was I running the risk of disturbing them if they found out, but even if they did not find out, I believed that God knew I had defied my parents, and that was sin.

At times in my life I have thought that my parents, teachers, or ministers were responsible for the religious repression that crushes so many anxious Christians. However, I know that they too were its victims. Anyone who has lived in a separatist tradition knows how hard it is to resist the world and set life aside. But anyone who has lived in a separatist tradition also knows that the pressures to conform are powerful, and the price of resistance can be rejection and isolation. In order to even question the tradition, one needs to have confidence that it is possible to survive outside of the circle that closes some in and others out.

I have disentangled myself from many of the claims that church made on my childhood. The arbitrariness of much of its behavioral restrictions has become clearer to me. With each step of testing I could see that the mere fact of keeping or breaking these rules did not distinguish good from bad people. As I have had increasing exposure to persons who do not feel the need to disavow the world in order to love God, I have become convinced that the world is not a prison. It is a garden. And both its nature and culture are ours to admire and enjoy. When we do, we sense God more clearly.

But second, and perhaps more important, I have now lived long enough to see how hard it is for me to be honest within the church. The company of the saints does not invite my honesty; I am afraid of them. The church may be a place where one celebrates shortcomings that have been overcome, but it is hardly a place to acknowledge the ones that are ongoing. To really grasp the meaning of the gospel I need to encounter it in life one small step at a time. I can go to the dark side of guilt all by myself, but I can only find the light of grace when I experience the love of others; the real love of others that is willing to embrace me honestly, as I am. The church can talk about it, but talk is no substitute for the experience of living. Grace has been most potent in my life outside of the church; guilt has been more potent in it.

It is in the world, not in the church, that I have been confronted on every side by the question, what is really important? And while I can not say a lot about it, steadily and more deeply I sense that *LOVE* is important. I know that it sounds strange and abstract stated that way. There have been times in my life when I would not have stuck around to hear any more from someone who started out that way. As a Christian I would have discounted it as humanistic. As an intellectual I would have discounted it as simple-minded, undefinable, and indefensible. But it is in face-to-face encounters with real people, it is in daily ways when I have seen love at work, or have seen how cold the absence of it is, that my mind has been changed.

Living has taught me that love is neither shapeless, soft-headed, or unintelligent. It is not artificial, egocentric, easy or vain. Rather slowly, and through a glass darkly, I have come to sense that it is the most faithful reflection of God's presence in the world. When love makes a difference I know that grace is touching down, and God is willing to be present in a form that I can understand. I know that it is good to be where this is happening, and I know that my spirit is well-cared for there.

As I have experienced what love means in my life (generosity, kindness, mercy, and forgiveness) it has changed me. It is not always there vividly, but it is there in brief glimpses and in a steady sequence. For me, a person who has spent a lot of energy in the pursuit of good and solid ideas, noble and durable principles, and just and righteous causes, this realization represents a sort of spiritual meltdown. As I come to understand that love is more fundamental than the systems of knowledge in which I once anchored myself, I am learning something new. This new genre of knowledge is more solid than what I have known before. And while it is not easier, it is simpler.

The simpler way makes ordinary events seem more important, and it makes important events seem more ordinary. The simpler way lifts the burden of taking everything so seriously, and at the same time it leaves room for taking whatever is here and now quite seriously. In all of this I am coming to realize that I know less and less with certainty. But I am also coming to trust more deeply that there are some things certainly worth knowing. These are the things that life teaches me wherever the way of love does God's work. This work is not bound in by the walls of the church. It is everywhere, and sometimes in the most unexpected places. Convinced of this, today I am a post-ecclesiastical Christian.

Epilogue: Reflections on Telling the Story

Telling a part of my own life story has been refreshing and helpful. It is heartening to scan the years and see that, what from day to day seem like ordinary and scattered events, do form a story.

At first as I wrote it seemed like a difficult project. I suspect I was in the mode of trying to inform someone else about the important details of my life. It was hard to know which details to focus on and in which order to present them. In fact, I experienced so much difficulty trying to assemble my story this way that I set aside the first few pages and decided to start over completely.

When I began again I decided to forget about an audience or reader and prime the pump of my own thinking. I began an inner dialogue in which I tried to say for myself what I feel are the important themes in my life. This got me started. As I proceeded with my inner dialogue it became clear to me that this dialogue is my story. If I want to tell someone something about who I am, the most authentic way is to disclose something of how I know myself.

There were some other things that became clearer to me as I wrote. Through the process of writing I came to know some things about myself in a way that I did not know them before. Sometimes when the writing was easiest it seemed to flow quite effortlessly from out of my thoughts. Especially when it was most effortless and natural I surprised myself here and there by the way I said things. It was not that I did not know what I intended to say, but I was surprised that an image or memory that was mine, but never before formed for words, was now transformed by words.

The process of writing also formed me. As I scanned my own life I came to a clearer sense of my own destiny. On a naive level I have always thought that having a destiny required grandiosity. How can I believe that I am special, that there are particular intentions for my life, that my life has a purpose in a particular time and place? Doesn't this lead to some kind of inflation?

In pausing to look at my life I came to realize—with great joy and relief—what a simple thing destiny is. What it first of all requires is that I embrace the ordinary contingencies of my life. I was born into a particular ethnicity through no choice of my own. I did not create it; I was formed by it. It was my destiny. I was born female; that is a fact, and it is a gift. It is also my destiny. My personality and disposition is bred in the bone. I can live through it or fight it, but I can not escape it. It is my destiny. I struggle with the particulars of belief, but there are also some realities that I can not deny because they are the sacred conditions of my life. These too are my destiny.

The facts of my life, which I see now are my destiny, are quite ordinary. They are not accomplishments; they are starting points. In living my destiny I let them be. Discovering that is a great relief. I do not have to find a destiny: I have one.

As ordinary as these contingencies of my life are, they also bear with them an element of mystery, because the full meaning of them is not yet clear. There is always more of them yet to be discovered. And there is joy and a deep sense of significance in this discovery. These conditions of my life are fulfilling, but I sense they will never completely be fulfilled as long as my life goes on. They are a continuing source of vitality and surprise.

The realization to which I came as I wrote is deeply rewarding for me. It makes me aware that even if no one were ever to read the pages

I have written, writing them would still have its own reward for me. For me the experience has already been good. At the same time, it is with pleasure that I share what I have written, because I can feel that it has come from me gently, and in sharing it with others I am sharing a part of my life.

3

A Hope and a Future
(Jer. 29:11 NIV)

Bonnidell Clouse

It is fitting that an educational psychologist begin her story with a quote from the father of educational psychology, Edward L. Thorndike:

> Obviously I have not "carried out my career," as the biographers say. Rather it has been a conglomerate, amassed under the pressure of varied opportunities and demands. Probably it would have been wiser to plan a more consistent and unified life-work in accord with interest and capacity, but I am not sure. Even in the case of great men, there is considerable evidence that the man's own interests and plans may not cause a better output than his demands from outside.[1]

Some of us have found ourselves in like circumstances. The plans that we made, the interests we wished to pursue, the specific areas of concern that we had in the past are not the plans, the interests, the concerns we are encountering at the present time. If one would

1. Thorndike, Edward Lee. 1936. *A history of psychology in autobiography,* vol. 3, ed. Carl Murchison, 263–70. Worcester: Clark University Press.

insist that the calling of the believer in terms of a life work is a once-and-for-all situation with details fairly well specified, and that what was felt in the past to be God's will for one's life is what one should be doing presently, the result often would be disappointment and disillusionment. Fortunately, this is not the case. God uses the pressures and demands of our daily existence to direct our steps. Many of us can say with the servant of Abraham, "I being in the way, the Lord led me" (Gen. 24:27 KJV).

My earliest plan for Christian service was to be a missionary, probably in Africa, although the location was not certain. This desire came partially from the unwritten, but nevertheless well understood assumption prevalent in many fundamentalist churches: that the value of Christian service is determined by its position within a hierarchy. This runs from lowest to highest value as follows: Christian lay person within the church, elder or deacon within the church, minister of the local congregation, evangelist, home missionary, and foreign missionary. This desire was also increased by the large number of missionaries who came to our church, visited in our home, and were a source of considerable interest and inspiration.

The Early Years

I was born in San Jose, Costa Rica, the second of three children and the only girl. My parents, Ranselaer Barrows and Lela Freeland, were serving under the Central American Mission at the time. They had met at Manaul School in Albuquerque, New Mexico in 1923, where Mother taught typing and shorthand and Father was principal of the school. As she was the prettiest of the single women on the staff, he decided she was the one he would pursue. Even as he admired her beauty, she admired his intellect. It seemed he could converse on any subject and would explain the constellations of the stars as they took long walks in the evening. "When did you learn all this?" she would ask; and he would respond, "When you were out partying and dancing."

Mother was not a Christian at the time. She had grown up in an affluent Canadian home where money was everything and education was nothing. Raised by servants, she seldom saw her parents, who were occupied with their three stores and thirteen farms. By contrast, my father grew up poor, but education was important as it prepared one to better serve the Lord. Coming from a line of ministers and missionaries, he had graduated from Wheaton the year before they met. When he explained the way of salvation to her she was immediately receptive and became an ardent convert. Together they decided to become missionaries. During their engagement she took a year of study at the Bible Institute of Los Angeles and he earned a master's degree at the University of Arizona in Tucson.

I was two years old when my parents returned to the states and do not remember Costa Rica. My father's health had never been good and the damp weather and a bout with malaria proved too much to remain in Central America. We came to California on a banana boat and took up residence in a community of homes owned by a Mrs. Suppes, who allowed returning missionaries two years free rent. It was her gift to the Lord's work. I've often thought what a saint she was.

My earliest recollections were of that place. I can still recall in detail the arrangement of the rooms, the people we knew, what we had to eat, and some of the conversations. I was three years old and much of what I remember was never told to me by anyone. My older brother and I were very close and we would go everywhere together. Our favorite place was halfway up the hill to where Mrs. Suppes lived. She had provided swings for the children to play on and we enjoyed it immensely. Once there was talk of a robbery in the neighborhood and mother quoted the verse, "Men love darkness rather than light because their deeds are evil." I was sure if we would write that on a piece of paper and put it on the outside of our door that anyone who would be tempted to steal would be so ashamed he would never enter our house.

Father worked at the Bible House of Los Angeles, but the pay was so low that there was not enough money even for food. Once a week a man would bring a dozen eggs and occasionally other food would appear on our doorstep. It was a pattern that occurred at other times and in other places during my childhood. One might say that God takes care of his own. One might also say that "the life of faith," as it has often been called, can be quite humiliating. That was the depression era, however, and many people suffered whether or not they were religious.

The years between four and seven were very painful ones and I have tried to shut them out of my memory. Our two years at Mrs. Suppes were up and we had to move. Mother was ill part of the time and unable to care for us. I was afraid of everything and stayed close to my older brother, Irvin. Sometimes a kind soul would invite us into her house and give us something to eat. When Irvin went to kindergarten I went with him. He was five and I was four and neither of us spoke English, but we soon learned and would talk English at school and Spanish at home. Since then we have both forgotten Spanish.

When I was five we moved to a Faith Home for Children where Father was the teacher for grades five through eight. It was a two-room school and I was in first grade in the other room. Although the home was established to take in unwanted children and care for them in the name of Christ, the children were often treated in a very cruel way. My brothers and I were safe from such actions because our parents were with us, but seeing even toddlers beaten for minor infractions was frightening. There were some bright spots, though. I read everything I could get my hands on, including Bunyan's *Pilgrim's Progress.* Mother helped me with the words I did not know. I also took a few piano lessons and practiced whenever I had the opportunity. "Thursday's child has far to go," mother would say. I accepted it as destiny.

Growing Up in Phoenix

We left for Arizona when I was seven. My father had been asked by a Leland Entrekin to come teach at Phoenix Bible Institute. We would be given a house and a monthly salary. The house turned out to be slum property barely fit for human habitation (the land is now part of Sky Harbor Airport) and the salary lasted one month. So Father began doing carpentry work to earn a living, as well as continuing to teach at the Bible Institute. I enrolled in second grade and enjoyed being the top student in the class and also the fastest runner.

I didn't enjoy, though, having to sit in the room all by myself while the rest of the class went to see a film. My parents forbid us from engaging in any part of school life other than the regular classroom. A film was especially suspect, as it might be a "movie," and movies were of the devil. My mother had rejected every part of her old life. This despite the fact that her brother was a movie producer and later became General Eisenhower's chief photographer during World War II. His wife was a movie star and I would sometimes see my Aunt June's name on the theatre marquee as I was growing up. But I knew I would never be able to see her in pictures. When I was four years old, she gave me a large cloth doll that I called "Poochie." Poochie was my favorite doll and just about my only toy.

My parents worked hard and were excellent role models when it came to personal integrity and a sincere desire to serve the Lord. However, no affection was ever expressed in our household, either physically or verbally. The only exception was that on occasion my father would tell my mother how attractive she was. Father was a thoroughgoing pacifist and never raised his voice to her or spoke unkindly to her. But to grow up in a home where seemingly no interest is shown by parents in their children, other than what they will become as adults, is not pleasant. It was not until I established my own home and had children of my own that I was delivered from the pain that it brought. I was very fond of my father, though. I thought he was the most intelligent and kindest person I knew. I loved his dry wit and would have a feeling of pride whenever we were together. We always got Sunday dinner ready and would joke as much as we worked.

The Bible Institute was housed in a large building in downtown Phoenix and a number of students lived there. Our family was assigned two rooms on the second floor, but later we moved to one of the basements where tires were stored. Phoenix was a sleepy little tourist town in the late 1930s; I walked across a number of vacant lots on my way to school. The two big events of the year were the rodeo and the circus, and everyone turned out for these. Father enjoyed teaching and talking with his students; mother made lists of what my brothers and I were to do each day, which included cooking, dishes, and cleaning. One of my jobs was to darn all the socks for the family.

Father had a Scripture verse for every occasion. If the topic of conversation was unpleasant, he would say, "Whatsoever things are true, whatsoever things are honest, whatsoever things are just, whatsoever things are pure, whatsoever things are lovely, whatsoever things are of good report; if there be any virtue, and if there be any praise, think on these things." If speech became peppered with too many adjectives or adverbs, it was "Let your yea be yea, and your nay, nay." When my brothers and I would quarrel, we could expect to hear, "How good and pleasant it is for brethren to dwell together in unity. It is like the precious ointment upon the head, that ran down upon the beard, even Aaron's beard: that went down to the skirts of his garments." When Father spoke we listened. The Bible was sacred and not to be argued with. Often at night after I went to bed I would hear my father walking back and forth in the living room quoting psalm after psalm. "The heavens declare the glory of God; and the firmament showeth his handiwork. Day unto day uttereth speech, and night unto night showeth knowledge. There is no speech nor language, where their voice is not heard . . ." And I would go to sleep.

If my father loved the Bible, my mother taught it like a drill sergeant. Time was spent each day learning Bible facts, having "sword drills" to see who could find a verse in the Bible the fastest, and of course memorizing passages of Scripture. By the time I was seven I had learned several chapters, King James perfect, including Joshua 1, Romans 8, and Hebrews 11, and was expected to recite them for company or church groups. It was embarrassing but I had to do what I was told. In retrospect I believe that, even though I should not have been asked to do this, nevertheless I owe my parents a debt of gratitude for teaching me the English Bible. It was a truly great gift, and one that has served me well both in my personal life and in relating Scripture and psychology.

We purchased a house three miles from downtown Phoenix outside the city limits when I was in the eighth grade. It was small for a family of five but to us it was beautiful. Father put his carpentry skills to work and literally raised the roof, making several rooms upstairs. Because of the heat, my brothers and I slept outside six months of the year. We would put our cots under the clothesline, drape mosquito netting over the line, and tuck the netting under the mattresses. Every eighth night the irrigation water would flood the yard. In the morning we would pull our cots three or four inches out of the ground and look for our shoes that had floated away. The government Indian School was two blocks from us, and we would ride our bicycles there to see the pigs and other farm animals. Adobe houses, vacant lots, huge sunflowers, and unshaved palm trees dotted the landscape. I loved Phoenix. Sometimes now I become nostalgic for it, but then I remember that Phoenix today is not the Phoenix I knew before World War II. A big city has taken over like a huge monster, gobbling the beauty of the place and destroying its tranquility. The last two times I was there, in 1965 and 1978, were for my parents' funerals. I was glad to return to the midwest as quickly as possible.

Wheaton College

I was told from the time I was small that I would go to Wheaton. Not only my father but my aunts and uncle had graduated from Wheaton, and I looked forward to the day when I would do the same. Because there was no money to send me, mother took small children into our home to care for when I was in high school. We kept them twenty-four hours a day, some for several months, others for as long as two years. When I wasn't studying for my classes I would help her feed them in shifts, bathe them, or wash the endless piles of clothes. We took good care of them and there were always one or two babies I would bond with and wish I could adopt. I loved children and decided I wanted a dozen. I will always be grateful to my mother for providing a way for me to go on to school.

At Wheaton I decided to major in Christian Education but soon learned it was not for me. I had no artistic ability with which to draw pictures of the events in the New Testament on long white sheets of paper that stretched the length of the room. Surely I could be a missionary and major in something else.

My sophomore year I attended Arizona State University in Tempe, taking the bus each day from Phoenix. One of my classes was in general psychology and I immediately took a liking to it. When I returned to Wheaton for my junior and senior years I had no doubt what my major would be. Psychology was what I wanted to study. It was a wise choice. No matter what area of psychology I studied, I was fascinated with it. Once when my father was looking over my notes he remarked that the psychology he took at Wheaton in the early 1920s was, as he put it: "one-third ethics, one-third philosophy, and one-third something like you are studying now."

At Arizona State I had taken a course on the Old Testament prophets from a Jewish rabbi. Rabbi Khron believed that Jesus was a great prophet, but no greater than Amos, who was the greatest of all. It was the first time I had encountered a religion that differed from my own and it shook me to the core. I couldn't talk with anyone at church about it because it would mean raised eyebrows, whispers, and prayers on my behalf on Wednesday evening. That would be too embarrassing and would devastate my parents. It didn't help that the Rabbi was gracious, intelligent, and quite willing for me to dialogue with him, whereas the minister of the church I attended was bigoted and narrow, even criticizing those of us who went to college because, after all, the Lord was coming soon and we should be spending all our time witnessing.

I broached the subject to Kenneth Kantzer, who was my Bible teacher at Wheaton that fall, and he gave me very good advice, including the suggestion that I attend a church where I could respect the minister intellectually. It also helped that I now was where I could respect my teachers for their abilities, and they believed in the Christian faith. A Christian college may not be the place for all Christian young people, but I have no doubt that it was providential that I be there at that critical time in my life.

I had excellent teachers at Wheaton. Besides Kenneth Kantzer I especially remember Russell Mixter for biology, Arthur Volle for tests and measurement, Paul Wright for geology, Lamberta Voget for sociology, and Philip Marquart and Jean Kline for psychology. Each one had a profound effect on my life and I am thankful for them. The daily chapel services at which President V. Raymond Edman often spoke were a source of inspiration as well.

With the encouragement of Dr. Marquart, several of us formed a psychology club. The "nifty class of fifty" had only two or three psychology majors, but we got others who were taking psychology to join us. We met once a month in the evening. That meant we had to reserve a room so it would be unlocked at the appointed time. One evening we found the room already occupied by people on their knees praying. Dr. Marquart paced back and forth becoming increasingly agitated, insisting that it was a plot by the college because—as he put it—Wheaton did not like the psychology department, nor did it want psychology taught on campus. That a group of young people who wished to pray had happened upon an unlocked room and proceeded to use it was not something that occurred to him. Whether there was any basis for his remarks I do not know, but the idea of possible persecution did serve to give us a sense of oneness and a feeling that we must be quite important indeed.

Dr. Marquart had been a psychiatrist in the armed forces and taught most of the courses in psychology. As a medical doctor he was especially gifted in the area of clinical psychiatry and did an excellent job with psychoanalysis, the Rorschach test, and case studies. He seemed uneasy around women and said that the girls in the dorm spent much of their time kicking each other and screaming, but once he got to know you he would begin to relax. I considered him to be not only an excellent teacher but also my friend. We continued to correspond for a number of years after I graduated.

During my junior year I spent increasing amounts of time reading the Bible and praying, both in the prayer room in Blanchard and in my dorm room at North Hall. I was captivated by the writings of the prophets, and as I read Isaiah, Jeremiah, Hosea, and Amos I would ask God to speak to me. I became especially moved by the dialogue between Jeremiah and the Lord, with Jeremiah questioning the evil in the world and God answering in terms of his own treatment by his chosen people. I could picture the desolate land with seemingly no one to care and the speckled bird that was mocked by the other birds. I could feel Jeremiah's terrible despair when he said he could no longer speak in the Lord's name and had decided to give it up. But then Jeremiah did an about face, realizing that this course of action was unthinkable. "For the word of the Lord was like a fire in my bones and I could not stay," he wrote.

Dedication to God's service surely means different things to different people. Each of us is unique and God calls us in a variety of ways. Going in front of the church after a service may be all right for some people but it never appealed to me. I had long been irritated with evangelists who ask the audience to "raise your hand if you know Jesus," or "stand if you want a closer walk with God," and I would keep my hand in my lap or continue sitting. I couldn't see what right they had to pry into my personal life, especially in public. But God's call to Jeremiah was different. This was One-on-one. No alter calls. No singing of twelve verses of "Just As I Am." This was just the Lord and Jeremiah getting it all sorted out. Regardless of the circumstances and regardless of the consequences, Jeremiah knew he had to serve the Lord. He had to do what God had called him to do. And then there was the wonderful promise given to Jeremiah: "For I know the thoughts that I think toward you," saith the Lord, "thoughts of peace, and not of evil, to give you an expected end."

The New International Version puts it even more beautifully. "For I know the plans I have for you," declares the Lord, "plans to prosper you and not to harm you, plans to give you hope and a future" (Jer. 29:11). HOPE AND A FUTURE. What could be more exhilarating? Seeking to know God's will, and to do it, brings with it a promise that is better than anything offered by anyone or anything else. Jeremiah's doubts had been my doubts, his hesitation my hesitation, his feeling of fire in the bones when he heard the word of the Lord my feeling of fire when I read the prophets, his decision to obey the Lord my decision to seek God's will and do it, his promise of hope and a future my promise of the best God had in store for me. Whatever the future would bring it would be a part of the divine plan. I knew God had spoken to me and I was satisfied.

The Clinical Experience

After graduating from Wheaton I obtained employment as a psychiatric aide at the Institute of Living in Hartford, Connecticut and remained there for two years. Dr. Marquart's interest in clinical psychology had had its influence on me and I wanted the practical experience of working with patients, knowing it would give a very different perspective than that gleaned from textbooks. The Institute of

Living is one of the oldest private neuropsychiatric hospitals in the United States, being founded in 1822, and has an excellent reputation. I worked on a variety of units, from the profoundly psychotic to the mildly neurotic, and found the experience invaluable. My shift was from seven in the evening until seven the next morning, four nights running with two nights off. I met many fine people, both staff and "guests" (as the patients were called), but I experienced something I had never encountered before. When a person's whole life revolves around an institution—including housing, food, friends, and work—the very thought of leaving brings apprehension and sometimes panic. Several of the aides who had worked there for years told me they wanted to leave but could not. I had heard of circus people feeling this way, but I had never seen it first hand or come close to knowing the phenomenon myself.

My salvation came in finding a wonderful Bible-believing church in Hartford, where the people were warm and friendly, and where there was ample opportunity to socialize. I joined an excellent young people's group and had a few close friends to go places with. I also belonged to a "girl's trio" and we had the fun of singing in a number of churches in the area. My best friend, Doris Johnson, helped me to make the difficult decision not to stay at the Institute. I will always be thankful for the choice people God sends into our lives.

The summer between my junior and senior year at Wheaton I had worked as an attendant at Southern Wisconsin Colony at Union Grove. This had given me the opportunity to know better the outlook of retarded teenage girls and women. One of the valuable lessons I learned from them is that one's self-concept is in large measure dependent on who you compare yourself with. I have never been around prouder, more arrogant people than some of the "educable" residents there. They could go to work each day doing the laundry or setting tables at the institution, visit with each other or dance to music in the evening, and plan their strategies for the next escape. They felt quite superior to others who were bedfast or unable to talk, and called those less fortunate than themselves "dumb old things." Interestingly, I was relegated to the category of "dumb old thing" when they found I was returning to college that fall. They could not understand how someone who was all grown-up would still be going to school, unless she was indeed a "dumb old thing."

My second experience of working with the retarded came after I left the Institute of Living. I had returned to Phoenix and obtained work at Arizona Children's Colony in Coolidge the summer of 1952.

This time I was with babies and small children and thoroughly enjoyed it. We worked twelve-hour shifts and even though it was strenuous, involving constant lifting and carrying, I liked the children and was repaid many times over by the look in their eyes or an outstretched hand when I came near. I would have stayed longer but I had saved enough money to go to graduate school and it was time to move on.

Boston

That fall I began a program at Boston University leading to a master's degree in psychology. I survived mainly on peanut butter sandwiches, walked several miles to and from classes, and spent my time studying. On occasion I would go out with friends or buy a pair of shoes, which were my weakness. The higher the heels the better, and if they were suede that was better yet. I met my husband a year later who told me that one of the first things he noticed about me was my yellow suede shoes. Yellow suede shoes was one of the best investments I ever made.

If my memory serves me correctly about sixty students were admitted to the master's program at Boston University and were placed in the same courses, which covered a wide range of subjects. The classes were thorough, demanding, and provocative. Standardized tests were also administered that had to be passed. An unexpected delight was that on one occasion Henry Murray of Harvard spoke to our Psychology of Personality class, filling us in on his latest research. When asked during the discussion period about the Thematic Apperception Test, he appeared irritated, remarking that he had designed the T.A.T. so many years before that he had forgotten what it was about.

An excellent InterVarsity chapter met once a month and included students from several area schools such as Boston University, MIT, and Harvard. It was good to meet with other young people "of like precious faith." We were served tuna and noodle casserole each time we met. It tasted wonderful. While at Boston I attended Park Street Church under the ministry of Harold Ockenga. I usually went to the early morning service so I could get back to my studies and then would return for one or two evening services. On occasion I would go across the street to Tremont Temple. Both churches had inspiring services and I have often thought how great it would be if every city had such a place for people to worship and reach out to those who do not yet know our Lord.

In the spring of 1953 I received the desired degree. I now wanted to teach in a Christian college as it looked less and less as though I would become a missionary. I figured the next best thing was to teach those who would be going to the mission field. The placement bureau at Boston University told me of other college openings, but I had no interest in pursuing a career at a secular school.

Bryan College

I signed a contract to teach at Bryan University that fall. Bryan College, as it is now called, is located in Dayton, Tennessee and was established in memory of William Jennings Bryan who died soon after the Scopes trial that took place there. Through Dr. Marquart I heard that Bryan needed a teacher in my field, so I applied. Judson Rudd, president of the college at the time, was coming to Boston to collect books for the library, and we arranged to meet. It was breakfast at Howard Johnson's, then church at Park Street. Dr. Rudd told me later that when he saw my Scofield Bible he knew I was the right one for the job. I found that to be an interesting criterion for the position but if it worked it was all right with me. My Bible was well worn at the time. I had received it several years before from a group of ministers who preached on Sunday afternoons at the Maricopa County Jail in Phoenix, where I played a small folding organ that had to be braced against the wall so it would not "walk" all over the floor. I had had the Bible all through college and for the three years since that time. What could make a better impression in the 1950s than a well-worn Scofield Bible when one wished to teach in a Christian school?

At Bryan I was *the* psychology and education department. I had to teach all the courses in both disciplines. I knew some areas of psychology, but not others, and knew virtually nothing about education. Being conscientiously inclined, I did the best I could, trying to stay one jump ahead of the students. My Scofield Bible was not sufficient for the task, although I remember a member of the board of trustees asking me in front of President Rudd if I taught psychology from the Bible. He expected a "yes" answer. It was a tense moment.

All students at Bryan were required to take a course in general psychology prior to graduation. It was in this context that I became better acquainted with a young man named Bob Clouse, who was a senior the year I came, and who sat in the back row of the class with some of his friends. We had dated a couple of times before he enrolled for the course and I knew from some of the other professors that he delighted in asking questions teachers could not answer. I let him know that the first time he embarrassed me in class would be the last time I would go out with him. He never said a word the whole term, something those who know him would find hard to believe. There were times, however, when his friends would ask difficult questions and I had the feeling that he put them up to it.

Bryan College in the 1950s had a myriad of rules typical of Christian colleges at the time. Seniors could chaperone a couple until sundown, faculty after sundown. We worked out our own arrangement. Bob chaperoned the two of us until sundown and I took over the duties after that. We may have conformed to the letter of the law but certainly not the spirit of the law. There were two of us and "three" of everyone else. Students had to be in their dorm rooms by 10:30 each evening and midnight on weekends. We were late getting back from Chattanooga one evening and when the dean of the school heard about it he was angry. He told me he had something to say to me, took me in his big fancy car down to the lake and said, "You don't have to worry about Bob Clouse anymore. I'm going to send him home." Why the dean couldn't have just told me at school was a mystery to me. It was an awkward time to send Bob home, though, because Bob had been elected student body president and had just received the faculty award for having the highest grade point average of any student in the school. This may be why the dean decided to give the job to the assistant dean who would then be the one blamed if objections were raised.

The assistant dean was a very affable young teacher named Joe Raffa. We shared an office and got along great. The dean did not specify the punishment to be given to Bob but rather told Joe "to take care of it." Instead of sending Bob home Joe took care of it by confining Bob for a week to the building in which he lived, except for going to classes and to work. The nice part about it was that I lived in the same building two floors up. We met on the steps halfway.

One morning Joe told me we had to talk. So he took me into the chapel at Bryan and in hushed tones told me that he and his wife had been praying that if Bob and I were meant for each other that God would reveal it to us. I was flabbergasted. Bob and I were only friends and had no serious intentions. Besides, why didn't Joe just tell me in the office? Why the hush-hush of the chapel? As Bob and I look back on it we sometimes wonder if we might not have gone our separate ways if everyone had left us alone. But with the dean trying to send him home and the assistant dean praying that God would reveal to us if our relationship should be permanent, we couldn't just walk away from each other, at least not at the time. Other faculty and students were beginning to talk and observe and predict how things would go.

They went well. We became engaged the following spring and were married a year later in June of 1955.

And They Lived Happily . . .

The week of the wedding we were in a serious automobile accident. Driving on Highway 30 from Winona Lake, Indiana to Mansfield, Ohio—where we were to be married in the Grace Brethren Church—we collided with a semitruck coming from the opposite direction. There was no way to know who was at fault. It was night and the road was narrow, curvy, and slick with rain. The front left wheel of the car was sheered off and the door came in on Bob's leg. I was rendered unconscious and came to the next morning. A nurse was bent over me taking glass out of my head and I asked her if Bob was alive. I was relieved to find that he was but was told I had asked that same question dozens of times that night; the doctors and nurses had grown weary of answering me. The left side of my face was smashed, I had a skull concussion, and three vertebrae in my back were cracked. The truck driver had found me walking along the highway and got me into the car until the ambulance came. The state patrolman who wrote up the accident and picked up our belongings scattered along the shoulder of the road said he did not know how either of us survived.

We had no business getting married in that condition. Bob walked with a cane, and my cut face, black eye, and bruises that showed through my lace wedding gown did not make for a very pretty sight. We had no car, nor could we have driven one. But my parents had come from Phoenix, my maid of honor (Doris Johnson) from Hartford, Connecticut, my bride's maid from northern Indiana, my brother Thornton and his wife from Wheaton, and the little flower girl and her parents (my brother Irvin and his wife) from St. Louis. It seemed we had to go through with it, even though the ceremony was cut short because it appeared Bob was going to faint. There was another snag as well. Our hospital stay meant we were not in Mansfield a sufficient number of days to get a license before the wedding. Bob's uncle who was a lawyer said he would take care of it. We assumed he did. Bob jokingly says we may have been living in sin all these years, and that would make our relationship even more interesting.

The night of the wedding everyone went to the church without us. I don't know how they thought we were going to get there. I guess they didn't want to be late and it was taking me too long to get dressed.

After they left, Bob helped me into my gown. Some out of town friends came by to ask the way to the church and we got a ride with them. Hundreds of people were there. I'm glad I didn't miss it.

Cedar Rapids, Iowa

The year was 1958 and the place was Cedar Rapids, Iowa. Pregnant with our first child I sat with my back against the arm of the sofa, my legs across the seat, and read *What Then Is Man?*[2] It was the first book I had seen that was a true integration of psychology and Christian faith. To say I was thrilled would be an understatement. Here at last was what I had been looking for years before. *What Then is Man?* developed from a symposium of theology, psychology, and psychiatry at Concordia Theological Seminary in St. Louis. Much of it was written by Paul Meehl who has served as president of the American Psychological Association and has received numerous honors, including APA's Gold Medal Award for Life Achievement in the Application of Psychology. Since my undergraduate days at Wheaton I had hoped such a book would be forthcoming.

At Wheaton, under the direction of Philip Marquart, some of us tried our hand at integrating a topic in psychology with Christian belief. Dr. Marquart had written on "basic anxiety," which he believed to be God-given to every person. Basic anxiety was the foundation of all motivation and worked for good when it turned a person to God, for ill when it led to neurotic behavior. He encouraged each of us to take a topic in psychology and endeavor to see how it related to Scripture or Christian theology. Our productions were meager at best but it set before us an exciting adventure.

In my mind one book would put it all together, and I had hoped to be the one who would write that book. Now someone else had already written it. That the field of integration is so vast that there is room for everyone, and the list of topics so numerous that one can pick and choose, was not something I was cognizant of at the time. I did know, however, that the articles and books I had seen up to that point that claimed to be an integration did not deliver what was promised. A presentation of psychological facts or theories followed by a few Scripture verses does not come close to the meaning of the term "integration."

2. Meehl, P., R. Klann, A. Schmieding, K. Breimeier, and S. Schroeder-Sloman. 1958. *What then is man?: A symposium of theology, psychology, and psychiatry*. St. Louis: Concordia.

On occasion I had had the good fortune of being with others of similar interest and would listen to their ideas. I remember one evening at Park Street Church in Boston when after a presentation on psychology at a young people's group, the speaker put three circles on the blackboard to represent Freud's id, ego, and superego and then proceeded to explain that the id represented sin in a person's life, the ego the intelligence God had given us to understand our world, and the superego the godlike portion of the personality. A listener then took the chalk, drew a large circle that encompassed the three on the board and wrote that all three were under sin; the id, ego, and superego are all examples of the old nature and in need of salvation. I was not sure at the time which position was correct although in reading *What Then Is Man?* it was spelled out that all three components of the personality are indeed under sin; the id being self-serving and impulsive, the ego inclined toward self-interest, and the superego used as an instrument of domination over others. The book is now in my office at the university, a symbol of the beginning of the fulfillment of an area of integration now shared with dozens of other psychologists who have penned their respective interests in relating psychology and Christianity.

We had moved to Cedar Rapids the spring of 1957 for Bob to pastor the Grace Brethren Church there. He had completed three years at Grace Theological Seminary in Winona Lake, Indiana and was ready to put his training to work. I contracted to teach first grade in the nearby town of Marion, but could not begin until after the birth of our child. I went to work when Gary was five weeks old. The next door neighbor took care of him during the day for the next few years, giving him the same love and training she gave her own son who was a few months older. I am eternally grateful to her. I taught in Marion for four years, attending summer school at Coe College in Cedar Rapids, until I had earned thirty hours of education credit to acquire a lifetime certificate to teach elementary school in the state of Iowa. Being a mother, a pastor's wife with all the duties thereof (including attending at least six services a week), and an elementary teacher kept me quite busy.

Bob was busy, too. Besides his duties as minister, he matriculated to the University of Iowa in Iowa City, about thirty miles away, and completed both the M.A. and the Ph.D. there. After graduating in 1963 he accepted a position teaching history at Indiana State University in Terre Haute; it was time to move again. I stayed in Cedar

Rapids for a few months to sell the house and Bob returned with a U-Haul at the end of the summer to move us to Terre Haute.

There is something very humbling about having all your possessions in one small truck. It makes you feel so little, so insignificant. All of your earthly goods are with you, traveling along the highway to a destination where you will begin a new life with new friends and new responsibilities. But seated between us in the front of the truck was a bright, beautiful four year old, our pride and joy, who made it all worthwhile. He had to cope with the disappointment of leaving his "other family" behind, but he too seemed eager to know what lay ahead.

Indiana University

After we settled in Terre Haute, I knew it was time for me to return to school. I had worked to put Bob through; now it was his turn to do the same for me. Indiana University was sixty miles down the road and I applied for their doctoral program in educational psychology. This seemed to be a logical choice as I now had a background in both psychology and education. I chose elementary education and psychology for my minor areas. Pregnant with our second child, I began classes. Both the pregnancy and the return to school were planned. I wanted another child and I wanted a Ph.D. As I was in my midthirties at the time it was not feasible to put off either. I knew that neither could be sacrificed for the other and that traveling time alone would take three hours a day. Consequently, I began with only two courses a semester, working up to a full load the last year while teaching classes every day as a graduate assistant.

Some of the women in the church were critical that I was going to school when I had a five-year-old and a new baby, but I had learned that one must do what he or she believes to be right. We did not feel we should let others play God for us. There is too much of that sort of thing going on, especially in religious circles. Besides, if fathers are not condemned for going to school or to work with small children in the home, mothers should not be either. Bob and I arranged our schedules so that one of us was home until Kenneth was about a year old. Again, we were blessed with an excellent baby-sitter after that time.

The first class I had at Indiana University was taught by Professor Clinton Chase who became my major advisor and chairperson of my doctoral committee. Dr. Chase was most helpful, and I owe the completion of the degree in large measure to his assistance and encouragement. Other excellent teachers were Larry Brown, Leo Fay, Stafford Clayton, Richard Turner, and Harold Shane. Numerous teaching positions were available in educational psychology when I finished my coursework in 1967, and I received several offers. However, it seemed best to stay near Indiana University until my dissertation was completed. I took a job at Indiana State University advising graduate students in elementary education and teaching courses in general psychology and child development. I was awarded the Ph.D. degree in 1968 and began teaching full time at Indiana State when the department of educational psychology was formed a year later.

Integrating Psychology and Christian Belief

Writing for publication came after I completed the doctorate. My dissertation was in the area of beginning reading methods for kindergarten and first-grade children and appeared in *Perceptual and Motor Skills*.[3] Papers that had been assigned at Indiana University were revised and subsequently printed in *Education*[4] and *Instructor*[5] magazines.

I had not lost sight of my desire to integrate psychology and Christianity. My earliest published attempts came with "Psychosocial Origins of Stability in the Christian Faith" for *Christianity Today*,[6] "Psychological Theories of Child Development: Implications for the Christian Family" for the *Journal of Psychology and Theology*,[7] and "Some Developmental Ideas of Jean Piaget" for the *Journal of the American Scientific Affiliation*.[8]

I was intrigued by the major psychologies, especially Freudian psychoanalysis and Piagetian developmental theory. "Ego and Superego Variables as Related to Moral Behavior,"[9] and "The Teachings of Jesus

3. Clouse, Bonnidell. 1971. Selected cues in the acquisition and retention of four meaningful C-V-C trigrams. *Perceptual and Motor Skills* 33 (August): 83–90.

4. Clouse, Bonnidell. 1971. Pressure groups and the public schools. *Education* 92 (September–October): 118–21.

5. Clouse, Bonnidell. 1971. Help children appreciate their language. *Instructor* 81 (December): 39–40.

6. Clouse, Bonnidell. 1970. Psychological origins of stability in the Christian faith. *Christianity Today* 14 (25 September): 12–14.

7. Clouse, Bonnidell. 1973. Psychological theories of child development: Implications for the Christian family. *Journal of Psychology and Theology* 1 (April): 77–87.

8. Clouse, Bonnidell. 1971. Some developmental ideas of Jean Piaget. *Journal of the American Scientific Affiliation* 23 (September): 104–8.

9. Clouse, Bonnidell. 1974. Ego and superego variables as related to moral behavior. *Journal of Psychology and Theology* 2:223–35.

and Piaget's Concept of Mature Moral Judgment,"[10] both published in *Journal of Psychology and Theology* in the 1970s, provided the opportunity to express my thoughts on these disparate orientations. The article on Piaget was reprinted in *Psychology and Christianity: Integrative Readings*[11] and requests for reprints came from professors all over the world.

Many variations of Freud's writings in the area of moral development can be found in the literature: Bruno Bettelheim, Robert Coles, Paul Meehl, Karl Menninger, and M. Scott Peck to name a few. Likewise, Piaget's *The Moral Judgment of the Child*[12] provided a basis for Lawrence Kohlberg's six stage sequence of moral reasoning that has in turn spawned an estimated 5,000 studies. The more I read in the area of morality the more interested I became. The Scriptures are the believer's basis for faith and morals, and although psychology does not deal with "faith" as such, it does deal with morality. This seemed a likely topic on which to base my efforts to contribute to the escalating interest in the integrative process.

I had in mind a book-length manuscript that would present the basic psychologies; give the philosophical assumptions of each; show how these assumptions translate to an explanation of how moral development takes place; apply each theory of moral development to the home, the school, and the church; and then see how each method is in accord with Christian theology. This meant I had to become as familiar with the literature in moral processes, as conceived by learning (behavioristic) psychologists and by humanistic psychologists, as I was in psychoanalysis and cognitive psychology.

At the undergraduate level I was teaching classes in human development. At the graduate level I was training students who were teachers and administrators in the schools to apply psychological theory to a variety of classroom problems. Consequently, the way I went about organizing the material for the book was already familiar and much of the content that would be included was known. Still, it took about four years to complete the writing. Teaching is only one of many tasks assigned to college professors. Furthermore, I had a family to

10. Clouse, Bonnidell. 1978. The teachings of Jesus and Piaget's concept of mature moral judgment. *Journal of Psychology and Theology* 6:175–82.

11. Clouse, Bonnidell. 1978. The teachings of Jesus and Piaget's concept of mature moral judgment. Reprinted in *Psychology and Christianity: Integrative readings,* eds. J. Roland Fleck and John D. Carter. Nashville: Abingdon, 1981.

12. Piaget, Jean. 1932. *The moral judgment of the child,* trans. M. Gabain. London: K. Paul, Trench, Trubner, & Co.

care for that provided interest and variety to my life and I was active in the work of the church. *Moral Development: Perspectives in Psychology and Christian Belief* was published in 1985 by Baker Book House.[13] I was pleased with the final product and with the book reviews that followed. I felt that at last I had fulfilled a long standing desire.

I have continued to write in the area of morality, although on occasion I will digress and pick up another topic. One example is the *Women in Ministry: Four Views*[14] book published in 1989. Bob has edited several "four views" books with InterVarsity Press, the best known being *The Meaning of the Millennium,*[15] now in its thirteenth printing. He asked if I would be willing to coedit the *Women in Ministry* book, as I had published two research studies on women and had also taught classes in the Women's Studies Program at Indiana State University. He felt that a psychological approach as well as a historical approach would strengthen the book.

The question of whether a woman should preach in the church was one that was of interest to both of us, and we had discussed it on a number of occasions. A little background on this is in order. Within a year of the time we arrived in Terre Haute in the early 1960s, Bob was asked to pastor a small Brethren church in the town of Clay City, thirty miles from Terre Haute. The church needed someone to preach on Sunday mornings, visit the sick, and perform weddings and funerals. It was to be a temporary arrangement, with the understanding that at any time either the church board or Bob could call it off, no feelings hurt. Bob agreed to serve on that basis.

When Bob would go to conferences or take a group of students to Europe, which he did every spring, there was no one to preach. One Sunday when the parishioners were discussing who should be contacted to speak, a woman who had been a member of the church for over sixty years suggested that the preacher's wife would be a good person to ask. As I was sitting right there, what could they say? The next Sunday I was in the pulpit and from then on, whenever Bob was out of town, I was expected to preach. If anyone had any objections, to my knowledge they were never voiced. Now after over twenty years of this arrangement it seems not to matter to the members of the

13. Clouse, Bonnidell. 1985. *Moral development: Perspectives in psychology and Christian belief.* Grand Rapids: Baker Book House.

14. Clouse, Bonnidell, and Robert Clouse, eds. 1989. *Women in ministry: Four views.* Downers Grove: InterVarsity Press.

15. Clouse, Robert, ed. 1977. *The meaning of the millennium.* Downers Grove: InterVarsity Press.

church which of us brings the message. As long as one of us is present, they are content. On occasion we are introduced to visitors as the pastors of the church. We have served the church for twenty-nine years and neither the church board nor Bob has ever suggested another arrangement. The people have grown to mean so much to us that we decided to dedicate the *Women in Ministry* book to them. The inscription reads:

To the Members and Friends of
the First Brethren Church
Clay City, Indiana,
whose fellowship has been our delight
whose faithfulness has been our inspiration
for a quarter of a century

In 1976 I was asked to serve as a contributing editor to the *Journal of Psychology and Theology* (JPT). JPT is an academically respectable refereed journal that serves as an evangelical forum for the integration of psychology and theology. A number of questions I have had have been answered by articles in JPT. It has been an honor to be a part of this endeavor. Another journal of a similar nature is the *Journal of Psychology and Christianity,* an official publication of the Christian Association for Psychological Studies, designed to provide scholarly interchange among Christian professionals in psychological and pastoral professions. I had the privilege of being the guest editor for the Winter 1991 issue on "Moral Development and Justice." I find it most gratifying to see so many young people who are pursuing the area of integration in a much more sophisticated way than many of us ever dreamed possible in the 1950s. These journals and others, plus a number of books and dozens of articles in other publications, show the growing interest in this field.

Relating Psychology and Christianity in the Classroom

The printed page is not the only avenue of expression in the integrative process. I have found that relating Christian faith to what I teach in the classroom is as natural as anything else I may do. For the teacher who is familiar with Scripture, using phrases from the Bible or giving examples from its passages is as easy as quoting any source one has knowledge of or giving illustrations from everyday experiences. This does not mean, of course, that I teach my psychology classes from the Scofield Bible or any other translation of Holy Writ. But it does mean that Freud's idea of innate passions and aggressive urges can be compared to the Christian doctrine of innate depravity, thus signaling our need for salvation; that Skinner's view of the human organism responding to reinforcers and punishers in the environment is informative in helping us to better understand the way God created us, and in turn provides the learning experiences that are optimal; that Piaget's cognitive developmental stages are basic to our knowledge of what children perceive at various ages, so that we can enjoy and appreciate each child at his or her level, and present those concepts, including the religious, that are most meaningful.

When giving Combs' perceptual view of intelligence and mentioning the symbolic or vicarious kinds of environmental effects that limit perception, the term "vicarious"—which is not known to some students—can be explained by using the example of the vicarious atonement of Christ and explaining what this means. Many of the students go to church and may have heard the word in this context. When lecturing on Erikson's seventh stage, the mature stage of generativity, and describing what Erikson meant when he said that unless a man loses his life in a cause he will not find it, one can pick up on the Scripture from which Erikson took this phrase and explain what Jesus meant when he told his disciples the same thing.

The possibilities are limitless. But it must be done in the context of the subject matter at hand, often as one of several illustrations given to demonstrate an idea or concept, and never in a laborious manner. I never really plan these types of statements, but because this is what naturally comes to mind, this is what is presented. It seems that psychology, perhaps more than most disciplines, lends itself nicely to such an approach.

It is the nature of state universities to be tolerant of varying ideas and concepts. Freedom of speech is prized and less regulation is imposed than in many institutions. I have profited from this in that it has given me the freedom to share my Christian faith. It is expected, of course, that one will have the same tolerance for those who disagree, and dialogue is always in order.

Students in my classes tend to come from conservative communities, and college opens to them a large variety of options. It is easy to become confused. Needed is someone who holds out to them the idea that the faith they have known since childhood still remains a viable and desirable option. Some are intrigued that my political and social views tend to be toward the liberal end of the continuum, but my religious views are bedrock conservative. If they ask about this I refer them to the life of Jesus. Our Lord turned the world upside down, showing kindness to women, children, and the dispossessed while calling down anathemas on those with power and money. Yet he said, "I am *the* way, *the* truth, and *the* life." When it came to the spiritual, no one was more orthodox than he. There is only *one* way to salvation and that is through our Lord Jesus Christ.

My joy comes from students who come to my office to share their faith in God, to seek encouragement, or to tell about someone they are trying to win to Christ. It comes from the occasional note penned at the end of a final examination, a slip of paper slid under the office door, or a letter in the mail after the semester is over saying how much it meant to have a professor who is a Christian and is not afraid to speak out. One student wrote: "I learned . . . that I need not feel self-conscious when I acknowledge my relationship with Christ"; and another: "You've given me the courage to stand for truth as a Christian in my class."

Little did I realize when I received my call to serve God while a junior in college that it would take me to a state university. But I have no doubt that this is where I should be. On occasion Bob or I have been offered a position elsewhere and some of the offers have been quite tempting. Perhaps someday we will serve in a different capacity or in a different place, but that remains to be seen. Again, we can say with the servant of Abraham, "I, being in the way, the Lord led me." I know now that the value of Christian service is not determined by its position within a hierarchy that runs from Christian lay person as the least favored to foreign missionary as the most favored. God uses people in all areas of life to do his will. Regardless of our line of work, we are privileged to serve him.

Sometimes students who have taken classes from both Bob and me, who see what different personalities we have and that we teach very different subjects, will ask what we talk about when we are together. I suppose the answer is that we talk endlessly about a host of topics: our children (and now our grandchildren), our work at the university, our many friends, how much our Christian faith means to us, how happy we are that we still have each other (especially in light of the fact that without a heart transplant in July of 1985 Bob would not have survived),* and what we can do to help the many people we know who are in need. We also engage in the kind of talk that

* The story of Bob's transplant was told in the March 1988 issue of *Christianity Today,* in which he was featured on the cover, and in the November 1989 issue of *Second Opinion.* It is scheduled for publication in book form by *Brethren Press.*

might be called "bantering." We seize on a word the other has said, give it a slightly different meaning or place it in a different context, and wait for the subsequent reaction. It is a form of ridiculous verbalization but usually ends with one or the other saying something that brings a flood of memories—usually pleasant events that are shared only by someone you have lived with for many years and whom you love and enjoy.

Varied Opportunities and Demands

At the beginning of this brief autobiography I quoted Edward L. Thorndike as stating that his career had been more a conglomerate than a consistent and unified lifework. This was because he was expected to respond to the opportunities and demands given him at the moment rather than follow his own long-range desires. But in the end, it seemed that it turned out just as well and the output was just as great.

All of us have demands placed upon us and all of us have opportunities as well. Let me fasten on a couple of opportunities not yet mentioned that contribute to the rich life I now enjoy.

First, Bob and I are sponsors of the African students at Indiana State and their friendship has meant a lot to us. On Thanksgiving Day our home is filled with townspeople, colleagues, and foreign students. The students who come are not only from African countries but other countries as well. We would like to believe that our profound interest and respect for people of all races and ethnic backgrounds has paid off, at least in part, in that one of our lovely daughters-in-law is from Malaysia.

Another opportunity is having the privilege of meeting and hearing well-known people in the area of psychology. David Elkind, J. McVicker Hunt, O. Hobart Mowrer, Robert Coles, Raymond B. Cattell, Robert Havighurst, and Charles Osgood have made presentations at Indiana State University. As my major area of interest is moral development and I have always had a profound regard for Lawrence Kohlberg and his cognitive-developmental theory of moral reasoning, an opportunity of a lifetime came when, through Kohlberg's personal friendship with my colleague, Professor Liam Grimley, Kohlberg spent two days on our campus in January of 1983. Bob and I were both on the committee that made the arrangements for Kohlberg and a friend to come and, as Larry did not wish to spend all his time with large groups, it was decided that he and his friend and Bob and I would have breakfast together. As there were just the four of us it gave me the opportunity to ask Professor Kohlberg a number of questions and to get a better feel for where he stood on several issues related to his ideas. I was also able to share with him some of the work that had been done at that time in relating his theory to Christian thought. He said he was not aware of this but seemed quite interested. Having the opportunity of getting to know this gentle, prince of a man, and hearing what he had to say was one of the most rewarding experiences of my life.

Bob often quotes the verse, "The lines are fallen unto me in pleasant places; yea, I have a goodly heritage." I realize how true this is for both of us. Part of my goodly heritage was having a father who loved the Bible and seemed to have the right verse for every occasion. The love of Scripture continues in our household and I am doubly blessed by hearing it again and again.

Days are spent teaching classes, attending meetings, and endeavoring to meet the deadline for the next manuscript. The list for continued projects is always long and includes in the near future another "four views" book, this one on "Law and Gospel," or how Christians relate the Old and the New Testaments, and an article using Kohlberg's stages on the value of human life to apply to who should be eligible for organ transplantation.

When I claimed God's promise four decades ago that his thoughts toward me "were thoughts of peace, and not of evil," I did not know the extent to which this would be fulfilled. I marvel that God has been so good. His plans were truly "plans to give . . . *hope and a future.*" And I know that the plans will remain intact for as long as he sees fit.

How Writing This Autobiography Has Affected Me

Being introspective by nature and often mulling over in my mind past events means that putting these events on paper did not bring any surprizes or startling revelations about myself. Writing things down, however, may give them a slightly different twist. Even as what we see is not an exact replica of reality, what we write is not an exact replica of experience. I was struck, however, by the tremendous changes that have occurred in the United States over six decades. In some ways it was a better world in the 1930s and in other ways it was not.

I had two major concerns as I wrote. First, I am a very private person and tend not to share my thoughts or my past with anyone. Before Bob's transplant, when it appeared he had only a short time to live, friends tried to get me to confide my innermost feelings, believing that I was working against myself by not sharing my burden with anyone. But that was not my style. At school I tried to keep my mind on my teaching and writing; when I was home I cleaned furiously. I kept wondering while I was writing this autobiography why I was willing to disclose so much about myself, much of it of a personal nature, to people who may not know me. I decided it really is easier that way. It is only embarrassing when you are with acquaintances who feel they know you well and register surprise when they find you are different than what they thought you were.

Second, I found it impossible to write about myself apart from my relationship with my family and, especially, my husband. I made a conscious effort not to express myself in this way but finally gave up, using the rationale that the assignment was to "remain true to my autobiography." I also remembered Robert Sears' article in the February 1977 issue of *American Psychologist* on "Sources of Life Satisfaction of the Terman Gifted Men," in which he found that "in spite of their autonomy and great average success in their occupations, these men placed greater importance on achieving satisfaction in their family life than in their work" (p. 128). It seemed to me that if this is true with them, why should it not be true for those of us of lesser notoriety.

Writing this autobiography has renewed my deep gratefulness to God and what he has done. I have no doubt that he hears and answers prayer and has our best interests in mind.

4

The Story of My Life ... Up to Now*

Paul C. Vitz

My earliest memories are from Minneapolis, Minnesota, where my family lived from 1937 until 1946. (I was born in Toledo, Ohio, in 1935, but I have no recollections of life there.) Minneapolis memories are somewhat jumbled, but some of the important ones follow. We lived in a house on West 50th Street and I remember many hours of playing with blocks, cars, trucks, and toy soldiers with two younger brothers (a third brother arrived in 1947). We invented a simple language spoken by a community of creatures called "Snurlings." I remember fishing at Lakes Calhoun and Harriet, hiding in forts made from old Christmas trees covered with snow (the winters were cold but dry and pleasant), playing lots of football with neighborhood boys, wandering along the banks of Minnehaha Creek.

My father had been married before and had five children by his first wife, who died. Janet and John, the youngest of the older brood,

* A shorter version of this account appeared in *Spiritual Journeys,* Boston: St. Paul, 1987 (rev. ed., 1988).

were teenagers when I was a child and lived with us, though John left to fight in World War II. I remember Janet as a kind presence in the family, and I recall roughhousing with John, especially when he came back on leave in his Army Air Force uniform, smelling of leather and cigarette tobacco.

But the ongoing core of my family consisted of my parents and us three boys: myself, Martin (a year and a half younger), and Robert (three years younger). My mother was, at the time, a full-time wife and homemaker, and my father was head of the Minneapolis Public Library. Every now and then I visited him at his office. Driving downtown we saw the tallest building, the Foshay Tower, dwarfed today by other buildings. The library was a big stone 1890s style edifice like many courthouses of the same period. My father was too old to serve in World War I and I only remember him with white hair. He was born in 1883 and raised in a small German-speaking town: New Bremen, Ohio. His father, Martin, was a minister in the German Evangelical and Reformed Church, and he eventually moved the family to Cleveland so that Dad (who was a precocious oldest child) could get a better high school education. My father was therefore older than other boys' fathers, impressive, somewhat distant, and "old-fashioned": in an important sense, premodern—or as I refer to him—a "preFreudian man." The German environment of his childhood and the classical education he had received in high school and college contributed to his somewhat formal, even courtly manner. His understanding of the mind was almost entirely rationalistic and will-oriented. Perhaps he had a seething unconscious (as modern Psychology says we all do), but I never saw any glimpse of it. He was a mildly affectionate man (of the pat-on-the-head sort), an occasional disciplinarian, and he always held to the highest personal moral standards. Moral rectitude certainly characterized him. He was a reliable and stable father, and I was always aware of his presence. He spanked us once in a while—always a somewhat scary experience. By the standards of today, he was certainly not demonstrative. But on the other hand, I can never remember any of us children having serious complaints about him, or anything but pride and confidence in him.

My mother, Alda Clayton Vitz, born in 1898, came from a very different background, although she was born and raised only a few miles from New Bremen, near the town of Jackson Center, Ohio. She came from solid English-American stock: Claytons, Hills, Blands were the last names. The first Clayton came over in 1776 and married an American girl in New Jersey whose last name was FitzRandolph. (The

FitzRandolphs sold a good deal of farmland to a then newly-established college called Princeton.) Mother grew up on a farm, which her family had homesteaded in the early 1800s. They were active members of the nearby country Methodist Church. She received a college education at Ohio Wesleyan (though her parents had only gone through the sixth grade), graduating in 1919. She was working in the Library in Toledo when she met my father. My mother was present almost all the time throughout my childhood and was a calm, kind, tolerant, but somewhat distant, mother.

I would describe the tone of our family life as pleasant, somewhat cool, and with a vague but clearly felt moralism. My parents didn't smoke, drink, play cards, or dance. (My father rather looked down on the fact that my mother's father had raised trotting-horses!) Gambling, obviously, was also on the forbidden list. All these things were seen as vaguely "Catholic"—things done by the Irish, Italians, and other Catholics—evidence of their moral inferiority to Western European Protestants, who ideally lived highly disciplined and socially productive lives. Our family life was rather austere in comparison with that of most of my contemporaries. Even Coca Cola was suspect—perhaps a hangover from the early days, in my Father's youth, when it contained cocaine!

In any case, the religious atmosphere in the house when I was growing up was generally Protestant, without any particular clarity or enthusiasm. Although my parents' way of life was in many ways impressive, it is important to mention that they never explicitly encouraged their children to follow it. A certain American notion of tolerance seems to have kept them from direct "interference" in our lives.

I also remember going to the University of Minnesota Natural History Museum in Minneapolis and being fascinated with the exhibitions of birds. (I think when you entered, at the top of the steps was a wonderful case with an American bald eagle.) Even living in the city, I had begun to be fascinated by birds and trees and the natural environment. I also recall the nearby Washburn Water Tower. (I remember eating a meatloaf sandwich with mustard as I sat on the lawn beside the base of the tower. When I returned home, I told my mother that it was the best sandwich I ever ate.)

It was a happy childhood that was somewhat suddenly uprooted and successfully replanted in Cincinnati, Ohio, in 1946, when I was in the middle of my fifth grade year. Here, my involvement in natural science grew substantially. I was interested in birds, trees, butterflies (which I collected), and roamed the hills near our home in

Clifton, a suburban part of Cincinnati. I spent a lot of time tramping the southern Ohio woods and fields. I got to know the floodlands where the Miami Rivers intersected the Ohio River. My long walks as an amateur young naturalist were a kind of communing with nature. Although I didn't know it, I was part of an old American tradition of nature worship, found in the writings of John Muir and earlier in Thoreau. I was emotionally repelled by any evidence of human intrusion into or destruction of the environment. To see a field bulldozed away for a new road or housing development deeply offended me. On my walks I always avoided people and, should humans break into my communing, I was irritated. Even in 1950, as a young Audobon Society type, I had all the basic ideas and feelings of today's Green Movement. If I am much less "green" today this is because nature is no longer my religion, and because my religion has so strong a focus on a person, and on other people.

I was a Boy Scout and became an Eagle Scout by fifteen. I did a lot of camping, specializing in winter campouts. I did a modest amount of reading: Sir Walter Scott, Mark Twain, James Fenimore Cooper, and stories about the North Country and Canada being among my favorites. When I was about eleven I spent a summer on my mother's family farm in Jackson Center with my father, and another summer (in 1951) with an older half-brother, Howard, in the Colorado Rockies, working construction. (He was a geologist with a mining company.) For someone who was to become a psychologist, my interests were certainly remarkably nonpsychological! But, then, my parents were in many ways premodern; psychology simply did not exist in my environment until I went to college. The only early "signs" that I can detect to suggest that I would one day be involved in the study of the psyche—or "soul"—are that, first, I always loved philosophical discussion and debate, and the intense emotional restlessness or *sehnsucht* that always accompanied me on my walks and often during even an ordinary day.

Though I have no memory of the event, I suppose the story of my life as a Christian properly begins with my baptism as a boy of about twelve in Cincinnati. A few months after arriving there our family began attending a Presbyterian Church. I went to the Sunday school with modest regularity, and during these years my parents often went to church as well. It was here that I was baptized.

My father, now the head of the Cincinnati Public Library, was urged by my mother to go to church. She felt that Dad's position in the community made this important. My father acquiesced without much resistance, though he seems to have been rather a sceptic or agnostic in fact. In all the years I knew him, I never spoke to my father about religion, nor do I remember his ever saying anything about his beliefs. In part, this was simply an expression of the fact that religion was not a central aspect of our family life. I didn't learn of my father's agnosticism until after his death when I asked my mother about it. In spite of his lack of belief, Dad eventually became an elder in the church, some time after I had gone off to college and was no longer living at home.

To the best of my recollection religion came up in our house only in three quite different contexts. For reasons that are obscure, Dad always said grace before dinner or other formal meals. This family ritual was accepted by us children without discussion as simply "the way things were done at the Vitz's."

There were also not-uncommon criticisms of the Catholic Church; antiCatholic attitudes were a regular though minor part of family talk. My father, like many no-longer-believing Protestants, kept his hostility to Catholicism intact after his own faith had gone. The third way religion came up was when my father talked about his family. Somehow he never tired of reminding us, with pride in his voice, that his grandfather Peter Vitz had come over from Germany in 1853 to become a minister. After some seminary study in America, Peter Vitz became a minister in the German Evangelical and Reform Church. Thus Peter Vitz was a kind of pioneer minister to the new German communities in the midWest (Ohio, Indiana, Minnesota). Rev. Peter Vitz had nine children: the five boys all became ministers and the four girls all married ministers. So Dad, who was born in 1883, was both the son and the grandson of ministers. Yet somehow he rejected his faith. How this happened no one seems to know.

Dad's father, Rev. Martin Vitz, died shortly after I was born. Dad once or twice suggested that his father's faith had weakened so that near the end of his life he was himself in doubt. Perhaps this was true. However, shortly after my father's death—he died in 1981 at the age of ninety-seven—I came across a letter written to him by his father at the time he and my mother were married in 1934. (One of my grandfather's last official acts was to marry my parents.) To his son, now in his fifties, Rev. Martin Vitz wrote a moving letter that ended in a presumably heartfelt "Yours in Christ."

There was always some tension between the Germanic character and background of my father, and the English mentality of my mother and her family. Though he was born and raised in middle America,

German was his first language, and he spoke German at home as a child. (My wife reminds me, however, that my mother made a mean German "springerle" cookie!) Over the years this tension largely resolved itself, but I gather that the German character of the Vitz household, plus the presence of the five children from his first marriage, were rather a shock and strain for my mother when she first married Dad.

Mother's religious background was country Methodist, although to her surprise she recently discovered that her early American ancestors were Seventh Day Baptists (yes, Baptists). However, as I mentioned, she never discussed her religious beliefs with me, nor with her other children as far as I know. In Cincinnati she did fairly often go to church: Presbyterianism was apparently the resolution of her Methodism and Dad's Evangelical-Reform background. Her attendance was more regular in the years after I left for college.

At Sunday school I learned parts of the Bible and small amounts of basic Christian doctrine, but precious little of it stayed with me, and in fact Sunday school had not much lasting impact on me. We did sing and hear hymns, carols, and gospel songs. I suspect that these had permanent effect and may have been instrumental in my later return to the faith. (I know this is true in my wife's case.) The positive emotional resonance of these songs, especially Christmas carols, is still with me.

There was also a youth group at church, but its meaning was primarily social: as a kind of introduction to dating, dancing, and indeed the early stages of "making out" (as it was termed in those days).

In retrospect, the problem with the kind of Christianity I grew up with is that it was *nice,* but just not very convincing. (No doubt my father's scepticism influenced my attitude.) Everyone was pleasant and friendly and relaxed. Religion as a deeply serious, challenging thing, however, was something I never ran into. To me Christianity seemed good, idealistic, a little vague, and hard to believe in. Considering how we were brought up, it is not surprising that one of my brothers is an atheist or skeptic; another shows no special involvement in religion and is what might be called a nominal Christian; the youngest has just recently become a serious Christian.

Beginning in the seventh grade I went to Walnut Hills High School. This was a college preparatory public high school with high standards. I worked moderately hard at my studies and did moderately well. But I was, at that time, primarily involved in football and in social life: I was elected to various class and fraternity offices, dated a good deal, and went steady in my senior year. All in all I enjoyed my years in Cincinnati very much: the city, its people, its homes and neighborhoods are still a part of me. It is my home town. Cincinnati—and the small towns and farms around it for a hundred miles or so—are, for me, the archetype of America. I still root for the Cincinnati Reds.

In the fall of 1953 I left Cincinnati to attend the University of Michigan. Here I chose to be a serious student and for the first time the life of the mind opened up for me. I plunged in, somewhat surprised to discover that much of the intellectual material I was being given was easy to master and some of it deeply interesting. Originally I was attracted to the natural sciences, but soon shifted to psychology as my major. It was a field in which I felt comfortable from the start: in part because it contains such a wide variety of intellectual approaches, ranging from natural science to social science, and from empirical research to philosophical issues. The breadth of the discipline, as well as the particular subjects within psychology, were appealing to me then, as they still are today. As a junior and senior I was in the Psychology Honors Program, working with John Atkinson on achievement motivation (need achievement, as in the research of Henry Murray, David McClelland, and also Atkinson).

In psychology and the rest of the social sciences the attitude toward religion varied from a grudging tolerance—and recognition of its importance in human culture—to active hostility and criticism, the latter being more common. I still remember a course in cultural anthropology taught by a Prof. Leslie White. In his lectures he often made criticisms of Christian positions and dropped scathing comments about various aspects of Christianity, especially Catholicism. He was an effective lecturer, and we all laughed at how foolish religion was. In retrospect, I see his arguments as brilliant superficialities.

Within psychology it soon became clear to me that all the major psychologists were atheists: from Wundt to Freud to Skinner. Psychology, like most of the other academic disciplines, operated on the assumption that religion was false—indeed, rather backward—and was in the process of disappearing, as science and modern thought advanced toward their inevitable worldwide triumph.

I quickly picked up this general attitude; it appealed to me at once. It allowed me to reject much of my background, to escape from my "provincial" past, and to join my new profession without any intellectual or moral liabilities from my nominal Christian upbringing. The reading of Bertrand Russell's "Why I am not a Christian" also eased my deconversion. His essay—with its ideal of a no-nonsense stoical pessimism in the face of a meaningless and implacable universe—seemed tough, manly, and noble: everything Christianity (as I understood it) wasn't. Thus, in my sophomore year, appropriately enough, I acknowledged that I was an atheist. There wasn't any big change in my life, since I hadn't been much of a Christian to begin with. My atheism quickly receded into the background of my life to be replaced by a general indifference toward the whole subject.

I was graduated from Michigan in 1957 and entered graduate school in psychology at Stanford University that fall. There the same skeptical attitude toward religion generally prevailed; indeed, if anything, it was even more explicit and pervasive than in Ann Arbor.

As I mentioned earlier, I had always had a deep sense of restlessness: an intense, unfocused searching. This ever-present longing is one of my earliest memories. I put much of this restless energy into studying hard to become a professor of psychology. As we would put it today, careerism became the religion of my life. Still, some of this nagging restlessness remained through college and graduate school, expressing itself most often in long evening walks—usually by myself—and many hours, especially in graduate school, writing poetry. Only since my conversion has this *sehnsucht* disappeared.

In graduate school my involvement in my career became intensified and my religious indifferentism continued. Stanford—even all California—from the late 1950s into the 1960s, seems to me to have been primarily a place of sunshine and secularism.

While at Stanford I enjoyed life in many ways, but as the years have gone by I have found myself disillusioned as I reflect on my time there. The psychology department was outstanding then (as now) and was ranked first in the country. But the faculty members were almost entirely focused on their personal careers. (It was from them that I learned to do likewise, though perhaps original sin could have managed on its own.) The honest search for truth was not high on anyone's list. I've learned since that this kind of narcissistic careerism characterizes academics everywhere. It means that much of the university's defense of itself in terms of such concepts as academic freedom, the marketplace of ideas, and the search for truth is simply hypocritical posturing.

During my Stanford years I was on the edge of what was later called the counterculture. Richard Alpert was my first faculty research advisor and was a friend for a while. A few years later Alpert and Timothy Leary became famous at Harvard for their LSD capers. Shortly after having to leave Harvard, Alpert became a kind of religious guru and took the name "Baba Ram Dass." At Stanford I lived near Perry Lane: on which also lived Ken Kesey, Alpert, and others of similar kind. I visited them fairly often, drove Alpert's motorcycle (before buying my own), and so on. This little world would later become something of a national phenomenon in the late 1960s. At the time it was already seriously involved in drugs and sexual liberation.

In 1962 I completed graduate school and took a job in the Psychology Department at Pomona College: a fine, small college in southern California. The next year I married Carol Royce, who had just graduated from Mills College, near Berkeley. Her background was secular Jewish. In many respects she was something of a hippie. She had long hair, wore beads and sandals, and had a good number of friends in the political and artistic counterculture. Finding Pomona attractive but somewhat limiting, we both wanted to move. I took a one-year postdoctoral fellowship at Stanford (1964–65) that I used to get extra training in mathematical psychology and to look for a university job. The opening at New York University looked promising and I took it. Carol was glad to go to New York because of her own interests, in music especially (she played the recorder). So in September 1965, after eight years in California, I arrived in New York with Carol to take an apartment in Greenwich Village near NYU.

In New York, my job at NYU started with research grants and publications developing at a good rate, but in a few years this slowed down somewhat because everything else in my life was falling apart. It was the late 1960s—do you remember, or can you imagine it? All around me in the Village and in the university world the new "lifestyles" were exploding. Radical politics, LSD and other drugs, the sexual revolution, radical feminism, Gay politics, the Peace Movement, Eastern religions . . . The world I had known as a curiosity in California had metastasized throughout the country. My marriage unravelled very painfully; Carol and I separated in 1966 and later divorced.

During this time I saw the peace and radical lifestyle movements up close. Although I had sympathy with some of the ideas involved, my general reaction was one of revulsion, in part because the personal lives and characters of the people involved contrasted so greatly with their ideals. Their lives were commonly mixtures of self-indulgence, rationalization, and often hatreds derived from personal experiences unrelated to the issues they espoused. Drugs permeated this new world, the result being that illusion and subjectivism were rampant. I learned that this was no place to find answers to my underlying and now growing sense of discontent.

On the other hand, the representatives of the status quo—for example, the U.S. government, big business, and the universities—came across as deceitful, unthinking, and above all, as weak and insecure. It was the weakness of the establishment leaders that the opposition sensed, and the counterculture closed in on them like wolves on old, sick animals. In particular, the university (the community of scholars) showed itself so without standards, so without the courage of their convictions, as to be a kind of joke. The last vestiges of my respect for academia collapsed as I watched the university leadership cave in to the various social, sexual, and political pressures. By the end of the 1960s and the start of the 1970s my secular ideals were in shreds. I kept my career on track, but it was slowed down by both personal and cultural crises, as well as by my growing awareness that a self-centered career was a pretty hollow thing to hold as one's highest value.

One of my concerns was my deepening disillusionment with the field of psychology itself. My research in experimental and cognitive psychology was no longer very satisfying on ethical grounds. This research was aimed at building scientific, testable models of human mental processes, such as pattern perception and pattern learning. The collective purpose of cognitive psychology is, someday, to be able to simulate the processes of the human mind. I came to the conclusion that such a goal was immoral; it was wrong to help create "human minds" to be used by who knew whom. (In addition, the goal itself of simulating the mind—even apart from the issue of who would control and use this "mind"—seemed morally ambiguous at best.) Of course, perhaps the goal was impossible, perhaps the mind cannot be simulated—but then, why waste one's life on such a task?

Even more disturbing was my growing understanding of how other parts of psychology, for example, personality theory and counseling practice, had contributed to the secular madness that was going on. I couldn't believe that people took such shallow notions as "self-actualization" and encounter groups seriously. Yet by 1970 these ideas that I had first met ten or fifteen years before were being received by millions of Americans with astonishingly wild enthusiasm.

In all this there was one bright spot. In September of 1968 I met Timmie Birge. (Her given name is Evelyn but she has always been called Timmie.) From the very beginning she seemed right, and so she has proven over the years. In early 1969 we became engaged; we got married that August. There was no mention of religion in our marriage vows. We made them up ourselves, carefully leaving out any reference to God (Timmie was a fiercer atheist than I, since by then I was mostly just indifferent). Timmie wore a white minidress with green shoes and stockings (this was the 60s!). But in spite of our rejection of him, God in his mercy blessed us from the start.

When was I first aware of God, or even of the possibility of God's presence in my life? Only looking back does it seem clear that the first fleeting conscious experience occurred in Paris in the summer of 1967. Early the first morning after I arrived I slipped out of the hotel and began wandering through the streets of the Isle de la Cité. (Like so many people, I loved Paris from my first minutes there.) By chance (?) I happened to walk into the Sainte Chapelle. Not knowing its fame, I was totally unprepared for its great beauty—a spiritual beauty. The early light streaming through its windows for a brief moment told me of someone else. Then it was gone, and to all appearances forgotten.

Three years later, in the summer of 1970, Timmie and I spent a glorious month in France. After a few days in Paris we rented a car and drove through Burgundy, the Auvergne, Provence, and the Haute Savoie. I was continually ambushed by the beauty of France. We spent much of our time visiting French cathedrals and churches. (This isn't strange for Timmie, since she is a French scholar, a medievalist by profession, but it is strange for a psychologist.) Somehow, seeing them, being near and going inside these churches, was a glorious yet comforting experience.

In the fall of 1971 our first child, Rebecca, was born. (We now have six: Jessica, born in 1974; Daniel, in 1977; Peter, in 1979; Michael, in 1983; and Anna, in 1987.) Being a father faced me with the concrete question of what I stood for. The question of what to teach our daughter—what values and ideals—could not be avoided. Even more important, having these children has radically changed my understanding about what is truly important in life. This transformation has been as significant as my conversion, and has been inextricably connected with it. It has been the shift from myself, and from things (for example, the environment), to God and to others, especially my wife and children. My own family are my neighbors—not exactly a brilliant interpersonal insight—but there it is! The complexity and time-consuming nature of family life still leave me rather bewildered, and no doubt I have much yet to learn in this important sphere.

By 1972, the collapse of my secular worldview and ideals was pretty complete; the need for an alternative was obvious. One of the symptoms was the frequency with which I got into intense arguments with my secular colleagues. More than one dinner party or other social event ended in unpleasantness. (I can still feel Timmie kicking me under the table—generally to no avail.) For example, my secular friends and colleagues were reliably smug moral relativists—or rather, they were relativists about *my* values—but they were unexamined moral absolutists when it came to their own secular or liberal views on morality. Actually, I have always credited an atheist former friend of ours with being partially responsible for my conversion (he would be much surprised to hear this). Once, in the course of a conversation, he exclaimed happily: "Oh, isn't it great to live in an age of decadence!" That remark alone moved me along several steps toward Christianity.

In the fall of 1972 I took my first sabbatical year. Although I had planned to devote it to research and to the further development of my career, the Holy Spirit apparently had other plans. I was unable really to focus on my professional goals, and the issue of life's meaning—of who I was and what I stood for—pushed its way to the forefront of my concerns. I began talking vaguely about possibly looking into going to some church, maybe sometime . . . Once we went to a nearby Presbyterian church where the sermon sounded just like an editorial from the *New York Times.* We didn't go back, but we were launched on our search for a church. In October I recall walking down Fifth Avenue and stepping, briefly, into St. Thomas Episcopal Church. This beautiful Gothic church appealed to me—no doubt it resonated with my experiences in France—but I didn't do anything about it until January 1973. Timmie was in Indianapolis with the baby visiting her mother. I was alone for the weekend and on Sunday, for reasons that I can't even recall, I went up to St. Thomas for the 11:00 service. I loved it. The gospel was preached clearly, indeed eloquently, in the context of an extraordinarily beautiful liturgy.

Words like "Evensong" and "Advent" evoked my English heritage. The people seemed familiar and reminded me of friends in Cincinnati (two of my closest had been Episcopalians, and our boy scout troop met for years in the local Episcopal church). The following week Timmie also agreed to come: our return to Christianity had begun. At first, our faith was weak and we felt strange, even embarrassed, about it. We hid it from our friends and relatives, as though it were a kind of leftover adolescent activity. I called us "closet Christians."

During this time certain books were critically important to me, especially the writings of C. S. Lewis and G. K. Chesterton. It was an enormous surprise and relief to me to discover that Christianity was not only intellectually defensible, but powerful! Indeed, I soon found that its intellectual variety and riches were so much deeper and more sophisticated than any secular framework that there was simply no comparison. As a consequence, my mind—my intellectual understanding—soon went through a momentous conversion. I began to grasp the essential character of Christian thought and to see clearly the weaknesses of modern secular positions.

I found deep satisfaction in the fact that the Christian view, with its firm acceptance of physical, psychological, and moral reality, allowed me to understand why I had been so disillusioned with popular contemporary ideology. Modernism is in its essential nature subjective, arbitrary, and nihilistic. It was a joy to steep myself in the wisdom and truth of the Scriptures and in the thought of the countless great Christians who have written over the centuries.

As my Christian intellectual understanding developed, I knew that I must change my professional and public life, not just my personal or private life. That is, I knew that my new Christian understanding of reality, especially the life of the mind, had to be applied to psychology: to the secular theories of the mind that were undermining so much of Christian thought. Exactly what this would require was unclear to me, but I knew I had to become a "Christian psychologist," whatever that meant. I had to give up my purely professional friends, my status in the department, my understanding of who I was. This realization was extremely painful, for it really meant jettisoning all of my career as it then existed. For example, I had to give up cognitive and experimental psychology and move into the fields of personality and motivation. Granted, my original interest in psychology had been in these fields, but I hadn't published in them, and of course none of my career had ever had anything to do with Christianity. Except for my maintaining a modest continued professional involvement in psychology and art, all else was changed. To add to the difficulty, at the time I didn't know one other person who was, or much less had become, a Christian psychologist. All I knew of were people who moved the other way: away from faith into secular psychology.

This abandonment of my previous career and professional involvement began in early 1973. It was a slow business, with occasional brief regressions, but by 1978 this "move" was largely completed. It was accelerated by the publication of my first book, *Psychology as Religion: The Cult of Self-Worship* (Eerdmans, 1977). This book began as a short presentation in 1975 to a small group of Anglo-Catholic Episcopalians. It was a critique of humanistic psychology, the kind of psychology so immensely popular at the time. The group liked the paper, so I expanded it somewhat and sent it off to some Dutch Reformed Christians that I hadn't even met. To my eternal gratitude, they responded very positively and sent it to Eerdmans. Before I knew it, I had a contract and not long afterward the book was published. From the start the book was well-received by many, and from the start it changed my life. I received all kinds of support in letters and personal contacts from fellow Christians all over the world. Although to this day I remain isolated in a secular psychology department at NYU, these contacts have kept my intellectual development and much of my spiritual life going for years.

As my understanding of Christian theology deepened, I quickly came into conflict with liberal theology which, it was obvious to me, was at best a compromise with antiChristian modernist thought, and at worst a thinly disguised denial of Christ. No doubt in the past the primary challenge to the faith has been rigid pharasaical theology, but today the moral danger is this modernist self-indulgent mush. As I was intellectually formed in the heart of the modernist and secular worldview—that is, in contemporary social science—it was easy for me to recognize these assumptions and ideas when I saw them creeping into Christianity. Unfortunately, the Episcopal Church was dominated by liberal thought, indeed so much so that many couldn't even see the fact. As far as they were concerned, liberal theology was the only possible way of viewing things. It was then that I first experienced the narrow-minded character of so many liberals. I still remember the remark made to me by a young Episcopal priest (his voice dripping with condescension): "You mean you actually believe in the *bodily* resurrection of Christ?" My awareness of the prevalence of liberal theology in the Episcopal church brought increasing dismay. In spite of the beautiful Episcopal liturgy, and the many fine individual Christians that I had come to know and love, it became clear to me that its basic Christian character was seriously compromised. I knew firsthand the hollowness of secular thought and values, to find them enthusiastically imported and on display in a Christian church was more than I could take. Emotionally the breaking point came the morning I read in the *New York Times* that the Episcopal bishop of New York had just ordained his first woman "priest": a practicing lesbian. In the very depths of my being I felt the faith betrayed, and the heart went out of my relationship with the Episcopal Church. In fact, after the ordination of women, the Anglo-Catholic cause within Episcopalianism looked increasingly lost.

Since I became a Christian, my basic motivating principle as a psychologist has been to use psychology to defend the integrity of the orthodox Christian faith. Here I simply must say that I am disturbed at liberal Christianity. I know and continue to meet many people with these positions, since they characterize much of the university world (insofar as it is Christian at all). I have had many painful (for me) conversations with friends, colleagues, and even relatives on these issues. I have found almost all such people easy to like, but the sheer lack of intellectual coherence in the liberal theological positions is to me shocking. This is combined with an attitude of "noblesse-oblige": a presumptuousness that blinds them not only to intellectual weakness, but to the self-indulgence of their religious position. For example, to call oneself a Christian and yet to deny the divinity of Christ! Or to reject obviously representative or important scriptural passages as inauthentic or nonbinding, while accepting others. It is rather like accepting the laws of addition, but not those of subtraction. Or, for example, to deny the obvious fact that in Scripture Jesus calls God his Father—not an androgynous "parent"—and does this many times; in fact, it is one of his most distinctive messages. Beyond all this is the liberal understanding of Jesus as a "nice guy." C. S. Lewis is right: either Jesus was God, or he was crazy (or worse)! There is no in-between ground.

What is particularly discouraging to me is that so many exChristians and antiChristians do not leave the Church. They continue to draw salaries and to hang on, like tapeworms, to their positions in Christian institutions. This is what I mean when I say they lack integrity. Give me an honest old-fashioned atheist anytime, or a new-fashioned sceptic. Give me a Pharisee (after all, the Pharisees gave us St. Paul, Nicodemus, and others), anything but these modern-day Sadducees!

Already, to our surprise, Timmie and I often found ourselves taking what would be called the Catholic position on issues under discussion. We found ourselves defending the bodily resurrection of Christ, arguing for the existence of the Devil, defending the creeds, opposing divorce, opposing abortion, even arguing against the legitimacy of contraception. By the spring of 1978 it was pretty clear to both of us that we were going to become Catholics; it was just a question of when: when each of us would overcome our remaining personal barriers. To me the Catholic Church seemed so strange, so ethnic; you know—Italian, Irish, Polish—somehow not quite American.

In May, Timmie decided to take the plunge and enter instruction. She was helped in her decision by a dear friend of ours, Helen Corbett, who had recently completed instruction and entered the Church herself. In late June I too started instruction. All this was during the last days of the pontificate of Paul VI. I had no illusions that the Catholic Church had escaped the modernist infection in a form that might be called "the American disease." But I knew that Catholic theology had remained true, and if I was to fight for the faith, then it would have to be in the Catholic Church.

In September of 1978 we began regular attendance at Catholic services, and we were both received in June of 1979 at St. Thomas More Church in Manhattan. At this Mass, at which we made our first Holy Communion, we were also married and confirmed. (Timmie, who was extremely pregnant with Peter, thought we might end the day with a baptism as well!) My sponsor was Rev. Benedict Groeschel, a Capuchin monk and priest who helped me greatly at this critical time. Timmie and I have in fact been blessed to know many wonderful and deeply impressive priests, and sisters as well. We give special thanks to God for Fr. Eugene Kevane and Fr. James Halligan. Their example—and prayers—have meant a great deal to us and our family.

Much of the delay between September 1978 and June 1979 was due to the time needed by the Church to resolve the question of my first marriage. On the basis of ancient precedent, Rome annulled this marriage as not having been sacramental. I was an atheist/skeptic at the time, Carol was not a Christian, and the ceremony was conducted by a Unitarian minister. In short, it was essentially a civil contract.

Preceding and leading up to my Catholic conversion were a series of religious experiences that caught me completely by surprise and greatly deepened my faith. The first three (there were four in all) occurred in a ten-day period in September of 1977. These dramatic, unexpected experiences were something like visions, all taking place during the day. The first one revealed to me the existence, power, and majesty of God. Let me describe it briefly. I had just awakened—it must have been around 6:30 in the morning. Suddenly I saw myself, as in a vision, looking up and seeing an enormous figure with a long robe standing in front of me. By "enormous" I mean that I felt as though I were at the foot of a fifty-storey building, looking up. I reached up to touch the robe and as I did so it turned into a great, huge curtain. The curtain then seemed to move off to the right as though it were opening before me. I was overwhelmed by the space. It was truly infinite in all respects. At first the space seemed completely empty except for a diffuse glowing light that permeated it. The light was associated with a quiet but awesome low hum. Even as I was viewing this great space I knew that I was in the presence of God, that I was being shown, if you will, the existence of God through this sign of his omnipotence and majesty. After a few moments I saw, in the center of this space, a tiny dot far, far away. I saw that it was moving toward me. At first it moved slowly, but as it got closer, it moved faster. At some point, when it was about halfway toward me, I saw that this dot was Christ on the Cross: it was a Crucifix. In this form Christ came closer and closer to me and then moved off in a curve to my right. Then I became aware that I was lying in bed and the light was coming in the window.

The other visions would be too long to relate here, but I can simply say that the second revealed to me the futility of purely cognitive inquiry with respect to theological issues—also the existence of Satan (I heard his laughter throughout the vision). The third experience was of the reality of sin, especially mine, and of the justice that sin should be judged. That is, I experienced being convicted of personal sin and evil, but there was, with this, no sense of condemnation; rather, I felt the absolute necessity of responding to the call for holiness.

The fourth and last of these experiences occurred on a weekday in late August, 1978, when I was praying in the almost empty Catholic Cathedral of Toronto. There in the midmorning I experienced in simple, dramatic terms both the reality of the risen Christ and my personal relationship with him. Along with prayer, reading, thinking, reflection, and Catholic friends, these experiences solidified my commitment to the Catholic faith.

One of the features of my conversion has been a changing understanding of the "ethnic" nature of Christianity. Part of the initial appeal of the Episcopal Church to me had been that it helped me recover my English and WASP roots. That is, part of the meaning of Christianity was its capacity to reinstate my ethnic identity in New York City at a time when nothing else did or could. In becoming a Catholic I further deepened my connection to Western culture and to the general heritage of Christendom both in the West and the East. (I have come to admire greatly the Eastern Orthodox churches.) Even more, one of the reasons why I found my conversion to Catholicism such a liberation was that it made me become part of the universal Church. There are Catholics everywhere, and in becoming a Catholic I sensed a new kinship with people in countries as diverse as

Argentina, Poland, and Zanzibar. I felt linked: united to millions of people of all nations, races, and cultures. It was exhilarating! A particular form of this new sense of expansion was the realization that Catholics cover the complete social spectrum: a Catholic may be a king or a truck driver, a millionaire or a peasant. To be a Catholic is not to be part of a particular social class.

A more recent understanding of the ethnic character of Catholicism has come from my experience of the Jewishness of the faith. In December of 1983, Providence provided me with a visit to Jerusalem. (I have not yet, alas, been to Rome.) In Jerusalem I was deeply affected by the Old City. Here I grasped the tough Jewish character of Jesus as well as the Jewish nature of the Church's beginnings. I believe this aspect of the faith needs to be more widely understood and cultivated.

People sometimes ask if I understood and agreed with every part of Catholic doctrine before I came into the Church. The answer is "no." I believed in the central doctrines, but I certainly didn't comprehend all Church doctrine at the time; I still don't. There was nothing I rejected, but there were things I didn't actively accept and believe in. However, I was, and am, confident that the Church is right, that she has been guided by the Holy Spirit, and I believe that in time I will grasp the basis for all her doctrines. So far, this has proven to be true. To take a human analogy: joining the Church is really rather like getting married to someone you love. When you get married you certainly don't know or understand everything about your bride—God forbid! But you are confident that as you get to know her over the years your love and allegiance will grow.

Throughout my Christian life I have remained in close contact and cooperation with many conservative Protestants, the kind that are probably best described as Evangelicals. These Evangelicals have been friends and supporters even more than all but a very few Catholics. I love and admire them and owe them a great deal. I pray that somehow I will be able to repay them. Of course, our important theological differences remain, but being with them strengthens my basic Christianity. Also, in some mysterious way, it increases my Catholic commitment. They inspire in me the hope that someday the Catholic Church in America will awaken from its slumber in the secular suburbs; that someday Catholics in large numbers, like these wonderful Evangelicals, will blaze forth in love for Christ and his Church and transform our society in the process.

As I said earlier, one of the exciting and unexpected things about becoming a Christian was to discover the power, beauty, and fundamental truth of Christian doctrine and its theological rationale. My secular training allowed me to recognize these properties of Christian intellectual life. But also, I soon recognized, after only a few months, how rich and unexplored were the connections between psychology and theology. The very concept of "person" derives from the doctrine of the Trinity, and from the idea of God as a person in whose image we are made. Psychoanalytic theory is rich in concepts and observations that enlighten and support the notion of original sin: the character of our fallen nature. The counseling process itself seems best conceptualized as speaking the truth in love.

It has also become clear to me that scripture and theology are the master framework, that they are the key to psychology, and not the other way around. Of course, I soon found and continue to find that translating such general insights into clearly formulated positions is not easy. There are many pitfalls where either the generalization was too superficial, or the independence of one or the other discipline was not maintained. It still remains very much to be seen whether my understanding here is correct or not, but it has been convincing to me, and my primary intellectual motivation. If I fail at the task, nevertheless it will have been an exciting adventure. Perhaps my basic understanding is flawed, or perhaps I am not up to the task. Regardless, I have greatly enjoyed working, wrestling, even fighting with this new set of problems and look forward to more years of the same.

Looking back on my life as a Christian, I can say that it has been filled with truly great surprises—the greatest being that I became a Christian at all: this is the first miracle. The second is that the same kind of conversion took place, at the same time, in Timmie as well; ours has been, and remains, a shared journey. Frequently in this journey my expectations and plans have been very painfully confounded, but the consequences of these "ego-strippings" have always been blessings. This Christian Odyssey is still far from over, and who knows what lies ahead? In spite of retrospectives such as this report, the prize lies ahead, and I pray, with St. Paul, to be able to finish the race.

5

My Pilgrimage as a Christian Psychologist

Siang-Yang Tan

In this autobiographical essay of my pilgrimage as a Christian psychologist, I will share my story chronologically under the following headings: (1) Years in Singapore (1954–73); (2) Years in Montreal, Quebec, Canada (1973–80); (3) Years in London, Ontario, Canada (1980–83); (4) Years in Toronto, Ontario, Canada (1983–85); (5) Years in Los Angeles/Pasadena, U.S.A. (1985–present).

Years in Singapore (1954–73)

I was born on October 25, 1954, in Singapore, which is located strategically in Southeast Asia. It is a modern, beautiful, clean, and green city-country, more officially called The Republic of Singapore. My father, Siew Thiam Tan, emigrated to Singapore from China when he was young. He worked hard in various odd jobs until he managed to become a businessman, running his own import-export business. My mother, Madam Chiow Yang Quek, was born in Singapore and married my father when she was still in her teens. My father had very little formal education (a few years in elementary school) in

China, and my mother had none. They had a total of seven children, in the following chronological order: Sien Chuan Tan (who is a stockbroker in Singapore, and married with two children); Siang Chik Tan (who is the managing director of an American firm in Singapore, and married with two children); Siang Yong Tan (who is a medical doctor and attorney in Hawaii, and married with two children); Daisy Gek Luan Tan (who is a school teacher in Singapore, and married with two children); Gek Hong Tan (who passed away in 1974 in Singapore); myself, or Siang-Yang Tan; and Gek Huan Tan (who is a newspaper subeditor in Australia, and single).

My mother was a homemaker, and with the help of a housemaid brought all of us up, while my father was the traditional breadwinner who provided for us materially in a middle-class, somewhat typical, Chinese Singaporean home. My father passed away of a stroke in 1976, while my mother is still living in our home in Singapore. She manages to do so on her own, although she has rented out a couple of rooms to women tenants, usually airline stewardesses.

I attended Saint Patrick's School and Saint Stephen's School while growing up in Singapore. They were Roman Catholic schools that provided me a sound education right up to what is equivalent to junior college level (or "A" levels). I was therefore exposed to the Christian faith through catechism classes and had always believed in God and in Jesus. I even went to a Roman Catholic church for Saturday evening or Sunday morning services from time to time. However, there was still a deep void of emptiness within me, despite outward success in academic achievement, sports (especially soccer), and relationships with many good friends, as well as with my family. As a young teenager I felt the void acutely and searched painfully and restlessly for the meaning of life and an answer to my fear of death.

I had two good Christian friends (Kim Lark Lim and Ee Keen Wong) who were my neighbors at this time. They witnessed to me and told me how I could be saved and find meaning in life through the Gospel of Jesus Christ. However, it was not until I had a couple of accidents in which I broke my left arm twice (the first time after falling off a bicycle: the second only two months later when I slipped and fell off a mossy pavement by the beach) that I considered Jesus Christ much more seriously. On August 12, 1968, when I broke my left arm the second time, I finally decided to receive Jesus Christ into my life as my personal Lord and Savior. I was "broken but made whole," and this dramatic conversion experience really changed or transformed my life. I was filled with the peace and joy of the Lord, and the void inside was no longer as acutely felt. My neighbors were delighted when I told them about my conversion, and they quickly introduced me to their church, an open Brethren church called Bethesda Katong. I was blessed by many fine and Godly people there, including Dr. Benjamin Chew who is one of Singapore's best known and beloved Christian leaders.

I became actively involved in the Sunday school and youth ministry of the church and learned much from the solid Bible teaching provided, for which I am still very grateful to this day. I was baptized in December, 1970, and thereby became a member of Bethesda Katong church. I also got active in Singapore Youth for Christ, which provided me with excellent ministry and leadership skills training. As a result of my YFC ministry and leadership experience, as well as the mentoring and training I received from YFC leaders like Donald Chia and Harry Quek at that time, I felt led by the Lord to obtain further training in clinical psychology so that I could counsel and minister to people more effectively. I had been exposed to some basic counseling and helping skills training through YFC. The local university in Singapore did not have a Psychology department in the early 1970s, so I had to go abroad for my university education and training in clinical psychology.

I went through a burnout experience in 1970, which taught me the need to set limits to my often hectic schedule of activities, as well as to live a more balanced life including regular exercise, sufficient rest and sleep, and good nutrition. My experience of burnout included a period of "the dark night of the soul," and being in the spiritual wilderness of dryness, lacking the deep sense of God's presence that I had always experienced since my conversion. It was a "Job-like" experience that was very painful emotionally, and I became more familiar with feelings of dryness, emptiness, depression, and fatigue. By the grace of God I experienced his healing touch and restoration and grew through this experience to a more mature and deeper relationship with him. My interest in helping people in emotional pain was also heightened as a result, and after much prayer and discussion with other Christian leaders, I sensed that the Lord wanted me to pursue a career in clinical psychology. I had other options like law or economics, but they did not seem to be the right ones for me.

I had long discussions with my father about my career choice, and by God's grace, he was willing to send me abroad for my university education in psychology. He did warn me about the danger of not finding a good job after graduation and returning to Singapore because psychology was not well developed as a profession then. He also somewhat regretted that I did not choose another career like law. I would have probably been awarded a prestigious Government scholarship, since I had excelled academically and was nominated for it. Academic achievement and awards were highly valued by him. My father graciously trusted my judgment and decision, however, and financed the early part of my university education at McGill University in Montreal, Quebec, Canada, from 1973–76, until the time of his death.

I chose McGill University not only because of its reputation, especially in the Commonwealth countries of which Singapore is a part, but also because my brother, Dr. Siang-Yong Tan, had graduated from medical school at McGill and he highly recommended the university to me. He informed me that the Department of Psychology in particular was an outstanding one at McGill. I therefore applied and was admitted for a B.A. program in Personality and Abnormal Psychology. I left Singapore in September, 1973, for Montreal and McGill.

Years in Montreal (1973–80)

I completed both my undergraduate studies in psychology (B.A., First Class Honors) from 1973–76, as well as my graduate studies in Clinical Psychology (Ph.D.) from 1976–80, at McGill University. I was blessed with two excellent mentors there: Dr. Ernest G. Poser and Dr. Ronald Melzack.

Dr. Poser was my academic advisor when I was an undergraduate; he also served as my major Ph.D. dissertation advisor. He directed one of the first clinical treatment and training facilities in behavior therapy in North America, called the Behavior Therapy Unit, at the Douglas Hospital Centre in Montreal. He also published a groundbreaking study in 1966 that showed that nonprofessionals (untrained college students) did as well as professional therapists in group therapy with schizophrenic patients.[1] While there are methodological flaws with this study, many others since then have provided further support for the effectiveness of lay or paraprofessional helpers. I have therefore developed a major area of interest and expertise in lay Christian counseling based on research like Dr. Poser's, as well as the scriptural injunctions to carry each other's burdens (Gal. 6:2) and to help one another out of loving concern.

Dr. Poser served as an outstanding model of the scientist-practitioner in the best sense of the term for me. He was trained himself at the University of London, with Professor Hans J. Eysenck as his

1. Poser, E. G. 1966. The effect of therapists' training on group therapeutic outcome. *Journal of Consulting Psychology* 30:283–89.

mentor for his Ph.D. dissertation in clinical psychology. Dr. Poser was Director of Clinical Training and Professor of Psychology at McGill, with an active research program, especially in the area of behavioral prevention. At the same time, he remained clinically active in therapeutic work with clients, as well as in the training of behavior therapists. He was also instrumental in helping me to receive a broad and balanced education in psychology, emphasizing the areas of neuropsychology and health psychology just before they became such significant areas of the discipline.

Dr. Poser was a genuinely caring and warm human being with great personal charisma, a sense of humor, and integrity. It was a real joy to work under his guidance and mentoring and to experience his support. He also had high standards that I found challenging and stimulating. For all this, and more, I will always be grateful. Dr. Poser left McGill several years ago and is now living in Vancouver, British Columbia, Canada, where he still teaches part-time at the University of British Columbia and has a part-time clinical practice.

Dr. Ronald Melzack, Professor of Psychology at McGill, is probably the best-known psychologist in the area of pain today.[2] He did his Ph.D. in experimental psychology under the mentoring of the late Dr. Donald Olding Hebb, former Chairperson of McGill's Department of Psychology and one of Canada's most distinguished psychologists, having been a former President of the American Psychological Association.

I am thankful to Dr. Melzack for his help, support, and guidance as my interim dissertation advisor for a year (1979–80) while Dr. Poser was away on sabbatical leave. Both Dr. Poser and Dr. Melzack provided invaluable input and mentoring as I conducted my dissertation research on "Acute Pain in a Clinical Setting: Effects of Cognitive-Behavioral Skills Training," which has been published.[3] My

2. Dr. Melzack is world-renowned for his gate-control theory of pain, which he first formulated with Dr. Patrick Wall and published in *Science* in 1965 (Melzack, R., and P. D. Wall. 1965. Pain mechanisms: A new theory. *Science* 150:971–79). Dr. Melzack has published widely, especially in the area of pain, including his classic textbook originally entitled *The puzzle of pain* (Melzack, R. 1973. *The puzzle of pain*. New York: Basic Books) and now revised and coauthored with Dr. Patrick Wall as *The challenge of pain* (Melzack, R., and P. D. Wall. 1983. *The challenge of pain*. New York: Basic Books). His theory has led to much fruitful research on basic mechanisms of pain perception and control, as well as new practical and helpful treatments for pain (Wall, P. D., and R. Melzack, eds. 1989. *Textbook of pain*. 2nd ed. London: Churchill Livingstone).

3. Tan, S. Y., and E. G. Poser. 1982. Acute pain in a clinical setting: Effects of cognitive-behavioral skills training. *Behaviour Research and Therapy* 20:535–45.

Tan, S. Y. 1982. Cognitive and cognitive-behavioral methods for pain control: A selective review. *Pain* 12:201–28.

earlier research work for my honors theses was in the area of behavioral prevention of psychological disorder, under the supervision of Dr. Poser and a graduate student of his named Lorne Hartman.

The other members of my dissertation committee were Dr. Irv Binik (formerly Director of Clinical Training at McGill), and Dr. George Ferguson (formerly Chairperson of McGill's Psychology Department), whose helpful suggestions were also much appreciated.

I am therefore deeply thankful to the Lord for providing Dr. Poser and Dr. Melzack as my mentors at McGill University. I count myself fortunate and blessed to have received such excellent training and mentoring and hope to pass this on to my doctoral students in Clinical Psychology at Fuller.

I completed my predoctoral internships, which were part of the A.P.A. accredited Ph.D. program in Clinical Psychology at McGill, in the following clinical settings in Montreal: Department of Psychology and Child and Adolescent Service, Allan Memorial Institute of Psychiatry; Montreal Neurological Institute; and the Behavior Therapy Unit, Douglas Hospital Centre.

At the Allan Memorial Institute (Summer 1977) my internship experience included psychological assessments of children, adolescents, and adults, individual therapy and behavioral assessments with adolescents, group therapy with children, and family screening or assessment. My internship training at the Montreal Neurological Institute (Summer 1978) involved mainly neuropsychological assessments of seizure or other neurological patients—preoperatively, postoperatively, and at follow-up. My final internship experience (Fall 1978-Spring 1979, half-time) at the Behavior Therapy Unit, Douglas Hospital Centre, included behavioral assessments and individual behavior therapy or cognitive-behavior therapy with adult patients. However, I was also fortunate enough to arrange for a special learning experience in psychoanalytically-oriented psychotherapy provided by Dr. Brian Robertson, M.D. (Psychoanalyst and the Director of Psychotherapy at the Douglas Hospital Centre), through a series of weekly seminars on a one-to-one basis with him that included watching videotapes of him doing therapy. My internship experiences therefore provided me with systematic training in a variety of clinical skills and a broad exposure to different clinical populations and problems.

As an undergraduate student I was also involved for two years (1974 and 1975) in a secular, student-run peer counseling group called Interaction McGill. Shortly thereafter, in 1976, I set up a Lay Counseling Service at Peoples Church of Montreal (part of Associated

Gospel Churches), which was my local church, and directed it until 1980 when I graduated with my Ph.D. in Clinical Psychology and left Montreal for London, Ontario, Canada.

A number of other significant events took place during my years in Montreal. The first was the passing away of my father in 1976 when I had just completed my B.A. (First Class Honors) in Psychology and was about to begin my Ph.D. program in Clinical Psychology. It was a sad event, especially since my father was only in his early sixties, and I was in Montreal when he died quite suddenly of a stroke (his second in a year), in Singapore.

The second was my marriage to Angela Woo on May 21, 1977, after meeting her through friends at McGill and dating seriously for over one and a half years. Angela majored in Economics and Accounting and graduated with her Bachelor of Commerce (Honors) degree from McGill in 1976. She is also a Chartered Accountant as well as a Certified Public Accountant (C.P.A.). I have the deepest love and appreciation for her and her crucial contributions in so many ways in my life and ministry, as well as in her own ministry. She was born in Hong Kong but emigrated to St. Jean, Quebec, Canada (close to Montreal) when she was young. Her parents, two younger brothers, an older sister, and her grandmother are also living in or near Montreal.

The final event that I should mention was another near burnout experience I went through in early 1979. It was a very stressful and hectic time of my life. I was doing my final, advanced internship, as well as beginning my doctoral dissertation research and preparing to write my doctoral comprehensive exams. I was also directing the Lay Counseling Service at Peoples Church of Montreal, and the Campus life Division (high school ministry) of Montreal Youth for Christ. Again, the Lord graciously helped me to restore balance in my life, and with Angela's love, support, and prayers, I was able to recover from this near burnout experience. Due to my high energy level (and somewhat perfectionistic tendencies, which I'm glad to say have been significantly tempered and reduced by God's grace over the years!), I am aware that I need to be careful of the danger of overextending myself and burning-out as a result. Angela has been a great help in this regard since she is less intense, more "laid-back" in general, and has put on the brakes when necessary.

Years in London, Ontario, Canada (1980–83)

I accepted a job in the Department of Psychological Services at University Hospital, affiliated with the University of Western Ontario, in London, Ontario, Canada, in the summer of 1980. Dr. Brian Shaw, a well-known cognitive therapist (trained by Dr. Aaron Beck, the founder of cognitive therapy), was the head of the department at that time, and he served as primary supervisor for my post-doctoral hours required for registration (licensing) as a psychologist in the Province of Ontario. Dr. Douglas Cann, also a graduate of McGill, was my secondary supervisor. I was registered as a psychologist in Ontario in November 1981 and gained valuable experience as a clinical psychologist in my three years at University Hospital.

My primary clinical responsibility was to serve as psychologist to the Epilepsy Unit in the Department of Clinical Neurological Sciences at University Hospital. I thoroughly enjoyed my years of working closely with Dr. John P. Girvin, Neurosurgeon and Co-Director of the Unit, and Dr. Warren T. Blume, Neurologist and E.E.G. expert as well as Co-Director of the Unit. I did some research in the assessment of psychosocial functioning of patients with epilepsy using the Washington Psychosocial Seizure Inventory, or WPSI, developed by Dr. Carl Dodrill,[4] as well as conducted an uncontrolled clinical trial of individual cognitive-behavior therapy with epilepsy patients for the reduction of seizures and psychosocial problems with encouraging or good outcomes.[5]

In addition to my clinical work with epilepsy patients, I conducted psychological assessments and therapeutic interventions with adult patients suffering from phobias, obsessive-compulsive disorders, anxiety disorders, depression, stress reactions and burnout, marital problems, pain (for example, headache and lower back pain) and other health and psychology-related problems. The major approach to therapy that I used was broad-based, cognitive-behavioral in orientation.

I also taught part-time in the Departments of Psychology, Psychiatry, and Oral Medicine at the University of Western Ontario, and was involved in supervising and training psychology interns and practicum students at University Hospital. Angela and I attended

4. Dodrill, C. B., R. Beier, M. Kasparick, I. Tacke, U. Tacke, and S. Y. Tan. 1984. Psychosocial problems in adults with epilepsy: Comparison of findings from four countries. *Epilepsia* 25:176–83.

Tan, S. Y. 1983. Psychosocial functioning of epileptic patients referred for psychological intervention. In *Advances in epileptology: 14th epilepsy international symposium,* 79-87. New York: Raven Press.

Tan, S. Y. 1986. Psychosocial functioning of adult epileptic and MS patients and adult normal controls on the WPSI. *Journal of Clinical Psychology* 42:528–34.

5. Tan, S. Y. 1983. Psychosocial functioning of epileptic patients referred for psychological intervention, 79–87.

North Park Community Chapel, a nondenominational evangelical church while we were living in London. I set up another Lay Counseling Service at this church, similar to the one I had established earlier at Peoples Church of Montreal. I therefore continued to be involved in the selection, training, and supervision of lay counselors in a local church context.[6]

Angela and I served as advisors to the Malaysian-Singaporean Students Christian Fellowship group at the University of Western Ontario, and were involved in student evangelism and follow-up. We saw several students become Christians, and had the joy of helping them grow spiritually. We also did some informal counseling and ministry with them.

We bought our first house in 1981 in London. Shortly thereafter the Lord gave us the gift of our first child, Carolyn Li Jun Tan, who was born on August 18, 1981. She has brought much joy and blessing to us.

In 1983 another significant turning point took place in my life. My pastor at North Park Community Chapel, Dr. William McRae, had just been appointed President of Ontario Bible College and Ontario Theological Seminary in Toronto, Canada. He was very pleased with the ministry of the Lay Counseling Service I had set up at the church. He challenged me to leave my secular job at University Hospital and the University of Western Ontario, so that I could use whatever spiritual gifts and talents the Lord has graciously given me to serve him and his Kingdom full-time, especially in the area of Christian counseling. After much painful reflection and prayer, Angela and I felt led by the Lord to leave London and a job I enjoyed, and moved to Toronto at the end of July, 1983, to teach at Ontario Bible College.

Years in Toronto (1983–85)

While in Toronto I worked full-time as Director of Counseling and Professor of Psychology and Counseling at Ontario Bible College, part-time as Pastor of the Malaysian-Singaporean Bible Church: a small, nondenominational evangelical church of about fifty people when I first started ministering there. I also established the Institute of Christian Counseling at Ontario Bible College in 1984, for

6. Tan, S. Y. 1981. Lay counseling: The local church. *C.A.P.S. Bulletin* 7 (1): 15–20.
Tan, S. Y. 1987. Training lay Christian counselors: A basic program and some preliminary data. *Journal of Psychology and Christianity* 6 (2): 57–61.
Tan, S. Y. 1991. *Lay counseling: Equipping Christians for a helping ministry.* Grand Rapids: Zondervan.

training lay or paraprofessional Christian counselors, including pastors and church leaders. A part-time, one-year course in lay Christian counseling consisting of a total of 108 hours of training was developed and made available.[7] The registration for this course was full, with an initial enrollment of about sixty people.

Just before I left London for Toronto, the Ontario Ministry of Health had awarded me a research grant of about $22,000 (Canadian) to conduct a controlled outcome study of group cognitive-behavior therapy with adult outpatients with epilepsy for the reduction of seizures and psychosocial problems. I was allowed to do the research study in collaboration with Dr. Joseph Bruni, Neurologist and Epileptologist, at the Wellesley Hospital and the University of Toronto School of Medicine. The results of this study have been published, showing little support for the efficacy of short-term group cognitive-behavior therapy for seizure control and the alleviation of psychosocial difficulties.[8] Further research, however, is needed, especially using either longer-term group cognitive-behavior therapy, or individual cognitive-behavior therapy with patients with epilepsy before more definitive conclusions can be made about the efficacy of this type of treatment.

I enjoyed very much my two years in Toronto, both in my teaching and work at Ontario Bible College and in my pastoral ministry at the church, which included regular preaching, teaching, pastoral visitation, and care. The Lord really blessed these ministries, and the church grew to about one hundred people by 1985. It was a real joy to work closely with church leaders like Danny Chia, Perry Soh, and their families. I also had a small, part-time private practice. My family and I had some financial struggles when we first moved to Toronto, primarily because of the high cost of housing, as well as a cut in my salary moving from a hospital position to a bible college teaching position. It was a good time to learn how to live by faith and to trust in the Lord more for daily provisions. We also learned how to live more simply and to give to others, like missionaries, who may have even less than we had then. These were precious lessons from the Lord who eventually more than adequately provided for us financially, as my part-time private practice filled up, and the church paid me for

7. Tan, S. Y. 1986. Training paraprofessional Christian counselors. *Journal of Pastoral Care* 40 (4): 296–304.

Tan, S. Y. *Lay counseling: Equipping Christians for a helping ministry.*

8. Tan, S. Y., and J. Bruni. 1986. Cognitive-behavior therapy with adult patients with epilepsy: A controlled outcome study. *Epilepsia* 27:225–33.

my pastoral ministry. Angela also had a part-time job managing the accounts of a hair salon company.

A significant event took place on July 31, 1984, when our second child, Andrew Hua Liang Tan, was born. Again the Lord gave us a special gift of life, and Andrew has been a real blessing and joy to us, as has Carolyn. They both have come to a saving knowledge of Jesus Christ as their personal Lord and Savior and enjoy attending church meetings and Sunday school regularly.

I was ready at this time in Toronto to give up my Psychology career and devote myself fully to pastoral ministry and the training of pastors, missionaries, and other full-time Christian workers and counselors, if the Lord so desired. It was a real struggle as I prayed over this issue, since I still wondered why the Lord had given me doctoral training at McGill University as well as invaluable post-doctoral supervised experience at University Hospital in clinical psychology, only to possibly "give it all up." But, I was willing to do what the Lord's will was, in his own way, place, and time. Angela was aware of my struggles and we prayed much together for the Lord's direction. I had jokingly said to her around this time that it may be a more ideal situation for me if I could teach at a place like Fuller Theological Seminary's Graduate School of Psychology, which has a Ph.D. program in Clinical Psychology and is fully accredited by the American Psychological Association. Little did I know then that the Lord was already working things out providentially for such a situation to happen, so that I could more fully use the gifts and training he had provided me so far in serving him and his Kingdom.

It began with my participation at the Annual Convention of the Christian Association for Psychological Studies (CAPS) in May 1984, in Dallas, Texas. I met Dr. Newton Malony for the first time, at this conference. He was Professor of Psychology and Director of Programs in Integration (of Psychology and Theology) at Fuller Theological Seminary in Pasadena, California. He informed me that Fuller's Graduate School of Psychology was looking for a tenure-track faculty member who had expertise in cognitive-behavior therapy and other areas, which fit my interests and experience beautifully! We corresponded, and in August 1984, the Annual Convention of the American Psychological Association was held in, of all places, Toronto! Dr. Malony and two other Fuller Psychology faculty members (Dr. Paul Clement and Dr. Winston Gooden) met with me for a three-hour lunch. I had just launched the Institute of Christian Counseling at Ontario Bible College and they saw the brochures and the kind of work I was doing in Christian and lay counseling. It was an exciting lunch together. I began to sense the Lord guiding us in our conversations, indicating the very real possibility of a move to Fuller in the near future.

Another providential turn of events took place in November 1984. I was invited to give a presentation of my research study on cognitive-behavior therapy with epilepsy patients to the Neuropsychology Interest Group at the Annual Meeting of the American Epilepsy Society, which took place in San Francisco! Dr. Archibald Hart, Dean of Fuller's Graduate School of Psychology therefore invited me to fly to Pasadena from San Francisco, to meet the faculty there informally and to present a talk on my work in lay Christian Counseling. He then formally invited me and my wife for interviews at Fuller for a tenure-track faculty position in January 1985. Without going into all the details, the final outcome was that I was offered a position as Assistant Professor of Psychology and Director of Practicum Training at Fuller's Graduate School of Psychology. Angela and I felt this was a definite leading of the Lord so that I could more fully pursue my interests in the integration of Psychology and Christian faith in a biblically-based, Christ-centered way. It would also allow me to make full use of my training and experience in clinical psychology. We therefore decided to accept the job offer at Fuller and moved to Pasadena, California at the end of July 1985. It was sad to leave Toronto and Canada, our dear friends at the church and the Bible college, as well as Angela's family. However, we had prayed much about this decision, and the Lord providentially guided us through this series of quite amazing events. We felt that the move to Fuller was definitely the Lord's will and hence the right thing to do. The Lord did not want me to give up Psychology after all, but I believe that the process I went through to yield my all to him was an essential one for the deepening of my relationship with him, and my obedience to his will, much like the Abraham and Isaac situation so familiar to all of us recorded in Genesis 22:1–18.

Years in Pasadena (1985–present)

Since we moved to Pasadena, California in 1985, I have served as Assistant Professor of Psychology and Director of Practicum Training (1985–86), then as Director of Training (including Internship Training) of The Psychological Center (1986–89), and more recently as Associate Professor of Psychology and Director of the Doctor of Psychology (Psy.D.) Program (1989–present), which is also fully

A.P.A. accredited, at Fuller's Graduate School of Psychology. I received tenure in 1990.

Fuller has been and still is an exciting, enriching, and challenging workplace for me. I have experienced a deeper sense of fulfillment as I have been able to use more of my gifts and training in clinical psychology as well as my experience in pastoral ministry. I also serve as Assistant Minister/Pastor in the English-speaking congregation at a Chinese local church called First Evangelical Church in Glendale, California, where Rev. Dr. Eddie Lo has been the Senior Pastor and Rev. David Clotfelter is the full-time Pastor of the congregation. I therefore continue to have a regular preaching and teaching ministry, as well as to be involved in doing some pastoral care and leadership training in the church, especially with a young adults group called Sonlite Fellowship. Angela has also been involved in leading an adults fellowship and a small group, as well as in Sunday School teaching with children. It has been a real blessing to work closely with Rev. Clotfelter, Rev. Lo, and his son John Lo who is the Youth Minister, in pastoral ministry in our church.

It has therefore been a busy and full life for us, but we are deeply thankful for our church and for Fuller. We have experienced the Lord's grace and blessings in many different and powerful ways. We have learned more about being seriously committed as radical disciples of Jesus Christ, in a disciplined way, including the regular practice of the spiritual disciplines (for example, the inward disciplines of meditation, prayer, fasting, and study; the outward disciplines of simplicity, solitude, submission, and service; and the corporate disciplines of confession, worship, guidance, and celebration) so crucial for our spiritual growth into greater Christ-likeness.[9] We have also experienced more deeply the anointing and power of the Holy Spirit, including a fuller appropriation of his spiritual gifts, fruit and truth, as we walk in the Spirit more closely with the Lord. Without the Spirit's enabling or power we will not be able to live the Christ-centered life or serve the Lord the way he would like us to. Prayer is a crucial means of knowing more of his power and enabling.

Angela qualified as a Certified Public Accountant (C.P.A.) in the summer of 1990, after taking the required exams. She had already qualified as a Chartered Accountant (C.A.) in Canada in 1979. She has been working full-time since 1989 as an Assistant Controller of

9. Foster, R. 1988. *Celebration of discipline.* Rev. ed. New York: Harper & Row. Willard, D. 1988. *The spirit of the disciplines.* New York: Harper & Row.

a fresh produce company in downtown Los Angeles. Both our children are attending a private school in Pasadena; this has allowed Angela the time and opportunity to return to her career full-time.

We lived in Pasadena from 1985–90 and moved at the end of November 1990 to neighboring Arcadia, where the Lord has provided us a spacious home in which we often have church or Fuller group meetings.

I will now share in more detail my work and pilgrimage as a Christian psychologist since coming to Fuller. First, I have enjoyed teaching a number of different courses that reflect my areas of interest as well as expertise and experience. In the School of Psychology, I have taught courses on Psychology of Learning, Cognitive-Behavior Therapy, Clinical Health Psychology and Behavioral Medicine, Biblical Theology and Christian Counseling, Foundations of Christian Therapy, and the Annual Fuller Symposium on the integration of Christian Faith and Psychology (with Dr. Rebecca Propst, who was the Fuller Lecturer in January 1991, and who spoke on the theme of "Christian Contributions to the Treatment of Clinical Depression"). I served as the Chair and one of three respondents of the Fuller Symposium in 1991. I have also taught a course in the School of Theology entitled "Training Lay Counselors in the Church," and another course in the School of World Mission entitled, "Pastoral Care in the Chinese Church." It has been a real enriching experience for me to teach courses in all three Schools at Fuller, and to interact with faculty and students as well as staff and administrators. In my first year teaching at Fuller, I audited Systematic Theology I, II, and III in the School of Theology taught by Dr. Colin Brown, Professor of Systematic Theology, and benefited much from this learning experience. Dr. Brown is also Associate Dean and Director of the Center for Advanced Theological Studies (CATS) in the School of Theology. In co-teaching an integration course (Biblical Theology and Christian Counseling) a few years ago—together with Dr. Donald Hagner, Professor of New Testament—I learned more about careful exegesis of biblical texts in attempts to develop a psychology or counseling approach that is biblically-based. I therefore have grown in theological knowledge, and have benefited immensely from interactions with my colleagues who are excellent theologians and missiologists in the other two schools at Fuller.

I have similarly learned much from dialogues with my colleagues in the School of Psychology who are experts in their respective fields, representing a wide range of interests and approaches to psychotherapy. As a result, I believe I have become a more well-rounded and balanced psychologist and therapist. While my approach to therapy is still basically broad-based, cognitive-behavioral in orientation, I now have a deeper respect for psychodynamic, existential, and systems perspectives. However, the foundational guide for me in my integration of therapeutic approaches (or anything else in psychology) and the Christian faith is the light of the Scriptures: the Bible as God's special and inspired revelation. I have therefore attempted to develop a more biblically-based approach to cognitive-behavior therapy that corrects and expands the secular version of such an approach, with eight major guidelines.[10]

Other areas of integration and research interest that I have developed over the past several years and published in, include: lay Christian counseling and lay or peer counselor training; health psychol-

10. The following guidelines are from S. Y. Tan. 1987. Cognitive-behavior therapy: A biblical approach and critique. *Journal of Psychology and Theology* 15 (2): 108–9.

1) Emphasize the primacy of agape love (1 Cor. 13), and the need to develop a warm, empathic, and genuine relationship with the client.
2) Deal more adequately with the past, especially unresolved developmental issues or childhood traumas, and use inner healing or healing of memories judiciously and appropriately.
3) Pay special attention to the meaning of spiritual, experiential, and even mystical aspects of life and faith, according to God's wisdom as revealed in Scriptures and by the Holy Spirit's teaching ministry, and not overemphasize the rational, thinking dimension, although biblical, propositional truth will still be given its rightful place of importance. The possibility of demonic involvement in some cases will also be seriously considered and appropriately dealt with.
4) Focus on how problems in thought and behavior may often (*not* always, because of other factors, e.g., organic or biological) underlie problem feelings (Prov. 23:7; Rom. 12:1–2; Phil. 4:8; Eph. 4:22–24), and . . . use biblical truth (John 8:32), not relativistic, empirically-oriented values in conducting cognitive restructuring and behavioral change interventions.
5) Emphasize the Holy Spirit's ministry in bringing about inner healing as well as cognitive, behavioral, and emotional change . . . use prayer and affirmation of God's Word in facilitating dependence on the Lord to produce deep and lasting personality change, and . . . be cautious not to inadvertently encourage sinful self-sufficiency (cf. Phil. 4:13).
6) Pay more attention to larger contextual factors like familial, societal, religious, and cultural influences, and hence . . . utilize appropriate community resources in therapeutic interventions, including the church as a body of believers and . . . "priests" to one another (1 Cor. 12; 1 Pet. 2:5, 9).
7) Use only those techniques which are consistent with biblical truth and . . . not simplistically use whatever techniques work . . . reaffirm scriptural perspectives on suffering, including the possibility of the "blessings of mental anguish" . . . with the ultimate goal of counseling being holiness or Christ-likeness (Rom. 8:29), not necessarily temporal happiness. However, such a goal will include being more open to receiving God's love and grace, and growing thereby to be more Christ-like, and overcoming mental anguish due to unbiblical, erroneous beliefs (i.e., misbeliefs).
8) Utilize rigorous outcome research methodology before making definitive statements about the superiority of cognitive-behavior therapy.

Also see: Craigie, F. C., and S. Y. Tan. 1989. Changing resistant assumptions in Christian cognitive-behavioral therapy. *Journal of Psychology and Theology* 17:93–100.

Craigie, F. C., and S. Y. Tan. 1989. Entitlement. *Journal of Psychology and Christianity* 8 (3): 57–68.

ogy and behavioral health; epilepsy; cross-cultural counseling, especially with Asians and Hispanics; missionary assessment; explicit integration in Christian counseling or psychotherapy; intrapersonal or personal integration and spirituality; the Holy Spirit and counseling; and the ethics of paradoxical psychotherapy.[11] I have chaired

11. Tan, S. Y. 1987. Lay Christian counseling: Perspectives, programs, and proposals. *Journal of Psychology and Christianity* 6 (2): 3–5.

Tan, S. Y. 1990. Lay Christian counseling: The next decade. *Journal of Psychology and Christianity* 9 (3): 59–65.

Tan, S. Y. *Lay counseling: Equipping Christians for a helping ministry.*

Tan, S. Y. 1991. Religious values and interventions in lay Christian counseling. *Journal of Psychology and Christianity* 10 (2): 173–82.

Tan, S. Y. 1992. Development and supervision of paraprofessional counselors. In *Innovations in clinical practice: A sourcebook, Vol. 11,* ed. L. VandeCreek, 431–40. Sarasota, Flor.: Professional Resource Exchange, Inc.

Tan, S. Y. 1993. Lay Christian counseling. In *Clinical handbook of pastoral counseling, Vol. 2,* eds. R. J. Wicks and R. D. Parsons. Mahwah, N.J.: Paulist Press.

Sturkie, J., and S. Y. Tan. 1992. *Peer counseling in youth groups.* Grand Rapids: Zondervan/Youth Specialties.

Sturkie, J., and S. Y. Tan. 1993. *Advanced peer counseling in youth groups.* Grand Rapids: Zondervan/Youth Specialties.

Clifford, P. A., S. Y. Tan, and R. L. Gorsuch. 1991. Efficacy of a self-directed behavioral health change program: Weight, body composition, cardiovascular fitness, blood pressure, health risk, and psychosocial mediating variables. *Journal of Behavioral Medicine* 14:303–23.

Mittan, R. J., R. A. Newman, and S. Y. Tan. 1988. Marriage rates and epilepsy. *Epilepsia* 29:686.

Helgeson, D. C., R. Mittan, S. Y. Tan, and S. Chayasirisobhon. 1990. Sepulveda epilepsy education: The efficacy of a psychoeducational treatment program in treating medical and psychosocial aspects of epilepsy. *Epilepsia* 31:75–82.

Tan, S. Y. 1989. Psychopathology and culture: The Asian-American context. *Journal of Psychology and Christianity* 8 (2): 61–75.

Tan, S. Y. 1991. Counseling Asians. *Urban Mission* 9 (2): 42–50.

Tan, S. Y. 1992. Counseling Asians. In *Healing for the city,* eds. C. W. Ellison and E. S. Maynard, 110–23. Grand Rapids: Zondervan.

Garzon, F., and S. Y. Tan. 1992. Counseling Hispanics: Cross-cultural and Christian perspectives. *Journal of Psychology and Christianity* 11 (4): 378–90.

Haynes, C. J., S. Y. Tan, and M. W. Baker. 1990. Missionary assessment: Norm comparison and prediction of perseverance. *Review of Religious Research* 32:173–78.

Tan, S. Y. 1990. Dealing with sin and reconciliation in psychotherapy: A biblical approach. *Journal of Pastoral Counseling* 25:72–79.

Tan, S. Y. 1990. Explicit integration in Christian counseling. *The Christian Journal of Psychology and Counseling* 5 (2): 7–13.

Tan, S. Y. 1987. Intrapersonal integration: The servant's spirituality. *Journal of Psychology and Christianity* 6 (1): 34–39.

Tan, S. Y. 1992. The Holy Spirit and counseling ministries. *The Christian Journal of Psychology and Counseling* 7 (3): 8–11.

Ridley, C., and S. Y. Tan. 1986. Unintentional paradoxes and potential pitfalls in paradoxical psychotherapy. *The Counseling Psychologist* 14:303–8.

and supervised over a dozen doctoral dissertations (both Ph.D. and Psy.D.) in Clinical Psychology of students and advisees at Fuller. I would like to express my deepest appreciation to them for the enriching and challenging experiences we have had together as we collaborated on research projects and studies. Research has been particularly exciting and interesting because of our basic faith stance that believes all truth is God's truth, and that God is the source of all true knowledge. His general revelation and common grace allow us to learn from good research, whether conducted by Christians or non-Christians. My doctoral students and I have been blessed to be able to collaborate on research projects with people like Dr. Robert J. Mittan who developed the Sepulveda Epilepsy Education program, and Dr. Stanley Sue who directs the National Research Center on Asian American Mental Health at the University of California, Los Angeles (UCLA), as well as with other staff members of the Center, especially Dr. David Takeuchi, who is now at the University of Hawaii.

While I believe that good integration of the Christian faith and psychology can and should occur in the conceptual-theoretical, research, and professional categories, it is my conviction that *intrapersonal integration* (that is, our own appropriation of faith and our personal integration of psychological and spiritual experience as Christians) is the most fundamental and foundational category of integration, without which, good integration in the other categories cannot be truly or fully achieved. Spirituality is a key dimension of intrapersonal integration. I feel that the Christian psychologist needs first of all, and above all, to be a Spirit-filled or spiritually mature person in order to more fully understand and appropriate truth, including "psychotheological" truth, since it is the Holy Spirit who teaches us all things (John 14:26) and who guides us into all truth (John 16:13).[12]

Tan, S. Y., and C. R. Ridley. 1989. Conceptions and misconceptions about the ethics of paradoxical therapy: Response to Hunsley. *Professional Psychology: Research and Practice* 20:139–40.

12. Characteristics of such deep, Christian spirituality include: (a) a deep thirst or hunger for God; (b) a love for God based on intimate knowledge of God that leads naturally to worship and obedience; (c) being filled with the Holy Spirit and yielding to God's deepening work of grace in our lives, and not to the flesh, requiring the consistent use of the spiritual disciplines; (d) acknowledging and using the gifts of the Spirit for God's purposes and glory, and manifesting the fruit of the Spirit and deeper Christ-likeness; (e) developing biblical thinking and a worldview that is consistent with God's perspective as revealed in the Scriptures; (f) being involved in spiritual warfare requiring the use of supernatural power and resources from God including the use of prayer and the Scriptures; and (g) being familiar with the "mystical" aspects of our faith like the "dark night of the soul." See Tan, "Intrapersonal integration: The servant's spirituality," 34–39.

With such Christian spirituality as a foundation, I feel that Christian therapists need to develop and use more explicit integration in Christian counseling or psychotherapy where appropriate. I have defined explicit integration as a distinctively Christian, biblically-based approach to therapy and counseling that openly and systematically uses spiritual resources (for example, prayer, the Scriptures, referral to church and parachurch groups) and deals with spiritual issues. It emphasizes the spirituality of both the therapist and client as foundational and integrates psychological therapy or counseling with spiritual guidance and direction in the therapeutic context. It should be used in a clinically sensitive, ethically responsible, and professionally competent way.[13] Nelson and Wilson[14] have specifically suggested that it is ethical for counselors or therapists to share their faith if therapists are addressing problems that would be helped by spiritual intervention, if they are working within the client's belief system (so that they will not force their own beliefs on the client), and if they have carefully defined the treatment contract to include spiritual intervention. My own practice as a licensed psychologist can certainly be described as one that uses explicit integration frequently. My part-time practice (ten hours or so per week) is conducted as part of the Clinical Practice Plan at Fuller's Graduate School of Psychology and The Psychological Center.

More recently, I have also been blessed and touched by the third wave of the Holy Spirit's ministry in non-Pentecostal contexts where his anointing and spiritual power and gifts have been more fully released and experienced.[15] This has happened primarily through the anointed and powerful ministry of my close friend Dr. Joseph P. Ozawa, who is also a licensed psychologist, as well as through helpful interactions with colleagues at Fuller like Dr. Chuck Kraft and Dr. Peter Wagner. I believe that the Holy Spirit's healing power and appropriate spiritual gifts (for example, exhortation or encouragement, knowledge, wisdom, discerning of spirits, healing, mercy) are crucial for an effective and anointed ministry as a Christian coun-

13. Tan, S. Y. Explicit integration in Christian counseling, 7–13.

14. Nelson, A., and W. Wilson. 1984. The ethics of sharing religious faith in psychotherapy. *Journal of Psychology and Theology* 12:15–23.

15. Wagner, C. P. 1988. *The third wave of the Holy Spirit.* Ann Arbor: Vine Books.

Kraft, C. 1989. *Christianity with power.* Ann Arbor: Vine Books.

White, J. 1988. *When the Spirit comes with power.* Downers Grove: InterVarsity Press.

Wimber, J., with K. Springer. 1987. *Power healing.* New York: Harper & Row.

selor or therapist.[16] Some important literature has begun to appear on this crucial topic of the Holy Spirit and counseling.[17] It is interesting to note that even Dr. Jerome Frank, Professor Emeritus of Psychiatry at Johns Hopkins School of Medicine has made the following comment: "My own hunch, which I mention with some trepidation, is that the most gifted therapists may have telepathic, clairvoyant, or other parapsychological abilities . . . they may, in addition, possess something . . . that can only be termed 'healing power.'"[18] The healing power of the Holy Spirit and His spiritual gifts in the context of effective Christian counseling or psychotherapy deserve much more attention and research.

The general effectiveness of lay counselors may be partly due to their being blessed with such appropriate spiritual gifts and healing power.[19] I am planning to do further research in this area with some of my doctoral students at Fuller. Spiritual gifts and power however can be best used and released in the context of spiritual maturity and the fruit of the Spirit characterized by love (cf. Gal. 5:22, 23). A theology of healing must also include an adequate theology of suffering in order to remain biblically sound and balanced.[20]

Another area that deserves more attention, study, and research is the general area of inner healing and deliverance, or exorcism, touching on the reality of evil and the demonic. There is some danger and

16. Tan, S. Y. Dealing with sin and reconciliation, 72–79.
Tan, S. Y. Explicit integration in Christian counseling, 7–13.
Tan, S. Y. Lay Christian counseling: The next decade, 59–65.
Tan, S. Y. *Lay counseling: Equipping Christians for a helping ministry.*

17. Gilbert, M. G., and R. T. Brock, eds. 1985. *The Holy Spirit and counseling: Theology and theory.* Peabody, Mass.: Hendrickson Publishers, Inc.
Gilbert, M. G., and R. T. Brock, eds. 1988. *The Holy Spirit and counseling: Principles and practice.* Peabody, Mass.: Hendrickson Publishers, Inc.
Ozawa, J. P. 1988. *Power counseling: Gifts of the Holy Spirit and psychotherapy.* Paper presented at the International Congress on Christian Counseling, Atlanta, Georgia.
Ozawa, J. P. 1988. *Prayer and deliverance in the healing of chronic disorders: Hope for the hopeless.* Paper presented at the International Congress on Christian Counseling, Atlanta, Georgia.
Tan, S. Y. The Holy Spirit and counseling ministries, 8–11.

18. Frank, J. D. 1982. Therapeutic components shared by all psychotherapies. In *Psychotherapy research and behavior change,* eds. J. H. Harvey and M. M. Parks, 31. Washington, D.C.: American Psychological Association.

19. Tan, S. Y. *Lay counseling: Equipping Christians for a helping ministry.*

20. Brown, C. 1985. *That you may believe: Miracles and faith then and now.* Grand Rapids: Eerdmans.
Coggins, J. R., and P. G. Hiebert. 1989. *Wonders and the Word.* Winnipeg, Manitoba: Kindred Press.

controversy in this area, but this should not stop Christian psychologists who are spiritually mature and gifted to explore and research it more thoroughly and biblically.[21]

In the professional and practice area of integration, I have benefited from discussions with my good friends Dr. Al Dueck from Mennonite Brethren Seminary in Fresno, and Dr. Stanton Jones and Dr. Richard Butman from Wheaton College and Graduate School, especially on the topic of psychotherapeutic practice and the Lordship of Christ. We presented a symposium on this topic at a CAPS National Convention a few years ago[22] and suggested that Christian counselors are called to the following virtues that are in contrast to those that might "pay off" in the professional world:[23] *compassion,* as opposed to isolation; *accountability,* as opposed to independence and autonomy; *transparency,* as opposed to impression management; *love,* as opposed to Rogerian positive regard (that is totally indiscriminate and must overlook evil and sin); *stewardship,* as opposed to profit maximization; *holiness,* as opposed to anonymity or wholeness; *wisdom,* as opposed to mere secular brilliance; and *integrity,* as opposed to mere ethical compliance. Above all, true deep spirituality should be the general characteristic of Christian counselors called by God.

Finally, I should mention that it has been a paradoxical but exciting experience for me to be heavily involved in the development of lay Christian counseling and at the same time to be deeply involved in professional training issues as well. I participated in the Rech Conference on Christian graduate training in professional psychology,[24] and have been one of Fuller's representatives to the National Council of Schools of Professional Psychology (NCSPP) meetings and conferences. Recently, I also served as a Member of the Program Committee for the 1993 NCSPP Mid-Winter Conference on Clinical Training in Professional Psychology, January 19–23, held in La Jolla, California, and as Program Coordinator for the Professional Issues in Counseling Track for the Second International Congress on Christian Counseling, November 11–15, 1992, held in Atlanta, Georgia. I

21. Tan, S. Y. Dealing with sin and reconciliation, 76.

22. Jones, S. L., R. E. Butman, A. Dueck, and S. Y. Tan. 1988. Psychotherapeutic practice and the lordship of Christ. Symposium presented at the National Convention of the Christian Association for Psychological Studies (CAPS), Denver, Colorado.

23. Jones, S. L., and R. E. Butman. 1991. *Modern psychotherapies: A comprehensive Christian appraisal,* 410–12. Downers Grove: InterVarsity Press.

24. Tan, S. Y., and S. L. Jones. 1991. Christian graduate training in professional psychology: The Rech conference. *Journal of Psychology and Christianity* 10 (1): 72–75.

continue to serve as a member of the Site Visitor Pool for the Committee on Accreditation of the American Psychological Association.

As professional psychology develops, it is imperative that Christian and cross-cultural perspectives be heard so that the field does not move in a direction that is completely secularistic, ethnocentric, elitist, and even antireligious or anti-Christian. I am thankful to the Lord for providing me and my colleagues at Fuller's Graduate School of Psychology many opportunities to make an impact on clinical and professional psychology in more Christian ways, including doing and publishing good research. I presently serve as Associate Editor of the *Journal of Psychology and Christianity,* and am serving or have served on the editorial boards of the *Journal of Consulting and Clinical Psychology, Journal of Psychology and Theology,* and *Journal of Pastoral Counseling.*

Since 1990 a key workshop that I have had the privilege of presenting, together with Dr. Ed Shafranske of Pepperdine University and Dr. Robert Lovinger of Central Michigan University, is an A.P.A. workshop on "Psychotherapy with Religiously Committed Clients," at its Annual Conventions. Interest in this area has grown significantly, as evidenced by the number of registrations at this workshop. Although there still are strong critics of religion, especially dogmatic religion, in the field of mental health,[25] American psychology has begun to acknowledge the importance of religion as a crucial dimension of human experience and diversity,[26] and hence of mental health and effective psychotherapy as well.[27]

25. Albee, G. W. 1991. Opposition to prevention and a new creedal oath. *The Scientist Practitioner* 1 (4): 30–31.

Ellis, A. E. 1980. Psychotherapy and atheistic values: A response to A. E. Bergin's "Psychotherapy and Religious Values." *Journal of Consulting and Clinical Psychology* 48:635–39.

26. Gorsuch, R. 1988. Psychology of religion. *Annual Review of Psychology* 39:201–21.

27. Bergin, A. E. 1980. Psychotherapy and religious values. *Journal of Consulting and Clinical Psychology* 48:95–105.

Bergin, A. E. 1991. Values and religious issues in psychotherapy and mental health. *American Psychologist* 46:394–403.

Bergin, A. E., and I. R. Payne. 1991. Proposed agenda for a spiritual strategy in personality and psychotherapy. *Journal of Psychology and Christianity* 10 (3): 197–210.

Lovinger, R. J. 1984. *Working with religious issues in therapy.* New York: Jason Aronson.

Lovinger, R. J. 1990. *Religion and counseling: The psychological impact of religious belief.* New York: Continuum.

Propst, R. L. 1988. *Psychotherapy in a religious framework: Spirituality in the emotional healing process.* New York: Human Sciences Press.

My pilgrimage as a Christian psychologist has therefore been a busy but deeply fulfilling one, especially since I joined the Fuller faculty in 1985. In the years ahead, I look forward to growing and developing even more as a Christian psychologist by God's grace. I also hope to continue to contribute to the integration of psychology and the Christian faith in a Christ-centered, biblically-based, Spirit-filled way, to the glory of God and for the blessing of many lives.

Postscript

Writing this autobiographical chapter has been a somewhat different experience for me compared to writing more technical or scientific articles for publication. I have had an opportunity to share more personal aspects of my life as a human being and as a Christian psychologist. In so doing, I have had a fresh view again of the "big picture" of my life and my pilgrimage as a Christian called by God to be a clinical psychologist. This has affected me in several ways.

First, I have been blessed afresh, with deep thanksgiving from my heart, by the sovereignty and gracious providence of a loving and faithful God who has guided my life in such amazing ways. Truly, great is his faithfulness!

Second, the uniqueness of Jesus Christ as Lord and Savior and the ultimate Answer to the deepest needs of human beings and the problem of sin, has rung out loud and clear. He has changed my life dramatically since my conversion on August 12, 1968, and continues to transform my life as well as many other lives. I am deeply thankful for his salvation, and for his love and grace that motivate me with compassion and caring to minister as a "wounded healer" to broken lives in a fallen world.

Third, the power and spiritual gifts of the Holy Spirit have touched my life and ministry in deeper ways in recent years. I am not only very grateful for such anointing and blessing, but I have been reminded to be faithful in using whatever spiritual gifts and power he graciously bestows on me for more effective ministry, for his Glory. I am motivated afresh to spend more time in solitude for prayer and deeper

---

Propst, R. L., R. Ostrom, P. Watkins, T. Dean, and D. Mashburn. 1992. Comparative efficacy of religious and nonreligious cognitive-behavioral therapy for the treatment of clinical depression in religious individuals. *Journal of Consulting and Clinical Psychology* 60:94–103.

Tan, S. Y. Explicit integration in Christian counseling, 7–13.

Worthington, E. L., Jr. 1991. Psychotherapy and religious values: An update. *Journal of Psychology and Christianity* 10 (3): 211–23.

communion with the Lord and his Word, and to continue to practice the spiritual disciplines with joy and celebration!

Fourth, I have seen the redemptive effects of my own suffering and struggles, especially with burnout, and am most thankful to the Lord for enabling me to experience his love, healing grace, and power through such experiences. I have also seen how he has used my pain to enlarge my empathic capacity for people who suffer and struggle with their own brokenness, demonstrating the truth of 2 Corinthians 1:3–4 over and over again.

Fifth, I have had a more integrated view of how I have grown and developed so far as a clinical psychologist. I have realized afresh how much I truly enjoy my work as a Christian psychologist with its many facets like teaching, doing research, conducting a part-time clinical practice, supervising students, doing administration (like directing the Psy.D. program), writing, editing, and publishing, attending and presenting at conferences, and so on. However, I have been reminded that a key priority for me is still to develop the integration of Christian faith and psychology in a Christ-centered, biblically-based, and Spirit-filled way. With God's help and by his grace I will continue to focus on this key priority in my life and work as a Christian psychologist in the years to come.

Finally, I have also seen the need for me to continually live a balanced life, including having enough time for my wife and children, as well as for the church as a supportive community of faith and as the larger family of God. Much as I love my profession of clinical psychology, it is not the be-all and end-all of my life. Whatever the Lord calls me and my wife and family to do for his Kingdom and Glory is whatever we want to do, for we know that life's greatest fulfillment and deepest blessings come from obedience to his will. The most important priority is therefore to seek the Lord and his Kingdom first (Matt. 6:33).

On an Equal Footing

Kirk E. Farnsworth

There is a cartoon, by Gary Larson, with a bunch of spear-carrying tribesmen chasing a couple of middle-aged looking guys who are either on their way to a costume party or desperately trying to get out of the jungle—in a hurry. The caption reads, "Couldn't resist, could you, Farnsworth! . . . Just HAD to reach up and honk the chief's nose!"

That just may be my real-life story. It's at least a part of it, as the following narrative will indicate. My purpose in telling my story will be to reveal my own journey through the jungle of life and also some of the "chiefs" whose noses I have felt inclined to honk. The territory I plan to cover will be in these areas: family, education, church, and career.

A few more words before I get started. First, I will be making a distinction between *chronicity* and *narrative*. I will not be developing a time line to simply catalog events from womb to tomb. Rather, I will describe events in each of the four areas listed above that give it texture and rhythm and develop a common theme or themes. I will of necessity be selective, and I will also be imaginative and honest. I will look for but not demand narrative unity.[1] A question I will be asking myself is: Is my life fundamentally constituted by a series of discrete events that make no sense? Or are the events linked into a story, a narrative unity, that grows out of a set of coherent and continuous themes and allows the events of my life to be meaningful?

Second, I will not be making a distinction between *love* and *work*, making them exclusive from one another in living and defining life. Freud did, but I will not. Love in our society is usually contextualized in the family and work in one's career. I have strongly resisted such separation all my life. Family life and career—love and work—have not stood apart from one another, separate and complete unto themselves. Nor have they stood together as the only, ultimate consideration of what life is all about. Rather, they have always been woven together, interdependent and mutually enriching. And, they have always been subsumed under something that is greater than the two of them together. A second question I will be asking myself is: What is that something that is greater than commitment to my family and commitment to my work?

A third distinction I will be making is in the area of integration. Since this is a book on how individuals have developed into mature Christian psychologists, I will be considering my development as a Christian and as a psychologist and my integration of the two. The distinction I have in mind is between *creativity* and *control*. By the latter I am referring to integrative imperialism, or the tendency of evangelical Christians to not accept psychology on its own terms but only if it is combined with its biblical counterparts or critiqued by its biblical conscience.

For example, much of what has appeared in the integration literature in our professional books and journals has been of a controlling nature:[2]

1. Construction of models for finding points of contact/agreement among psychological findings and theories, Bible verses, and biblical principles.
2. Critiques of the models, to protect the privileged position of the Bible in any pursuit of truth.

1. See Hauerwas, S. 1990. *Naming the silences: God, medicine, and the problem of suffering*. Grand Rapids: Eerdmans.

2. From Farnsworth, K. E. 1991. Christian counseling that is more than Christian in name only or just a field of dreams. *Journal of Psychology and Theology* 19:376–81.

3. Critiques of the psychological findings and theories from a Christian worldview perspective or by point-by-point comparisons with Scripture, to protect the church from corruptive secular influences.
4. Creation of systematic Christian approaches to the understanding of the human person, for example a Christian psychology, utilizing a predetermined set of biblical control beliefs.

That is one side of the integration picture: protecting the church and the privileged position of the Bible and controlling psychology. I would like, however, to look at what I have contributed to the creative side of the integrative enterprise. By this I mean the extent to which my work has been innovative and unique, without a prior agenda. Has my story been one of control, of building my own "field of dreams," telling myself that if I build it, if I lay down the guidelines for God to speak through psychology, he will come? Or has my story been one of listening to God, of hearing him say, "I have *already* built it. *You* come"? The third question I will be asking myself is, How has God spoken to me, and how have I creatively found ways to respond?

Family

I was born in Iowa in 1940. My parents, older brother, and I lived there, in a small rural community, until he and and I went away to college in the 1950s and my folks retired and moved to California in 1973.

Iowa was where extended family was. Dad's parents lived a block away and one of his two older brothers half a block away. Mom's mother lived twenty-three miles away, along with one of Mom's two older sisters. It's interesting to me that my wife's situation was very similar: her parents still live in the same small town in Wisconsin, backyard-to-backyard with the property where her dad was born and raised. His mother lived in that house and his two older brothers nearby until they died.

I'll start by reminiscing about my two granddads. I never met Grandpa Teeple. He was killed in a car accident three years before I was born. He'd been drinking. Grandpa Farnsworth was a drinker too. He had a built-in oak liquor cabinet above the bathtub—very practical man. He also chewed tobacco, but lived until he was ninety-six.

Grandpa Farnsworth was also a very predictable man. He kept the same hours at the family bank until he was eighty-five. He even walked the same route to work and home at noon and night every day. He was also very tight financially and had a mean streak as a disciplinarian. His oldest son ran away from home and none of his three sons graduated from college. He and his second wife (the first died right after marriage from a gun accident) lived simply, with apple pie and homemade bread on the menu almost every day.

Granny (Dad's mom) was a refuge for me as a youngster. I could always stop in for homemade honey cookies (they had their own bees) and peanut butter sandwiches with honey on top. I also enjoyed going through their old stuff that kicked around: they never threw anything away. Even though she and Mom didn't get along very well in later years, I never entered into that conflict. For me it was a foundational period of negative associations with alcohol, strong feelings regarding unfairness and meanness, and a positive sense of stability and home as the center of the world.

My other grandma certainly reinforced my feelings about home. I loved to visit her, watch her kill a chicken for lunch and let it flop around headless in the yard, play cards with her (she let me cheat), and play croquet in her yard. We'd go over there practically every Sunday. She would visit us frequently; it was fun to be sick in bed when she was around, because she'd act out funny roles and talk in German to make us laugh.

Mom was the disciplinarian, and she was tough. Used to spank us with the wooden spoon she made bread with. Then one day we got one of those paddles with a ball on the end of a rubber band connected to the paddle so you could keep hitting the ball as it came back to you. It soon broke and Mom converted it into a spanking paddle. My brother, Greg, and I retaliated by drawing pictures on it of an Amazon-like creature chasing two little innocent-looking cherubs (just like in the Gary Larson cartoon). That was not a wise thing to do: we paid. In my mind this was not abuse, but it did give me some strong feelings about overdoing discipline.

Mom was also a major source of fun in the family. She was a cutup who truly enjoyed having a good time. She could take a lot of kidding, about her weight, about some of her baby-talk expressions, about some of her goofy golf shots. I even gave her a nickname that has stuck to this day: Muz. She loves the name, although she probably has forgotten that it came from those spanking days and stood for muscles.

Dad was typical for his generation: work as number one priority (but not around the house), putting his boys through college as number one goal, and angry outbursts on an annual basis after letting it build up all year long. He would take verbal karate chops around home for months at a time and just stuff his anger. Then about once a year he'd lose it and really blow: chair-above-head style. He never struck Muz, but he surely didn't manage his anger well. Dad was dominated by his dad, who kept him at lower middle-class wages for years in the family bank. They had gone through the Great Depression, and Granddad's goal was financial security. Dad's was the same, which evolved into an all-encompassing goal of passing every penny possible on to his boys. His occupation and vocation in life was to manage his money. And he did it alone. Muz didn't even know his salary; not that she didn't ask—no, demand—to know what it was. She'd say, "We need a new refrigerator." He'd say, "You can't get one." "Why not?" "We can't afford it." "How much do you make?" "I won't tell you." "You tell me or I'll get a divorce!"

And on and on it would go like that. Greg and I would look at each other and ask, Why? I was beginning to formulate some pretty negative impressions about money. But Dad was not just about money. He was also about funny. He had a great, low-key sense of humor. He'd just crack us up with quips and comments. It did become a problem, however, when he got older and he thought his grandchildren were laughing *at* him. He kind of came around full circle, becoming pretty cranky just like his dad in older age.

Greg was a great big brother (three years older). We ran in different circles but were quite close. We shared many of the same interests. Everything he did, I did. I even took on his expressions and tried to dress like him. Partly because of Greg's success in high school, I changed dramatically between eighth grade and high school (more on that later). I wanted to achieve like that too.

We had great family vacations, when Muz could pry Dad away from his job. One year we took an excursion to Colorado in our old 1941 Buick Century, where every stop we got gas, oil, and smokes for Dad. Interesting thing: Dad quit smoking one day, from two packs a day to zero, and never went back to it. He took up eating fish bait instead. The family joke is that on one of our Yellowstone trips, we were fishing in a little stream without proper bait, using cheese instead. Dad wasn't fishing but stayed back in the car. When we returned for more bait he was just finishing a cheese sandwich he'd made with all that nice cheese he'd discovered. He didn't know we were using it for bait and had finished it all up. We've laughed about that for years.

I was kind of a nonconformist as a little kid, but in a quiet way. In fourth grade I took a girl to a matinee and sat there with my arm up over the back of her chair, aching so badly I thought it'd drop off. Greg, unbeknownst to me, was a few rows back and reported it all to our parents. I got a talking to. I loved to play pool and tried the corner pool hall one day—just one time—and sure enough someone saw me go in and reported it to my folks. I got a talking to.

I used to love to throw snowballs at moving targets: loft them high and long and let moving vehicles run under them for a big splash on the windshield. One day my throw was a little too direct, and it went through the side window and hit the driver in the ear. He chased me all over town in his truck. And there was this girl from my third-grade class that I hit in the ear one time with a precision throw from across the street. She told her parents. I really got a talking to that time.

I also had a compassionate side. I would bring home a stray dog, befriend the outcasts at school and help the older folks in the neighborhood. It was my idea to take a meal over to the old hermit living across the street from Grandma's and to mow our neighbors' lawn free of charge when they were gone. And I was the only one who didn't laugh at old Nellie Heinspeter walking down the middle of the street in her anklets and tattered dress. I cried when her house burned down.

Education was the arena for most of my life until I got married. But that's my next topic after this one. Family really became my focus and the home-as-center-of-my-life theme took on even greater meaning when I married Rosie and we had our three children: Craig, Eric, and Kristi.

I think my immediate family is just as important as my family of origin was in impacting my development as a Christian psychologist. Rosie has had an immeasurable effect on my growth as a Christian, as I will detail at some length in a later section. And in raising our children together she made some brilliant psychological moves, especially with our foster children (we had five over the years), that I could come back to later and say, "Oh yeah, that's just the way you should have done it." But before I witnessed her actions and before I had consulted the books in my library, I didn't have a clue. She simply demanded fairness and honesty, consistency and age-level appropriateness, pulling one's weight and doing one's best with what God has given you—of all our children, and of me.

God really did bless us with three wonderful children. Each has fully developed his or her God-given talents and been a pleasure to be around. It's hard not to start bragging about their many achievements, but I will say this. All three went through the secular educational system without "hurting their faith," as many Christians fear. From preschool through graduate school, they have demonstrated that God abides with his own who are faithful to him and that we are indeed called to be in the world, not of the world. The American Legion School Award, given annually to the eighth grader who best exemplifies courage, honor, leadership, patriotism, scholarship, and service—for God and country—symbolizes what I am talking about. All three of our children won that award. And to make it even more special, the award ceremony was held each time on our wedding anniversary.

All three contributed greatly to team efforts (I'll go ahead and brag). Craig won the Big Gun Award in track and field, at one of the finest high schools in the State of Illinois, two years in a row, elected by his teammates as the major team contributor for the year. He carried that team to heights it had never gone, running four middle-distance races—two of them anchoring relays—every meet. His efforts enabled others to qualify for the State Meet, where he was the first in the school's history to win an individual medal. He was also a co-captain on the soccer team as it began its road to respectability. And it didn't end with high school graduation. In college, Craig qualified for the TAC Junior National Meet (for eighteen-year-olds and under) and was an Academic All-American twice. I could identify with his exploits: *high standards, excellence in performance, and one-of-a-kind.*

Eric too was an outstanding scholar-athlete, also in track and soccer. Again I could identify: *little brother following big brother.* But Eric, as I had, strove for individuality. He too became one-of-a-kind by balancing athletic excellence, particularly in soccer, with being a National Merit Scholar and a very popular, all-around good guy. In college he almost single-handedly kept the soccer program alive, was selected as one of fifty college students in the first Leadership America program, and won a Truman Scholarship in addition to receiving full-ride scholarships through graduate school at Princeton University.

Not to be outdone, Kristi also received a full-ride college scholarship and is presently in graduate school at Cornell University on a scholarship. I view these scholarships as the product of hard work. They were earned. In that sense, Craig, Eric, and Kristi have all paid their own way, and I believe they have gotten a better education for it. Kristi too was a scholar-athlete (and musician, like her brothers—all played brass instruments). And what a team member. After her first year, as a junior, at her new high school after we moved to Washington, she was elected by her teammates Most Inspirational both years in cross country and again in track. She qualified for the State Meet in both. Although Kristi resembles her brothers in so many ways, she too has found her own identity. She was selected as one of fifty college students in the first American-Soviet student cultural exchange program, initiated by Reagan and Gorbachev, and parlayed it into an opportunity to hand out Christian literature. She has a gift of evangelism that does not challenge but invites the seeker to a relationship with the Lord, and she balances that with a well-thought-out challenge to male dominance wherever she sees it: both inside and outside of the church. In the Lord there is no dominance. She wants to serve the Lord and *will not accept any artificial barriers* to being all that he wants her to be. Again, I can identify.

Education

My first memory of school is walking down the sidewalk in front of our house and waving goodbye to Mom on my way to kindergarten. Leaving was painful, but I got used to it, walking/riding that exact same route for the next twelve years. My second memory is not being able to spell my last name: it was too long. My third memory is the best: the girl sitting in her fur coat in the desk next to mine. Same gal I later took to the movie, that ill-fated day my brother "reported" on me.

My best friend, Jimmie, was my total focus in those early days. Learning in school was a pain. Outside school we had great times playing guns, riding bikes, playing ball, and swimming in the buff in the Turkey River. We also had b.b. gun fights and stole our parents' cigarettes for little smoking orgies under the bridge on the dirt road to Baldwin's Hill. I swore a lot and really tried to be one of the boys.

But something strange happened on the way to high school. Kind of like Dad and smoking, I went cold turkey on all that stuff, which meant of course not palling around with Jimmie anymore. Later I realized I had enjoyed and resolved a classic chum relationship, as described so beautifully by Harry Stack Sullivan.

Literally overnight I got serious about grades, training for athletics, practicing my cornet, trying out for everything and singing tenor in the choir (good grief). I just took off: I never got anything other than an A on my report card from then on, graduated valedictorian of the school's largest class up to that year, with a 4.0 grade point; won varsity letters in football, basketball, track, and baseball; got a One rating with my cornet solo at the State Music Contest three years in a row, as well as getting One's with ensembles and vocal solos; made the All-State Band one year and Orchestra the next; got a One at the State Speech Contest in humorous declamation and a one-act play; joined every honor society there was; and on and on.

How can I explain the turn around? It was not a religious conversion. It was not forced. I think I saw what was happening with my friends and compared it with what my brother was accomplishing and just decided to strike out on my own and go for some of the goodies.

The downside was that I went for all of the goodies. My high school life was totally self-centered and self-serving. College changed all that. I started in industrial engineering at Iowa State University, because Sputnik had just gone up and I was good in math and science. Or so I thought. First grade in Engineering Drawing: F! I didn't even print my name right. Must have still been too long. I worked like crazy to get my grade up to a C and looked for a way out.

One of my brother's fraternity brothers shared a paper with me that he had done on industrial psychology. As I read it, I thought what a great transition that would be: more people-oriented but still salvaging my first quarter's credits. So I went into the Student Counseling Service and took the Strong Vocational Interest Blank. Wouldn't you know, I scored only average on the psychologist scale. But that did not deter me, nor did my C in the Introduction to Psychology course I took that quarter. Later I realized the norming on the psychology scale was based on experimental psychologists exclusively, and what I thought was people-psychology actually registered high on the social service scales. Why wasn't psychology there? Later I also realized that the Strong is not a social-change instrument but only a social-mapping instrument. It (the Strong-Campbell now) tells what is, not what should be.

That was my first experience of the natural science/human science tension in psychology, and the Intro. course was my second. I didn't like it. Not enough stuff on people as real live people. Not enough on helping hurting people. Just rats and statistics and experiments with people doing dumb things like rotary-pursuit and memory-drum tasks. Too much manipulation, too elitist about the kind of information about people that was worth knowing. And, of course, the really interesting chapter in the book was the last one. We never got to that. It's still like that.

I joined a different fraternity than my brother's. This was a major event in my identity formation. For the first time I was really on my own—sort of. We played in the University Band together—Greg first chair and me down the line—and saw each other during NROTC drills once a week. That was about it, but still there was a family presence during my first year.

Fraternity life was good for me. The Phi Delt house was a huge improvement over the dorm, or "brick armpit" as we referred to the biggest one, Friley Hall. The whole Greek system at Iowa State (thirty-three fraternities, twelve sororities) was very positive, with much more of an emphasis on educational and extra-curricular achievement and community service than on partying. It was within the fraternity context that I discovered others than myself and got in touch with that compassion again. The only office I found myself desiring was that of pledge trainer. He was the only guy who was allowed to befriend the entire pledge class, be available to them, counsel them, advocate for them. I loved that, and I think I was good at it.

The theme of helping others followed me through graduation when I was also commissioned an officer in the U.S. Navy, and into the naval service. More on that later, under "Career," but being a division officer on a ship homeported in Yokosuka, Japan, gave me lots of opportunities to lend a helping hand—or a listening ear.

Counseling was definitely the career for me, so I went back to Iowa State and entered the masters program. It was at that time that I broke the financial umbilical cord with my parents. They offered to pay my way, but I figured I'm married and have one child, I have Navy Reserve pay and an assistantship (the first one Iowa State had ever given in the counseling area) and I'm doing this on my own. I had grown up in the Navy. It also became very obvious to me, quickly, that the responsibilities I had as a Navy officer prepared me very well for graduate school. Half the students in my entering class couldn't make it. They wanted to know what to read by Friday, but we were told only what we needed to learn and when we needed to learn it by. That was usually by the end of the quarter, and we would meet in the meantime for discussions on a variety of topics. It was just like the Navy: here's a problem/project, come back in a month with it solved/completed.

I enjoyed graduate school, and went on for a Ph.D. because the courses at that level intrigued me. Also, my committee urged me to do so. My first publication came halfway through graduate school—in *Psychological Bulletin* no less.[3] Because it was the premier professional journal at the time some faculty members were actually jealous of me. They needed publications like that; I didn't. Not yet, anyway. It was my first introduction to professional competition and jealousy and began for me a theme of being an outsider, which developed into being a gadfly, and finally a prophetic witness.

Two books that I encountered during my coursework really opened my eyes and helped me begin to steer a course in psychology that seemed to be the person-centered psychology I always thought existed but could never find. The first was Abraham Kaplan's book *The Conduct of Inquiry*.[4] Kaplan helped me clarify and accurately understand the language of behavioral science. Suddenly "dustbowl empiricism" wasn't exactly all I had thought it was.

The other book, edited by T. W. Wann, was titled *Behaviorism and Phenomenology*.[5] In it Sigmund Koch, Robert MacLeod, B. F. Skinner, Carl Rogers, Norman Malcolm, and Michael Scriven debated everything from "Behaviorism at Fifty" to "Toward a Science of the Person" to "Phenomenology: A Challenge to Experimental Psychology."

The behaviorism-phenomenology conflict was one of my intellectual tensions at that time. The other one was a tension between psychology and Christianity. The problem did not have to do with conflicts in what each was saying about the human person so much as the fact that I was rigorously studying the one but not the other. Or at least it seemed. In reality, by God's grace, I was learning far more in my church and from books purchased at the local Christian bookstore than I ever imagined. The writings of Francis Schaeffer and John Stott were particularly helpful in creating a balance for me.

The Psychology Department had a forum for working out tensions such as these. I remember Leonard Ullmann coming to preach to us that schizophrenia was a myth. He was at the vanguard of the behav-

3. Farnsworth, K. E. 1966. Application of scaling techniques to the evaluation of counseling outcomes. *Psychological Bulletin* 66 (2): 81–93.

4. Kaplan, A. 1964. *The conduct of inquiry: Methodology for behavioral science*. San Francisco: Chandler.

5. Wann, T. W., ed. 1964. *Behaviorism and phenomenology: Contrasting bases for modern psychology*. Chicago: University of Chicago.

ior modification movement, when that term still meant something. It was exciting to hear his humorous stories about getting mental hospital patients to feed themselves and quit hoarding pillows. And Jerome Frank, of *Persuasion and Healing* fame, came by to convince us that voting for Barry Goldwater in the coming presidential election would be an utter tragedy. O. Hobart Mowrer (*The Crisis in Psychiatry and Religion*) stood in—or I should say sat in—and gave us, in one of his last public lectures, an impassioned plea to put some guts back into the spiritual side of helping hurting people. I took all three of them seriously.

My master's thesis was titled "Analysis of Criteria for Counseling Outcomes." It was a straightforward experience, and I got it published after completing my Ph.D., in the *Journal of Clinical Psychology*.[6] I was very much interested in finding a way to evaluate the effectiveness of what I planned to spend my life doing. There had been no definitive study up to that point, and none has been done to this day, but I kept trying.

My first proposal to my doctoral dissertation committee was to evaluate psychotherapy using the methods for criterion development that I had been working on. They shot it down; take too long, they said. We want you out of here as our first Ph.D. in counseling psychology so we can begin the process toward APA accreditation. My second proposal also went nowhere: an evaluation of the milieu therapy in the Day Treatment Center for schizophrenics at the VA Hospital where I was interning. So I decided to play ball, or play the game, and whomped up a proposal for doing a factor analysis of the women's form of the Strong (the men's and women's forms were later combined into a single, "unisex" form). Dave Campbell (of Strong-Campbell fame) and I had the same major professor, Ed Lewis, and he (Campbell) had several years earlier gone on to the University of Minnesota and collected all the data I would need. The connection of my major professor made getting access to the data easy and really shortened the process. Everyone was happy.

Happy, that is, until my oral defense of the finished product. Let me give a little background. A year or two earlier another dissertation had been done factor analyzing the men's form of the Strong to see how many orthogonally independent vocational interests men have. Computer technology had not been capable of the calculations

6. Farnsworth, K. E., E. C. Lewis, and J. A. Walsh. 1971. Counseling outcome criteria and the question of dimensionality. *Journal of Clinical Psychology* 27:143–45.

needed for such a study until then. Indeed, my statistician said it would have taken one hundred statisticians one hundred years to work out by hand the 400 x 400 correlation matrix that my study needed. Well, the other study did not find a religious interest factor for men. But mine did for women. Why?

I discovered that the women's form had eleven religion items and the men's form only four. During the oral exam, Wilbur Layton, well known in the psychological measurement field and very protective of the Strong, stated flatly that the inventories simply reflected the *fact* that women have much more interest in religion than do men. I came back with, "How can men register a similarly high interest in religion if there are so relatively few items to load up on such a factor? Was it not possible, in fact probable, that the possibilities for a man to pursue a religious career based on the results of such a test were severely limited by the conceptions of those who selected the items to include in the test?" Not a smooth move, honking the chief's nose in an oral defense.

Dr. Layton shot back, "If you include that in your dissertation, I will not sign it." I said, "All right, but I will include it when I get my dissertation published." Which I did the following year, in the *Journal of Applied Psychology*.[7]

The clinical side of my graduate education was not quite so stormy, but it again carried the theme of being the first one. I spent a year as a counseling intern at the Student Counseling Service and the following year, the final year of my graduate program, as an intern at the Day Treatment Center at the VA Hospital in nearby Des Moines. I was the first one from our program to obtain an internship in an outside clinical agency.

At the University, my supervisor was David Mills, who for years, until just recently, was the director for ethical affairs for the APA. My supervisor at the VA was John Crites, from the University of Iowa, one of the big names in vocational psychology at the time. The chief psychologist at the VA was S. J. Williamson, a black psychologist who had participated in the famous restaurant sit-ins during the infancy of the civil rights movement. I will never forget sitting with him for most of the day, just the two of us, in the Hospital auditorium watching the TV account of Martin Luther King's death. As we

7. Farnsworth, K. E. 1969. Vocational interests of women: A factor analysis of the women's form of the SVIB. *Journal of Applied Psychology* 53:353–58.

talked, or rather I listened to S. J., I began what became an ongoing interest in the richness of black psychology.

My very first client at the Counseling Service was suicidal, so I got initiated right away. My first three months at the Day Treatment Center were primarily consumed with figuring out who was staff and who was patient. When I got that straight I then moved on to the realization that I definitely did not want to work with either population again. On the positive side, I had actually accomplished what I took the VA internship for in the first place: to gain a basic understanding of schizophrenia, something I could not grasp just from reading books and listening to lectures.

I received my Ph.D. in counseling psychology from Iowa State University in August, 1968. My education was just beginning.

Church

During graduate school was when I began to grow as a Christian. Just like my children, I had never experienced Christian education at any level, except Sunday school, which was for me a total waste of time. Now, after having taught at two state universities and three Christian colleges, I have to say that I am not persuaded that Christian education is as good as many claim or that secular education is as bad. I hear reports all the time about parents who are mortified that little Johnny's faith will be deep-sixed unless he gets a Bible-centered education all the way through. And of course the public school gets nothing but scorn and ridicule.

I say hold on just a minute. One: if a child's faith is so shaky that it must be protected from reality, then maybe it should be tested, and thereby strengthened. Two: if you don't like the public schools, then do something constructive, like teach there or volunteer there or serve on the school board: we did. And don't forget the Christian teachers and administrators who work there; they really appreciate the support. Three: how we approach schooling with our kids tells them volumes about how to approach life, through faith or through fear.

Let's go back and take a look at what faith was like for me when I was growing up. My family belonged to the Congregational Church in town. I remember incredibly boring sermons, singing in a lousy choir, and great potluck suppers. I remember praying often in high school for God to help me do well and do the right thing, and I even started reading my King James Bible with a little study guide: that lasted almost a year. What I do not remember is hearing or reading about Jesus Christ as a personal Lord and Savior.

When I went off to college, I was morally fit and intellectually prepared to just keep right on doing what I had been doing so well. I attended the Collegiate Presbyterian Church all four years and was enthralled by the pastor's sermons. Again, not a word about Jesus Christ as personal Lord and Savior.

Then during the summer after my sophomore year, I met Rosie. We were working at George Williams College Camp at Lake Geneva, Wisconsin, and took an immediate liking for each other. I remember her asking me one night if I was a Christian, and I said of course I was. I had in mind two reasons for saying that: I was a Christian, according to anything I had ever heard about what being a Christian was, and the bottom line, I wanted to keep dating her. But she didn't stop there. She explained that Jesus had died for my sins, and that no one could come to the Father but through him. That hit me pretty hard, and I wept.

After a delightful summer I went back to college with a burning question: was she right? So I enrolled in an Old Testament survey course and, more importantly, read the New Testament for the first time. I found that it agreed with all that Rosie had said; they were both saying the same thing. They were either both right or both wrong. I decided that I must do this on my own, and mustering all the integrity I could, I decided I would not make a decision for Christ to save a relationship. I had to decide one way or the other, though. That much was clear.

So I did, but hesitated to tell her because I did not want her to in any way think I had made a decision for Christ to please her. But she picked up a change in my letters and in other subtle ways that I didn't even notice. She took it as a confirmation, for she had asked the Lord to reveal to her one way or another where I was in relationship to him and saw my change as an answer to that prayer. To me, it meant we were on an equal footing at last.

But we were not. That became most evident to me right after we were married. I had graduated from college, been commissioned an ensign in the U.S. Navy, gotten married, and here we were in Japan—all in a three-month period of time. We were sitting in our little Japanese house in Zushi, several miles from the Navy base in Yokosuka, and were about to eat dinner. I wasn't sure why we had to say grace before every cotton-picking meal, but Rosie had a much stronger and far less frivolous frustration. It had to do with giving. She put it to me like this: "You say we can't give, and I have been giving monthly support to several missionary groups since my days at Wheaton. Does this mean that I must stop obeying God just because I got married?" The line had been drawn.

I thank God to this day that I had not been raised in a church that fed me a male dominance theme that would have demanded that I take over the spiritual leadership and that if she would submit on this point everything would turn out rosy. That would have been absolutely nuts. Me, a babe in Christ, preoccupied with everything but growing in Christ, leading a mature Christian? I know today that, had I stuck to my guns, we would not be giving any more than possibly a grudging 10 percent, after all other needs and wants were taken care of. And even worse, I would have broken my wife's spirit and quenched the Holy Spirit in her life.

I did not think about Ephesians 5 at the time, but I believe I hit it on the head: mutual submission (equal footing by another name). I just did it first. The Bible doesn't say who goes first, it just says do it. The more I learn about the type of servanthood exemplified by Jesus, I know I did the right thing.

God has blessed our family mightily, all the while teaching all of us who the real Lord of our family is. He has taught me how to be a servant leader and what headship and authority really mean. Headship is a position and is a given. Authority is the power of the position and is granted. Headship, to be consistent with servanthood, involves giving up personal privileges, just like Christ, and building others up in Christ. Authority, when it is exercised with a servant attitude, is granted by those over whom it is exercised. It is earned, and it is based on trust and mutual accountability. Headship is not ruling, and I do not have authority just because I'm a man.

Giving was not easy for me. My family history had been one of not giving really at all and protecting against the future by saving everything. Further, the male myth modeled to my generation was that a real man puts his kids through college. No two ways about it. My first step in breaking my bondage to that myth was when I turned down my dad's offer of money for a master's degree. The second step was actually many little steps every time we were faced with a commitment to give and limited resources. We had committed to the Lord, after Rosie's insistence, to give first, at the beginning of each month, 10 percent of the figure we needed to basically live on, and an increasing percentage of each additional $1,000 after that, all the way to 100 percent if the Lord so blessed. Let me tell you that was tough. It not only stood against everything I thought I knew about money, but how could I tell the kids we couldn't afford something when with my old accounting (read nature) I knew we could? How could we keep giving like that and still put food on the table after moving expenses took us down to nothing?

We moved from Japan to Iowa to New Hampshire to Illinois to Washington. Every single time the temptation was almost unbearable to suspend our giving or at least cut it back for the year or two it always took to get back on our feet. But we never did, and we always had food on the table. And the thought always came back to me about all those people we have helped support. Had their needs scaled back just because ours had increased? Didn't they need to eat too? I was learning.

We have been blessed so we could be a blessing to others. Yes we have given sacrificially, and always as the Lord has provided, and he has provided in so many ways beyond the money involved. Probably the greatest blessing to me has been the release from the male money myth mentioned above. I did not have to gear my entire life to putting my kids through college. When they were young sometimes I would lie awake nights in a cold sweat thinking about that. But by putting my complete trust in the Lord and his provision, I let go of the cross-generational sin of bondage to money and put my energies into parenting and setting my family life on a higher plane than my career. I think the results speak for themselves, and I praise God for it. In the area of male provision alone, he just blew that myth right out of the water: as I indicated earlier, our children all have gotten scholarships all the way through. Craig, five-year undergraduate program and two years of graduate school; Eric, four-year triple major and two years of graduate school; Kristi, five-year undergraduate program and two years of graduate school. Does $250,000 sound close?

Meanwhile, back in graduate school. I believe that is where I really began to catch up with Rosie in spiritual maturity. We attended the Evangelical United Brethren Church and, as I mentioned before, had an upbeat Christian bookstore in town. Through adult electives and excellent Christian literature, my theological education really took off and actually began to catch up with the psychological side of what would become for me an abiding career interest. The key to the process, I believe, was developing a daily discipline of Scripture study. Henrietta Mears's wonderful book got me started,[8] and Scripture Union's "Encounter with God" series has kept me going to this day.

8. Mears, H. C. 1966. *What the Bible is all about: An easy-to-understand survey of the Bible.* Glendale: Gospel Light.

The theological/psychological balance I was beginning to experience began to express itself through both my writing and speaking endeavors. My entry into the popular Christian literature was with three different articles in InterVarsity's *HIS Magazine;* the third was also included in a book of readings titled *Guide to Sex, Singleness & Marriage.*[9] I followed those with a piece on male filters in *Daughters of Sarah* and another in *Free Indeed.*[10] Then the *Alternative Celebrations Catalogue* asked me to do a chapter on consumerism, and *The New York Times* picked it up and interviewed me for an article (WBZ Radio in Boston hooked me up all the way from Illinois for a live interview on the topic).[11] Then I wrote a very well-received article for *The Other Side* on family living based on biblical simplicity, and another on institutional integration for the *Christian College News* that was picked up and reprinted by several Christian college publications across the country.[12] My most recent publication was another article for *The Other Side* based on a chapel talk I gave at Wheaton College on institutional lifestyles.[13]

I will walk through my publishing activity in the professional Christian literature in the next section. In addition to writing I have also done lots of speaking in both the popular and professional arenas. Beginning in 1970, I have spoken for numerous special church events, Pioneer Girls regional meetings, Christian Association for Psychological Studies conventions, University and college symposia, InterVarsity staff retreats and state conferences, college and seminary chapels, American Scientific Affiliation conventions, biblical feminism seminars, an American Association of Christian Counselors regional conference, radio interview and talk shows, public school

9. Farnsworth, K. E. 1971. Love that heals. *HIS Magazine* 32 (1): 11–13; Farnsworth, K. E. 1972. Find yourself loveable. *HIS Magazine* 32 (8): 28–31; Farnsworth, K. E. 1974. The myth of the machine: That steam-pressure talk about sex is a lot of hot air. *HIS Magazine* 34 (5): 28–30; Farnsworth, K. E. 1974. The myth of the machine. In *Guide to sex, singleness & marriage,* ed. C. S. Board. 1974. Downers Grove: InterVarsity.

10. Farnsworth, K. E. 1976. The male filter. *Daughters of Sarah* 2 (3): 8–10; Farnsworth, K. E. 1978. Moral ciphers and male filters. *Free Indeed* 1 (2): 22–26.

11. Farnsworth, K. E. 1978. The psychology of consumption: How to kick the habit. *Alternative Celebrations Catalogue,* 4th ed., 98–100; They're taking the $ out of Christmas. *The New York Times,* 3 December, 1978.

12. Farnsworth, K. E. 1980. New families for a new king. *The Other Side* 16 (12): 14–19 (reprinted in *Christian Living,* 1981, 28 [6]: 2–4, 7); Farnsworth, K. E. 1983. No integration of faith and living, no committed Christian institution. *Christian College News,* 7 January: 1–2.

13. Farnsworth, K. E. 1985. Living justice: Rethinking our individual and institutional life-styles. *The Other Side* 21 (8): 30–33.

special education and continuing education seminars, a national conference on faith and learning, a Mennonite student and young adult services workshop, a live TV interview program, Christian College Coalition psychology conferences, a Salvation Army regional young adult retreat, single parents retreats, church secretaries retreats, managers retreats and seminars, a National Conference on Church and Family workshop, and the first International Congress on Christian Counseling.

Many of these speaking engagements have been with my wife. Our topics have included couples' relationships, family living, biblical feminism, living simply, and parenting. Much of what we do is model the interaction of both of us presenting and answering questions and perhaps even disagreeing on a particular topic. One of our most satisfying experiences was teaching a course in our home, an old farmhouse with chickens and sheep in the yard, bee hives, and a 100 x 180-foot garden, while I was at Trinity College. It was on voluntary simplicity and alternate Christian lifestyles. We did that for six summers, teaching students how to cook creatively with vegetables, bake bread, live off the land, be creative with throwaways, conserve nonrenewable resources, consume wisely, and give proportionately. It was fun.

But probably our least satisfying experiences have been in the organized church. One issue just keeps popping up: what women cannot do in the church. One instance among many stands out in my memory. It was while we were attending a Conservative Baptist church in New Hampshire. They needed a Sunday school superintendent, and the nominating committee came to me to fill it. I said no, but my wife was both interested and qualified. They came back with, "Why not do it together?" I said, "No, she can handle it herself just fine."

There seemed to be a hidden agenda, which became clearer with their next suggestion: "What about if she serves with the former superintendent and his wife?" "Why?" "Well, your wife can do the work, he can make the announcements from the pulpit and his wife can be there as the chaperone." They as much as said that! I could not believe it, and Rosie was crushed. What a bunch of demeaning messages, not the least of which was that she could do the job alone only if she were a man, qualifications notwithstanding. Her tearful response was, "The only thing that would make the difference would be if I shaved in the morning." A line had been drawn again and I realized that to be helpful on this issue I must submit again.

Well, they were desperate and let her have the job after all that. She did an exemplary job and blazed a trail for all the other women in that church as well. I knew, though, that we'd face this sort of thing again, so I chose to submit my service in any church from then on to hers. In other words, if she would not be allowed to serve in some way, then I would not either. I even broadened it to include all women: I would volunteer to speak from the pulpit the very next week after the first woman did, and I have kept my word. I know what it feels like to stifle a gift—I have not been speaking much from pulpits—but I have also been able to show little children in nurseries that they are important enough for men to care for and women are important enough to participate in ministries that change lives, not just diapers, and to serve the Lord's supper, not just church suppers.

As I am writing this section, it is becoming obvious to me that the church has not been the principal source of my wife's and my learning to walk the Christian life. Nor did we turn over the responsibility for our children's growth in the faith to the church. We always kept it within our family, as we believe we are told to in Scripture. Further, it is clear to me that "the church" has not been synonymous for us with the *local* church. Recounting our experience is not a matter of chronicity, of just going from one local church story to the next based on where we moved to next. Rather, our story is one of critique and commitment, of putting all things to the test and holding on to the good (1 Thess. 5:21), wherever we are. Our story is furthering the kingdom by bringing an awareness of kingdom issues to whatever local body we are a part of.

Mutual submission, servant leadership, sacrificial giving, God's provision, women's ministry—these are kingdom issues. We weep over those local churches that run roughshod over them, blindly following the leader but not the Lord, even after the glory of the Lord has departed. We therefore maintain and will continue to maintain a prophetic witness to further God's kingdom. Our desire is not to promote disunity but to bring honor to the Lord when what is being done does not square with Scripture. Our method is always, we hope, to reason together and speak the truth in love.

Career

While the church has not been the source of my spiritual growth, it has been the context for it. The same has been true for the jobs that I have had. Starting with the Navy, my place of employment has been a place of growth through conflict, not from overcoming barriers to personal advancement, but from seeing flaws in the system and addressing them. Conflicts have always been opportunities and I have grown immensely by confronting them, often on behalf of other people (colleagues, students, and so on). There have been costs, of course, usually in the form of being cast as somewhat of an outsider. To a point that has been fine with me. I am a team player, but I do not respect, for example, an arrogant group of insiders who can do no wrong, who are accountable only to themselves and who continue to accumulate and retain benefits even during hard times when others are being laid off.

I do not see privilege in Scripture. I see equality among believers. Perhaps we could call it a theology of equal footing, as we read such passages as these: "For he who is least among you all—he is the greatest" (Luke 9:48b NIV); "As it is written, 'He who gathered much had nothing over, and he who gathered little had no lack'" (2 Cor. 8:15 RSV). Those two sentences say it all. Whatever context I am in, I will always strive to give witness to the servanthood mentality of being least and the stewardship mentality of not gathering too much. Surely, all believers must come to realize that in God's eyes there is no privilege in being first, and that it is our Christian duty to make sure that those who have little do not have too little. I believe it is God's desire that we all share an equal footing in life, and not that some have privileges and some do not.

I have also brought a critique mentality to every job that I have had. But I must make a distinction between being critical and critiquing. I see critique as an honest evaluation, a God-honoring approach to making things better; being critical is being judgmental, which just makes them worse. Al Dueck, also writing in this volume, has been a real inspiration to me in the development of a critique mentality. His example and my own experience have shown me how to evaluate without being judgmental and that the God-honoring approach is the one that is based on the servanthood mentality of being least.

Meanwhile, back to peacetime Navy duty in Japan. We lived in a little Japanese house in Zushi, had our own car, and the ship was in port over half the time. In many ways it was like a two-year honeymoon. When we did put to sea it was exciting, but it was even more exciting to come back home. We would go to Hong Kong for R & R once a year and visit many of the ports in and around the South China Sea at times in between. I volunteered for everything on those essentially goodwill trips: spoke in schools, took tours with local government officials, dined at Kiwanis geisha parties. I usually just walked around, camera at the ready position, mouth hanging open, just enthralled by the sights.

But the greatest sight of all—I will never forget the vividness of the details—was when we steamed up Tokyo wan (bay) on a beautiful autumn afternoon, Mt. Fuji off the port side, coming home after a six-week tour to Singapore. We were all in our dress whites, blushing from "channel fever," anxiously looking for our dependents on shore as we turned into the port of Yokosuka. And there they were. Walking toward us as we docked, with our light blue Ford Falcon in the background, was Rosie in the red dress she had made, carrying baby Craig, whom I had never seen. As she walked up the gangplank, carrying that beautiful little boy, my mind snapped a picture that will hang there forever.

On board ship (USS Jupiter, AVS-8) I successfully qualified as Officer of the Deck (OOD) Underway and in Port, served as Ships Officer and Combat Information Officer, then Cryptosecurity Officer, Communications Officer, and finally First Lieutenant. The Executive Officer was a tyrant who totally controlled everyone's actions while aboard ship. No one could deviate from his plan or venture an opinion. We were so restricted that when a crack finally appeared in our corporate straightjacket, we just exploded through it. It was about a matter so trivial that it is almost unbelievable that in our minds it was essentially mutiny. What happened? He had decided that tacos, which we all dearly loved, were not dignified enough for wardroom meals! To a person we stood up to him and bucked his authority (honked his nose, so to speak), and he put tacos back on the menu.

My first trip to sea was during Typhoon Karen, the one that leveled Guam in the summer of 1962. I have never seen anything like it. The Chief Engineer and I had calculated the ship's righting arm to be 47 degrees: the amount of roll to either side we could sustain and make it back to an upright position. Well, we were out in the middle of this thing, pitching and rolling like crazy. I happened to be on the bridge at the time, just hanging on. I noted the clinometer at one point, and it hit 48 degrees to starboard. The ship just hung there and shuddered and shook. Slowly it came back, and as I took a deep breath of relief, it rolled over to the port side and hit 48 degrees again! I was petrified. It groaned and creaked all over again, but it came back. The old rust bucket had come through.

My last trip to sea was two years later. I was the OOD for getting underway and entering port, and it was my job to make all preparations for the ship getting underway. The Jupiter was leaving for the

U.S. after being homeported in Yokosuka for more than ten years. It was a gala ceremony indeed: geisha girls dancing on the pier, the homeward-bound pennant streaming from the fantail, fireboats steaming around shooting water into the air and CINCPACFLT (the admiral in charge of the Pacific Fleet) on board. When the lines were singled up and I had asked the admiral to depart the ship so we could get underway, I remember thinking, "It's been good, but this is sayonara for me too. I'm not making this a career."

During those two years I had developed some good administrative skills by working with Navy regulations in a variety of billets. I confirmed my desire to pursue a career in the social services by working with Navy personnel as a division officer. And, I had developed a strong distaste for the emotional wear and tear from being gone for a week, home for a week, gone for a week, home for a week, and confirmed my suspicion that advancement up the career ladder in the Navy was very political and tied as much to one's superior officer's personal preferences as it was to job performance. I decided to go to graduate school and pursue a career in counseling.

After graduate school I began my counseling career at the University of New Hampshire Counseling and Testing Center. I got licensed right away and within a year became the Assistant Director. The Director, Bob Congdon, became a good friend and somewhat of a mentor. Our staff was very community-oriented, passionately processing issues of the day and our own conflicts at three-hour weekly meetings, and once- or twice-yearly all-day retreats at one of our homes. I was the token Christian; we had a token homosexual, token feminist—everyone had an ideology. But I have to say this: it was one of the most caring groups of people I have ever been a part of anywhere.

I remember the morning our main receptionist came to staff meeting and sobbingly told us that her husband, on the faculty at UNH, had come home the night before and told her he was in love with his lab assistant and ordered her out of the house. She told us how she had competed with girls and women all her life and had committed herself in marriage to only one man for the rest of her life, and now he was gone. She had no one. We all sobbed: she had us.

A couple of years after that one of our other receptionists had a psychotic break, and one of our staff members—probably the best behavior therapist I have ever known—wanted to talk to me. As we sat in his office, he just poured out his heart. He said he wanted me to know that he and his wife had been active in the free-love movement and the receptionist's troubles were because of that. He and she had had a sexual liaison and things had gone from bad to worse. He hadn't told me before, he said, because he knew I would see his behavior as wrong, and he didn't want to hear that. He knew it was wrong too. I was saddened, for both of them as well as for the apparent fact that my Christian witness for all the years I'd known him, showing him the sufficiency of Christ, had created a barrier between us, not an invitation to the kingdom.

I was also deeply moved to share with him the power of such temptations on me, too, every day I came to work, and the huge threat they were to my number one priority, my family. We wept together. I know this opened a door for him, because at an ensuing staff meeting he shared an openness to Christ for the very first time. As for me, I had a door slammed in my face when I went to the next Monday noon faculty Bible study and made the request of them that they pray for me to persevere in the face of those strong temptations. The leader, an elderly professor, said, "That's not what Bible study is for. We don't do that here."

Another pressure point for me was dealing with suicidal students. I had evolved into the on-call therapist for the University Hospital, and I got involved in some pretty bizarre situations there. Outside the hospital too, like the gal who kept me on the phone at home late one night while she was dying from an overdose. Fortunately, I recognized the background noise and got the campus police there in time. But I was spooked for months afterward every time the phone rang. In another situation I had to do a little detective work just to make contact. We had received a letter addressed to the whole staff saying something important was in a certain book in the library. I went over and checked it out; inside was a crumpled suicide note. I called her, and when she came in she just sat curled up in a corner of my office, week after week. Slowly we worked her out of that, and she wrote me this note:

> I wanted to sit down and think a couple of things out with you. Because sometimes you know what is going on inside of me better than I do. And, what is even better, you know that sometimes I know even better than you.
>
> People keep telling me, My dear, you have a split personality—known in the jargon as simple schiz. A kid could get so he really believed it. So, when someone comes along and says, Listen, I really think that you have a lot of control over things, naturally that person has got to be of questionable character! Who in hell can tell a split kid that he is capable of responsibility? What in hell right do you have to tell me I can

> run my own life? You're supposed to tell me I'm too sick. When someone tells a kid like that—a dumb, two-peopled kid—that he has control, a lot of stuff happens inside. Maybe, just maybe, I'm not schizy, and maybe things don't have to get gray and weird.
>
> At first I thought you were a bastard just like all the rest, ready to hit me. You could have hurt me a couple of times—you didn't. You could have dug out some psych. tests or made me uneasy by asking me about some things I have done—but you didn't. And besides that, you play musical chairs when I'm uncomfortable. Those are kind of trusting things. You could really hurt me. But, I trust you.

It was a long haul with that "two-peopled kid," but she made great progress. A year after we terminated, I was riding my bike home from work and a car whizzed by and came to a screeching halt a hundred feet ahead of me. Out of the car she leaped. She came running up to me and wrapped her arms around me. "It's so great to be alive," she said. "I'm student teaching in Massachusetts and I love it."

I love feedback like that, and usually it comes just as unexpectedly. The third case I want to cite started just about as bleakly. It was one of those dark New England late afternoons in December, and this gal came into my office and settled down on the floor in front of one of my floor-length windows. She just stared out into the darkness: not a word. Well, I decided to join her on the floor in front of the other window. I had nothing to say either. But I did put a hand on her shoulder. Soon she slowly got up and settled into a chair and began to talk. She had been looking out the window at International House, where just the night before she had spread-eagled herself naked on her bed and taken on all comers: six in all.

Understand that this young woman sitting in front of me departed drastically from every definition of beauty that existed in our culture at the time. This was not a matter of sex for her nor could it have been entirely a matter of sex for her violators. For her it was an act of self-punishment for the trash she saw herself to be. Her father too had violated her forty-nine times. She had the deepest sense of self-loathing and worthlessness that I had ever seen.

Gradually she too worked her way out of it. She was so happy with herself one day that she walked into our session made up and dressed to look pretty. I had to bite my lip to keep from laughing. She looked awful. But something much more important was going on inside her. I didn't really see it until several months later. One Sunday I was setting up chairs in the church we were helping get started in Durham, and in she bounded, not trying to look pretty, but she was radiant. As she engulfed me, she cried out, "Brother Kirk, praise Jesus!"

I was flabbergasted. I said, "This is wonderful. We have to get together and critique what happened." When we did, she said one thing stood out more than all the rest, and it happened that very first night she came to my office. I had touched her—touched garbage—and hadn't flinched. And I was the first one—the first one—to touch her without hurting her in some way. Then during some of our final counseling sessions, as we talked some about the Lord she had begun to put it all together. "As you did it to one of the least of these my brethren . . ." (Matt. 25:40 RSV).

These were very formative years for me. I was pursuing Gestalt Therapy with gusto, attending workshops conducted by Laura Perls, from the New York Gestalt Institute; Joe Zinker, from the Cleveland Gestalt Institute; and others, and coming very close to signing up for the professional program in Cleveland. I began devouring everything I could find on the phenomenological movement in psychology and came very close to accepting a position in the psychology department at the mecca, Duquesne University in Pittsburgh.

I also began developing and publishing in the relatively untouched field of integration (equal footing by yet another name).[14] Dick Bube's conception of confusion of categories gave me a great starting point. Bube saw the Bible, a data base, being related by author after author directly to a scientific discipline, as in this statement: the Bible disproves such and such scientific theory. This mistake is prevalent to this day. The correct comparison is between theology and science, not between one of them and the object of study of the other. By comparing theology and science, not the Bible and science, we bring a balance to the integrative task, because human error can be acknowledged on both sides of the equation (not just the psychology side). My contribution was to bring balance to the experiential and cognitive aspects of the integration process. Up to that point the literature was almost exclusively conceptually oriented; a real field of dreams of thought, not action. My emphasis on what I called embodied integration was, I believe, more biblical: it put walk to the talk.

These were frustrating years for me. When it came time to be promoted to Associate Professor in the Psychology Department, they

14. Farnsworth, K. E. 1974. Embodied integration. *Journal of Psychology and Theology* 2:116–24; Farnsworth, K. E. 1975. Psychology and Christianity: A substantial integration. *Journal of the American Scientific Affiliation* 27:60–66.

weren't going to include my articles in Christian publications in the review process. But I insisted, because they were a part of me and I wanted to be evaluated for who I was. Further, I wanted to make it as a Christian psychologist in a secular setting. After an extended review, I was promoted. Meanwhile we were going through some real trials at the Counseling Center. The Vice President for Student Affairs was pushing for creation of an administrative hierarchy that contained a new level of managers just under him. Not only was it unnecessary, in our opinion, but the money would have been far better spent hiring service providers that we desperately needed. I became a leader in what turned into a prolonged battle, with our whole staff threatening to quit and set up our own shop elsewhere in town. We were fighting for the students, and they and we ultimately lost.

I figured it was a good time to take a sabbatical. My application was accepted and arrangements were made for a postdoctoral fellowship at Fuller Seminary. It was a great learning experience, being exposed to formal theological study for the first time. Soon after I arrived at Fuller, I realized I wouldn't be going back to UNH. This was opening up a new area of my life, one that I had only glimpsed teaching part-time for the previous couple of years at Gordon College in Massachusetts, and I was pretty excited about it.

Clark Barshinger had ignited my imagination just before I went on sabbatical about working at Trinity College in Illinois. His vision was a psychology department that taught psychology as a human science and had as its primary goal the education of students as persons, not as wannabes: I wannabe in graduate school when I get outa here. My colleagues at UNH thought I was crazy to go to a little "nowhere" school, but I knew it was the right thing to do. We moved there in 1975.

The Department of Psychology really took off. Within a few years it became the largest department in the College. I was also involved with the Counseling Service, as Director, and within just a couple of years we were seeing one-third of the entire student body. In those early years the faculty was really excellent across the board. But Trinity had a dark cloud hanging over it that periodically rained destruction. From my experience of being counselor to several faculty members and administrators, and being totally involved myself, I saw the clearest demonstration of the negative effects of top-down management I have ever seen. I will not get into personalities here, but the carnage of those years in other people's lives had a deep and abiding effect on me. And it certainly affected the College as well, as one good person after another left and Trinity continued to destroy itself from the inside.

I stayed on for a few years, "honking the chief's nose" while continuing to build my career around my family. I scheduled all my classes so I could attend all of our children's school events, day or night. We also attended most of the extracurricular events at the College: basketball games, soccer games, cross country meets, band and vocal concerts, student recitals, and "country fairs." We even helped the students start a recycling center and ate as a family in the cafeteria once in awhile. I know the students appreciated our involvement, and I really enjoyed seeing students in class the next day or even the same day and remarking about these other aspects of their lives. It brought a real *whole*someness into the classroom. I will never forget the athletic banquet one year when all the students and coaches spontaneously rose and gave me an ovation of appreciation.

Integration of faith and learning had to have a lived-out component to it, and I really tried to model that. Not just conceptual, but embodied, not just in the classroom, but also in outside activities, not just in the words of Scripture, but also in relationships and recycling. And not just the individual but the institution as well.

My emphasis can be seen in the name of the Faith/Learning/Living Institute that we started at Trinity for Christian college faculty from all over the U.S. It ran for several summers and was a great success. My emphasis could also be seen in my growing advocacy of institutional integration at that time. From my experience of the institutional chaos referred to above, I was feeling the weight of the need for redeeming institutional structures as well as individuals. An institution with all Christian employees was not necessarily a Christian institution!

Four books were fueling my fire: Hendrik Berkhof's *Christ and the Powers*, Wendell Berry's *The Unsettling of America*, Walter Brueggemann's *The Prophetic Imagination,* and Katharine Bushnell's *God's Word to Women.*[15] As far as my own writing, I was getting very interested in integration models and wanted to make a con-

15. Berkhof, H. 1977. *Christ and the powers,* trans. John H. Yoder. Scottdale: Herald; Berry, W. 1977. *The unsettling of America: Culture and agriculture.* New York: Avon; Brueggemann, W. 1978. *The prophetic imagination.* Philadelphia: Fortress; Bushnell, K. C. 1923. *God's word to women: One hundred Bible studies on woman's place in the divine economy.* North Collins, N.Y.: Ray B. Munson.

tribution in that area.[16] The response I have gotten has been very gratifying. In the non-Christian professional literature, I had earlier published an article in *Psychotherapy: Theory, Research and Practice,* which contained a significant amount of material by Jacques Ellul on prayer and the Apostle Paul on despair.[17] I was surprised and pleased that Eugene Gendlin, the editor, accepted it as submitted, without revision. Another article, in the Christian professional literature, dealt with the issue of professionalism, and that too received an excellent response.[18] Finally, a Trinity colleague, Wendell Lawhead, and I published a book on a Christian approach to careers.[19] It was the first workbook InterVarsity had ever published, and they did a beautiful job. Both Trinity College and Wheaton College have used it as the text for a life planning course, others have required it for the entire freshman class, and several seminaries and churches have used it on an ongoing basis. Also, it has been translated into Chinese.

In 1983 I gladly accepted a position at Wheaton College as a professor of psychology. The highlights of my relatively brief stay there concerned two books and a chapel talk. The first book was the product of a very generous faculty development grant and resulted in a critique of psychological methodology, theological methodology, and integration methodology.[20] The back cover quotes Newt Malony as saying, "Destined to be a landmark in the integration enterprise . . . that will deeply inform present as well as future generations of Christian psychologists." I certainly hope so. The second book was created for

16. Farnsworth, K. E. 1978. Models for the integration of psychology and theology. *Journal of the American Scientific Affiliation* 30:6–9; Farnsworth, K. E. 1981. *Integrating psychology and theology: Elbows together but hearts apart.* Washington, D.C.: University Press of America; Farnsworth, K. E. 1982. The conduct of integration. *Journal of Psychology and Theology* 10:308–19; Farnsworth, K. E. 1982. Responses to "the conduct of integration": An appreciative reaction. *Journal of Psychology and Theology* 10:334–36; Farnsworth, K. E., J. M. Alexanian, and J. D. Iverson. 1983. Integration and the culture of rationalism: Reaction to responses to "the conduct of integration," Part 2. *Journal of Psychology and Theology* 11:349–52.

17. Farnsworth, K. E. 1975. Despair that restores. *Psychotherapy: Theory, Research and Practice* 12:44–47.

18. Farnsworth, K. E. 1980. Christian psychotherapy and the culture of professionalism. *Journal of Psychology and Theology* 8:115–21.

19. Farnsworth, K. E. and W. H. Lawhead. 1981. *Life planning: A Christian approach to careers.* Downers Grove: InterVarsity.

20. Farnsworth, K. E. 1985. *Wholehearted integration: Harmonizing psychology and Christianity through word and deed.* Grand Rapids: Baker Book House.

Wheaton's 125th anniversary.[21] One faculty member from each of several academic departments was chosen to participate, under the editorship of Art Holmes. Each of us wrote a chapter on integration in our discipline and then rewrote it after being critiqued by each of the other authors. It was an exciting process and an excellent product.

The same group of professors was then asked to do a chapel series on justice. Mine was the final talk, titled "Living Justice." I applied the Prophet Jeremiah's admonition to not boast in one's wisdom, strength, or riches, but rather in the practice of loving-kindness, justice, and righteousness (Jer. 9:23–24), to the issue of institutional integration in general and a critique of Wheaton College in particular. At one point, much to my surprise, I received a standing ovation from a large group of people in the audience. What a privilege it was to give what amounted to a valedictory to college teaching and receive such a response both then and in the weeks that followed.

I say valedictory because I was being recruited at that very moment by CRISTA Ministries, a not-for-profit Christian conglomerate in Seattle. As it turned out, we moved to Seattle within three months. This was a definite leading of the Lord, not just a career move. In fact, we have never made a career move as such, but always a move based on the Lord's leading. Our best check on that has been that it was never my idea alone, but in every case the Holy Spirit has convicted Rosie and me independently and at the same time that it was what we should do.

It was a real step of faith to leave academia after seventeen years and enter into a management position at a level totally new to my experience. Actually, I have come full circle and am applying all of my previous educational and professional experiences. I am a vice president for the CRISTA Ministries corporation and the Executive Director of CRISTA Counseling Service; I see several clients each week; I host a twice-weekly live call-in radio show; I have taught for the Fuller Seattle Extension; and I continue to have ample opportunities to speak and write. Also, we live on five acres and have sheep and bees again (and I ride the ferry across Puget Sound every day to and from work).

The integration of ministry and business has been a marvelous experience these past eight years. We have turned around a stag-

21. Farnsworth, K. E. 1985. Furthering the kingdom in psychology. In *The making of a Christian mind: A Christian world view & the academic enterprise,* ed. A. Holmes. Downers Grove: InterVarsity.

nate, debt-ridden counseling ministry by developing and following a clear mission statement, ministry objectives, and an annual strategic plan, and by positioning ourselves as totally professional and thoroughly Christian. Also, we evaluate our services utilizing Jeremiah's three criteria of loving-kindness, justice, and righteousness, and have a significant ministry to the poor through our Wellspring Fund, which is funded by individual donations and foundations. The Lord has truly blessed us. We have grown remarkably in the past few years to six locations with twenty-two therapists seeing over 4,000 different people yearly, 20 percent of whom qualify for Wellspring funds, and with an annual budget of 1.5 million dollars.

My numbers have not been as impressive on the publishing end of things over the same period of time. After having several articles included in the *Baker Encyclopedia of Psychology* (on consumerism, interest measurement, phenomenological psychology, phenomenological therapy, and vocational counseling), I got away from writing for several years.[22] Then the *Journal of Psychology and Christianity* requested an article on validating religious experience and I responded with a methodology for putting it to the test and holding on to the good.[23] That article pulled together a lot of things that I have been working on for a number of years.

My current interest is in writing about servanthood, pulling together what I have learned from working in the organizations I have described above and teaching courses in organizational psychology; what I have learned as a husband and father, and teaching courses and seminars on family living; and what I have learned from being a therapist for twenty-five years and teaching undergraduate and graduate-level courses in therapeutic psychology. Servant managers, servant parents, and servant therapists: that is what my life is all about.

Wrapping It Up

As I look back at the three questions I asked at the beginning of this project, I believe some answers have emerged from my narrative. First, I do believe I achieved *narrative unity.* It was so obvious to me as I wrote that I could not just provide a chronological account. I don't live like that. I live through interaction of interconnected

22. Benner, D. G., ed. 1985. *Baker encyclopedia of psychology.* Grand Rapids: Baker Book House.

23. Farnsworth, K. E. 1990. Understanding religious experience and putting it to the test. *Journal of Psychology and Christianity* 9:56–64.

themes that provide meaning for my life. I found those themes to be quite coherent and very consistent.

I also found myself unable to separate love and work. Family and career were interlocked at every point. I was pleased with that. In answer to my second question, I would have to say that a *sense of vocation* is that greater something that subsumes under it commitment to both my family and my work. Furthering God's kingdom as my vocation was evident to me throughout all the four areas I covered: family, education, church, and career.

Thirdly, I was very pleased to see my *creativity* in the area of integration all laid out in one place. In answer to my question regarding how God has spoken to me and how I have responded, I was surprised to see ample evidence of both in each of the four areas. I can honestly say my story has not been, "I'll build it; you (God) come."

It also struck me rather forcefully how all my life I have sought *significance* and striven to be unique in whatever I do. That has prepared me and energized me for being both a servant leader and a prophetic witness. Another fundamental theme is *compassion*, which has prepared me to take up a career of helping others, to have a strong sense of justice, to take up the cause of women in ministry, and to affirm mutual submission in my marriage. The latter has created a context for learning about simple living, sacrificial giving, and God's provision.

Another theme is *balance*, and that is why I find integration in every aspect of my life, whether it be integrating psychology and theology, balancing the tension between business and ministry, or raising children. My whole life is in fact embodied, or wholehearted, integration. A final theme is *critique*, where I have challenged forces of insignificance and powers of imbalance all my life. That mentality has provided me with a context for growth, and although I have taken my lumps, it has been worth it. God has been good.

A Privileged Calling

C. Stephen Evans

Who do you think you are, C. Stephen Evans, to write an autobiographical essay? What makes your life distinctive enough to warrant telling others about it?” I am afraid that the answer is “Probably nothing at all.” My life has been a very ordinary one in most respects: a conventional upbringing, education, career, and family. No great crises or dramatic episodes punctuate its rhythms. Perhaps the only justification for writing my story is precisely its ordinary quality; the lack of much that is unique or idiosyncratic may allow me and those who read to focus on the universal dimensions of human life that we share. The one oddity of my story's inclusion in this volume is that I am not a psychologist, but a philosopher with interest in psychology.

In any case, I shall proceed, emboldened by the fact that I was asked to do this, and by a hope that even if no one else finds the essay valuable, it will be very helpful to me to write it. Though I think too much introspection a dangerous thing, I also believe there is great value in periodically taking stock of one's life, seeing where one has been and where one would like to be going. For me this is an opportunity to do just that.

I shall organize my story in several sections that have a certain chronological order. That order is, however, not precise, since the different dimensions of my life that I want to consider separately exist simultaneously. I shall proceed in the following manner: I begin with my beginning—early family and church experiences. Next I shall write about my education, focusing particularly on my undergraduate experiences at Wheaton College. I shall then proceed to say something about my career as a scholar and teacher, and conclude with some thoughts about my family and personal life and my spiritual struggles as an adult. The overarching themes that will (I hope) tie these disparate narratives together are the themes of providence and vocation. I am a follower of Jesus Christ, and I do believe that as his follower I have a calling. It is a calling that I cannot fulfill through my own unaided efforts. It is God's providential care that has made it possible for me to discern that calling; it is God's providential care that has made it possible for me to fulfill that calling to the degree that I have.

Early Family and Church Experiences

Roots

My parents were both from rural northwest Georgia. They moved to Atlanta during the Great Depression. My only sibling, an older sister, was born in 1941; I followed eight years later. I think that because of this large age gap, I have some of the characteristics of an only child. Though my sister and I are now close, we were not particularly intimate when I was a child.

Neither of my parents came from well-to-do families; however, relative to the extreme poverty of the rural South of that era, I suspect their families were not particularly bad off. I heard the usual stories of poverty from that era: Christmas meant getting an orange or other piece of fruit as Santa's present; summers were made to be shoeless; helping out at home meant hours of back-breaking work picking cotton. I am sure that my own relatively privileged and affluent upbringing does not allow me properly to appreciate the difficulties such poverty entails. Nevertheless, I think my parents' memories of childhood were largely happy ones. My father had to drop out of school after the eighth grade to help out on the farm, yet he has often spoken with nostalgia of the baseball games he played as a child, even though the sole ball owned by anyone in the group had to be restitched each night.

Both of my parents' families were impressive in different ways. My mother's family placed a high value on education. Her father, who combined schoolteaching (in a one-room schoolhouse, where my mother later taught as well) with farming, was the only person in a sizeable area with any college education; he had completed Young Harris, a junior college in North Georgia. Somehow he was able to see that every one of his eight children completed high school plus at least one year of postsecondary education. Thus my mother completed a year of college at West Georgia, which enabled her at that time to obtain a teaching license. One of her brothers actually completed a Ph.D. and eventually became the chairman of the psychology department at East Carolina University. My mother's people constituted a warm and intimate family, with perhaps a goodly share of arguments and even flashes of temper, but the kind of family where everybody knew that there was an underlying love so that the people yelling at each other would be embracing and reconciled a few minutes later.

My father's family had less formal education but always struck me as equally bright and thoughtful. There were teachers among the eight children of that family as well. Most impressive about this family, however, were the personal qualities: the love and commitment the family exhibited. I will never forget the way my aunts and uncles visited my grandfather on a daily basis when he had to go to a nursing home, or the seemingly endless love and care showed to each member of the family as the times of decline came for several in turn. When I wish to conjure up an image of what steadfast love, loyalty, and commitment mean, many memories of those people come quickly to mind. They were, and those who remain still are, simple, God-fearing people; the kind of people who really are the strength of a nation.

There were times in graduate school and later when I was tempted by the dazzlement of cultural sophistication, tempted to accept the unspoken assumption that the people who really count in life are the people who know all about the latest figures mentioned in *The New York Review of Books*. However, any temptation to measure the worth of people by such worldly measures was, I believe, successfully counterbalanced by those memories of my parents and their families. I feel very humbled when I compare my own achievements with the personal virtues of these people.

Parents

My father was and is a quiet man; he does not express himself often in words. He is a man of deep emotions, however—unafraid to cry, unafraid to hug. I always felt loved by him. He worked long hours, driving a city bus. It was a job he did not enjoy, and yet he worked fifty, sixty, even seventy hours a week to provide for his family. In those days the city buses were operated by a private company and bus drivers' salaries did not compare with those of municipal systems today; my mother was a teacher, but teachers in those days in Georgia were paid abysmally. Thus money was always tight, even in a "two-income" family. My father also worked hard around the house. He not only did the usual "male" things like yard work; I clearly remember him doing dishes, and with a vacuum cleaner in his hand. I am grateful for the example.

Though he worked long hours my father did make time for me. I treasure the memory of going to Atlanta "Cracker" baseball games (often when my Dad was driving a bus to the game), and Saturday fishing trips to my Uncle Bill's small, well-stocked lake near Marietta. Though I have not cleaned a fish since I was a teenager, I think I still remember how, as I recall evenings in the back yard dealing with our catch.

My mother's teaching career resumed when I was four or five years old. With her one year of college she was eligible only to be a "long-term supply" teacher, which meant she was paid the rate of a substitute even though she had a regular classroom. She taught third, fourth, or fifth grade. I commuted with her to Chattahoochee (one of the first words I learned to spell) Elementary School, a school in a very poor area. I can still remember my shock when I went home with a friend and discovered his home lacked indoor plumbing. I enjoyed school there and quickly discovered I had a talent for such work; in fact, I skipped second grade and was troubled in school only by boredom. I mainly lived for our lunchtime softball games; a game for which I had little ability. I was usually saved, however, from the ignominy of being the "last one picked" by the fact that I was good friends with many of the better athletes.

When I was around eleven, my mother lost her job because the school system decided to insist on a full four years of college. She was able to gain a new position outside Atlanta in Smyrna, on the condition that she work toward her bachelors degree. So my mother embarked on a college career, with two children and a full-time job.

How she was able to take evening courses, summer courses, take care of kids and husband, cook and clean, escapes me. All I can say is that my mother was a remarkably strong woman. The side benefit of her attending college was that I got to go to college with her, quite literally. After school we would take the trolley downtown to Georgia State University. After a cheap hamburger for dinner, my mother would attend class, while I stayed in the University Library. I believe it is here that I acquired most of my education, especially of history, psychology, and sociology. (My mother majored in sociology since there was no education major there at the time.) I was learning little in school at this time; by my eighth grade year I had stopped doing homework altogether. High school seemed a complete joke, but I loved reading my mother's textbooks, and I was fascinated by the library. There was no systematic plan in my education here; I am not even sure if I knew how to use the card catalogue, though I suppose I probably did. I simply browsed until I found a book that fascinated me, and would read until class time was over, usually between 9:00 and 10:00 p.m. Then home for another day on the trolley, or perhaps to be picked up by my father just getting off work.

The rest of my education was supplied largely by the city public library—to which I often went by bus on Saturday mornings, returning with six or seven books ranging from dog and baseball stories to historical fiction and light literary classics—and the church library. I have always loved reading, and to this day often read late into the morning hours when I am engrossed by a book; I just don't have the self-control to stop when I can read "just one more chapter." I think I understand some of the dynamics of addiction from this; I'm just lucky I developed what might be called a "positive addiction."

When I think of my parents I am profoundly grateful to God for giving them to me, or rather me to them. I know that most of what I am can be traced to them, including my spiritual identity, which I will discuss in the next section. I could of course mention things that irritated me then and even now; I regret that I was not allowed to attend dances. I still feel conspicuous and self-conscious on a dance floor with my wife, who loves to dance. However, such irritations are truly insignificant when I think of the enormously weighty goods my parents bequeathed me.

Church

The most significant thing my parents gave me was a Christian upbringing. They were committed and devout, and I knew their faith was serious and real. We attended several Baptist churches in turn. In two of these my father, who had an excellent voice but no musical training, sometimes served as "minister of music." These were churches where the term "fundamentalist" was regarded as a badge of honor and an important indicator of genuine Christianity. (It was not until I was in college that I discovered that the term "fundamentalist" had become a term of abuse.)

The most important of these churches was Colonial Hills Baptist, pastored by Paul Van Gorder, later of the Radio Bible Class and Day of Discovery Programs. There at the age of six, at the close of a Sunday night service, I responded to an altar call and prayed with the pastor to give my heart to Christ. I still regard that night as the night of my conversion. I know well now how little I knew about Christianity then. I also know how much my faith has changed (I hope deepened) over years, and how many times it could have been derailed if there had not been a reaffirmation of that initial commitment. Nevertheless, that night, of which I have a remarkably clear memory, gave my life a direction. It was there my walk with Jesus began.

Colonial Hills was a large church, and typical of many fundamentalist churches of the period. There I absorbed dispensationalist theology and learned to study the Scofield Bible. I experienced "revival" services, an annual missionary conference, and endured a four hour "watch-night" service on New Year's Eve.

I have many friends with similar fundamentalist upbringings who have deep scars. Some of them even shared my experience of Colonial Hills. Churches such as that one, which lie on the margins of society, attract more than their share of unhealthy individuals, and some of the kids I grew up with endured some truly sick experiences. However, I think Colonial Hills served me well on the whole. There I was taught the essentials of the gospel: salvation by faith through grace alone. Sin is real and pervasive but forgiveness and healing are offered through a relationship with Jesus Christ.

It's true that the emphasis of the theology may have been a bit skewed; there was little sense of the biblical concern for the poor and social injustice. But I acquired much that is sound and helpful: a good knowledge of the Bible through Sunday school and Van Gorder's consistent exegetical preaching; a strong sense that to be a Christian one must be willing to break with one's culture and its values; a firm understanding that a commitment to Christ was an absolute one that relativized all earthly relationships. Much of this was reaffirmed in my high school, which had many Jewish students and almost no other evangelicals, and which deepened my sense that to be a Christian one must be willing to stand alone if need be. Some Christian peers were provided by the weekly citywide "Youth for Christ" rally, though even here too I felt myself to be something of an outsider.

One aspect of Colonial Hills that I do regret was one of which I was completely ignorant at the time. That was the racism of the church. I discovered later that, despite supporting a Bible Institute to train blacks for ministry, my church at that time excluded blacks from membership. (I was glad to hear some time ago that the church has now had a service of repentance publicly to ask forgiveness for this.)

Perhaps this is a good time for me to digress and say something about my experience of racism, growing up in the segregated South of the fifties and the Civil Rights Movement of the fifties and sixties. It seems to me that there were two kinds of racists in my early days. There were people who genuinely hated blacks and other minorities: these were the kinds of people who formed the Klan. There were others who simply absorbed the institutional racism and social attitudes of the time without these attitudes taking any deep personal roots. Now the racism of the latter type may have been just as harmful as the former, but I think it was less spiritually destructive in its holders than the first. Thus, when those whose racism had merely been a matter of cultural ethos found themselves in a changing culture, they were themselves able to change. Many simply abandoned their beliefs in the inferiority of others.

I am thankful that in my own milieu the former type of racism was rare. Thus, even though my family and church people would have approved of segregation, I knew that I would have been harshly reprimanded for a racial slur or epithet. The word "nigger" was not allowed in my house. After all, we knew black people were God's children too, and in fact we knew many blacks and had cordial (if unequal) relationships with them. Thus I found it relatively easy (in fact, liberating) to discover that segregation was mistaken and that Christian people could be on the side of racial equality and reconciliation. I can in fact date this discovery with some precision. It occurred during my sixth grade, when Dennie Peteet, the headmaster of the small Christian school I attended that year, required us to write an essay on "segregation versus integration" and then flunked me when I argued for segregation. I had repeated in an unthinking way the arguments I had heard all my life. My teacher demolished them. I rewrote the essay arguing the opposite view and received an "A." I am grateful to him, both for the moral education and the demonstration of the value of logical argument.

Education

As I have already said, I received little that resembled an education in high school. Probably the greatest thing of value I got from high school lay in being on the cross-country and track teams. Here I not only learned to run and enjoy running, I also learned a lot about hard work and self-discipline, and I made friends who were thoughtful and interested in ideas.

Wheaton College

My real education resumed when I left for Atlanta as a homesick seventeen year old to go to Wheaton College. It's lucky for me I had a friend from Atlanta as my roommate, otherwise I might have just gone home. The Chicago area in general, and Wheaton in particular, struck me as incredibly dreary when I stepped off the train, suitcase in hand. I missed the hills, I missed the South, and I was soon to miss the gentle winters and beautiful early springs. In fact, in many ways I have never reconciled myself to living as a "yankee." Nevertheless, going to Wheaton was a wonderful experience. I learned that the interior life, the life of the mind, was as beautiful as any landscape of dogwoods and azaleas.

I had always had an intellectual bent. It was always assumed that I would go to college, and in fact, I can remember wanting to become a college teacher as early as the age of ten. I had read C. S. Lewis and some other books my sister brought back from college while still in high school. It was probably that intellectual bent that propelled me to Wheaton rather than Bob Jones or other fundamentalist schools that many in my church attended. In any case, it was at Wheaton that I discovered that my vocation included, as an important dimension, being a Christian scholar: more specifically, being a Christian philosopher.

As a raw freshman I was expected to read a book in preparation for orientation, *Education at the Crossroads,* by the French neo-Thomist philosopher, Jacques Maritain. I took the assignment seriously, but I could make little sense of the book. During orientation the entire freshman class was assembled in the chapel to hear a lecture by a philosopher, Stuart Hackett, explaining this work. Hackett took his assignment seriously and prepared an incredibly erudite lecture. I sat in stunned disbelief for an hour, not understanding a word the man was saying. I decided immediately to sign up for a philosophy course with this man; I wanted to know if the world he knew about and I didn't was one I could make sense of. So I took a course in ethics from Stuart Hackett and fell in love with philosophy.

I had always loved history and intended to be a history major. (I kept up a double major in history and philosophy until my senior year, when I finally yielded completely to philosophy.) It is perhaps not too surprising therefore that the course in philosophy that most captivated me was the history of philosophy. This course at Wheaton, taught by the renowned Arthur Holmes, was already a legend. It is difficult to describe the excitement and vitality of the history of ideas as Holmes plunged from Thales onward through the classical Greek philosophers, medieval and modern philosophy, and on to the Babel of the twentieth century.

Holmes not only lectured well, but really gave of himself to the students. A select group of us were privileged to attend extra sessions held in his home, for which we were expected to write rather lengthy papers. He spent long office hours helping students sort out their lives as well as their thinking. He will always be for me the model of a great teacher.

What Holmes did for me was not merely to complete the process of turning me on to philosophy, which Hackett had begun; he also was the first person to articulate for me, in a way that I understood, the Christian concept of vocation. He told me that I had a calling; I was called to be a disciple of Jesus Christ and I needed to think about how God might want me to invest my life in a strategic manner "for Christ and his Kingdom" (the motto of Wheaton College). He convinced me that there was special need for Christian scholars, and even more specifically, for Christian philosophers, to labor in the academic vineyards.

The vision I caught from Holmes was not simply to be a Christian who was also a philosopher. It was a vision of Christian scholars whose faith functioned *internally* to their scholarly work. When human beings think and do research, they do so as whole people, bringing with them their deepest values and "world-viewish beliefs," to use a Holmesian phrase. Though Christian philosophy was not monolithic, it was nevertheless possible for it to be distinctive, and possible for committed Christians to do work of high quality that was an expression of their faith. It is this vision that has inspired almost everything I have done as a Christian philosopher, including the thinking

I have done about the human sciences in general and psychology in particular. Later on, this vision was articulated and nourished for me by reading Nicholas Wolterstorff's little book, *Reason Within the Bounds of Religion.* There Wolterstorff talks of authentic Christian commitment, that complex of beliefs, attitudes, and actions that God expects from me personally as a follower of Jesus Christ; a commitment that necessarily will shape the way I think and the conclusions I draw as a scholar. That is the vision that I had absorbed years earlier from Arthur Holmes.

Of course my vocation as Christian scholar was not a generic one, but one to Christian philosophy. I believed (and still believe) that if Christians were to make a difference in the intellectual world, they had to pay serious attention to philosophy. Many of the problems Christians had in the intellectual world, problems dealing with science and even doubts about miracles and revelation, were at bottom philosophical in nature. Christians in all the other disciplines would be strengthened by the articulation of a Christian worldview.

Graduate School

So off to graduate school in philosophy I went. I considered seminary for a time, perhaps motivated somewhat by the threat of Vietnam (though I hope not). However, the decision was easy for me when I received a prestigious national fellowship from the Danforth Foundation for graduate study. The competition for this was fierce, and I interpreted my good favor as a nod from providence that this was a door I should enter. My worries about Vietnam were eventually solved; I developed an ulcer, perhaps from worrying about Vietnam, that gave me a health exemption.

I chose to go to Yale. With a Danforth in hand I probably could have gone most anywhere, but I wanted a place that would be, like my teacher Holmes, open and appreciative of many different schools of philosophy, and Yale was famed for its pluralistic approach. In some ways it was not a good choice. Yale's pluralism had led to squabbling; the squabbling hurt what had been a great national reputation. But on the whole I got from Yale what I needed. I got my Ph.D., of course, the union card one needs to teach in a U.S. college or university. More important, however, was that the Yale ideal worked for me. I really did become a pluralist and something of a generalist, interested in and appreciative of both the "analytic" philosophy dominant in England and North America, and the existentialist and phenomenological traditions then popular on the continent of Europe.

One characteristic of my professional life that began at Yale was a combining of scholarly and more "popular" work. At the same time that I was churning out typical graduate school papers, I was also working on my first book, *Despair: A Moment or a Way of Life,* which was a very personal response as a Christian to the existentialist authors. (That book, amazingly enough, is still in print after twenty years, in a revised version under the title: *Existentialism: The Philosophy of Despair and the Quest for Hope.*) Since that time I have continued to try to write for both scholarly audiences and generally educated readers. I believe that God has given me a gift for writing clearly, and I think scholars have an obligation to share what may be of value in their thinking with the larger public.

Career

My time at Yale went fast. In the spring of 1972, at the end of three years, I had completed all the required course work, passed the foreign language exams, and had an approved dissertation proposal, for which I had begun serious reading. I was also bored with being a student and anxious to get out into the "real world." During spring break of that third year I was in the midwest, visiting with my in-laws, when I received a call from Trinity College in Deerfield. At the last minute, a philosophy professor had bailed out on them, and they were looking for a replacement for the fall. Since I was only an hour away, I thought I would go and talk to them. I thought it might be fun to teach for a year, and wound up accepting the job.

My intention at the time was to return to Yale at the end of the year, and Trinity understood that. I still had a year of Danforth Fellowship money to use, and of course I had a dissertation to write. I didn't intend to let the dissertation slide completely during the year though, so I continued to work on it, and—much to my surprise—actually finished it late in the school year. How this happened I am still not entirely sure, since I probably had the heaviest teaching schedule of my career, and, typically of many first-year teachers, worked harder at preparing my courses than I ever have since. I don't think of myself as particularly industrious, though I must have worked hard that year. I do, however, have a "completion complex." I hate leaving things unfinished, and I do have a gift for writing quickly. When I am working well, I can turn out five to ten pages in two or three hours.

So there I was at Trinity at the close of the academic year, with a finished Ph.D. dissertation and no real reason to return to Yale. It was much too late to mount a serious search for a university position; in any case the job market for new teachers was dreadful. I had always felt a calling to teach in a secular university. Though I had loved my own experience in a Christian liberal arts college, I never intended to teach in one, except on a one-year lark. Nevertheless, I decided to stay at Trinity.

My two years at Trinity were wonderful ones. Ed Hakes, who was the Dean, had assembled a fine group of young faculty: people like Doug Frank, John Woodbridge, Ken Shipps, John Carter, and my fellow philosopher David Schlafer. I can remember lots of interdisciplinary conversation and a lot of fun. It was the early seventies; students still had long hair and were willing to take risks. My perspective on the evangelical wing of Christianity grew sharper, and I began to see that I had a gift for working with students who, like myself, may have come from Christian backgrounds but whose faith needed room to grow.

My second year at Trinity I got an offer from Wheaton. It was attractive; my own gratitude and love for Wheaton was strong. They wanted an early decision, which allowed me no time to mount a search for the kind of job I thought I wanted. I decided to return to my alma mater for the fall of 1974. I believe now that the decision to work in Christian institutions was right for me. During the ten years I spent on the Wheaton faculty I matured as a person and as a Christian scholar. No one knows the future, and it is conceivable that someday my original dream of teaching in a secular university may yet be fulfilled, though it is not one I long for anymore. However, I think my fragile vocation as a Christian philosopher was nourished in the Christian college in ways that would not have been possible in a university. In the university I think I would have succumbed to the need to do what I needed to do to secure tenure; I would not have had the freedom or security to work on the things I wanted to work on. I struggle with temptations to seek worldly renown and prestige instead of consistently seeking first God's kingdom. Perhaps God did not allow me to be tempted in ways that might have made the struggle an impossible one for me. His providential care does not allow us to be tempted "beyond what we are able," which is not to say that the temptations I have been given have always been resisted.

Kierkegaard

My early years at Wheaton were rich ones, particularly for the interaction with students that was provided. It was a privilege to be at Wheaton for ten years and come to know so many wonderful students, and I am thankful for the chance to share some of my life with these people.

Soon after I came to Wheaton, I decided I was floundering professionally. The demanding teaching load of the liberal arts college and the isolation from the well-known philosophers I had been able to encounter in graduate school threatened a slow intellectual atrophy. Someone, I don't remember who it was, gave me some sage advice. I was told to pick some major figure in the history of philosophy and concentrate my scholarly efforts there. It was easier to "stay up" in a limited area of the history of philosophy than in "hot" fields like philosophy of science or epistemology. Besides that, the discipline of working with a major philosopher would be beneficial in many ways. One should know one philosopher's writings *really* well. That philosopher could provide a reference point for addressing many issues, whether that philosopher's views were insightful or mistaken in interesting ways.

I decided that perhaps I would concentrate on Søren Kierkegaard, the nineteenth century Danish philosopher/theologian. I had always loved Kierkegaard; the first philosophical book I had really enjoyed in my first class was *Purity of Heart Is to Will One Thing*. My doctoral dissertation, which dealt with the question as to whether religious beliefs could legitimately be shaped in part by "subjective" needs, had treated Kierkegaard extensively, along with William James and Immanuel Kant. However, Kierkegaard presented problems as well. He wrote in Danish. Should I learn Danish? Could I learn Danish?

To answer these questions, my wife and I went for a visit to Howard and Edna Hong, renowned Kierkegaard scholars and translators, at St. Olaf College. The Hongs were gracious and invited us for a tour of their Kierkegaard Library at the college and for dinner. Howard and others of the St. Olaf philosophy department actually read my dissertation. Howard explained that he himself, contrary to my opinion, was not a native speaker of any Scandinavian language. He had learned Danish as an adult. It was possible to learn Danish, and I should do so, if I was serious about Kierkegaard scholarship. I decided to try to learn Danish, and to attempt to somehow get the funding to go to Denmark. On our way home from this visit my wife and I mused about how much we loved St. Olaf. Wouldn't it be great if by some miracle I could someday come there to teach? That was in 1975.

So I began to learn Danish. Incredibly, my wife actually learned the language with me; I don't know if I would have succeeded without her help. We worked on Danish every day at lunch time for almost two years. Grant funding came through from the Marshall Fund of Denmark and the Wheaton Alumni Association (at the time Wheaton had no sabbatical program), and in the late fall of 1977 we were off to Denmark.

Our nine months in Denmark were memorable. We both became proficient in the language. I wrote the first draft of my book, *Kierkegaard's Fragments and Postscript,* which earned me a modest reputation among Kierkegaard scholars. We made many wonderful friends and generally fell in love with everything Danish, including their pastry, which they call "Viennese bread" and tastes nothing like what we call "Danish." One way in which I feel my life has been specially privileged has been the opportunity to periodically "go away" for a year during a sabbatical, leave, or visiting professorship. Those times have always been special for my family, and we have always made special Christian friends who have remained a part of our lives.

Psychology

The return to Wheaton from Denmark was hard. After the glories of Europe, the Chicago area seemed dull and flat, and the legalism of Wheaton's rather close and inbred evangelical community wore on us. I began to chafe, though I still loved working with Wheaton students, who always provided a very rich sense that I was doing something worthwhile with my life. Nevertheless, after one particularly disheartening conflict with the college, I leaped at the chance to get away again, this time as a visiting professor at Western Kentucky. The offer came out of the blue immediately after I had taken a pretty hard and undeserved knock. I took the timing of this offer as providential, since at the time I was considering getting out of teaching altogether if I had to remain at Wheaton. I am sure I was influenced by the example of a colleague who was named "teacher of the year" but who was so dissatisfied with the situation at Wheaton that he resigned to change careers!

During the year at Western Kentucky I reflected and prayed about my future, and I began to think seriously about a career change to psychology. I had always been interested in psychology as a philosopher. An aborted doctoral dissertation had been a comparison of the theories of the person in Kierkegaard and Gabriel Marcel. My actual dissertation had dealt with the legitimacy of allowing psychological needs to influence one's religious beliefs. My first book after arriving at Wheaton was *Preserving the Person,* a philosophical look at the human sciences that had come out of a "faith-learning seminar" paper I had done, and a course on the philosophy of the person I was teaching to Wheaton undergraduates. Now I began to think that I might want to go back to graduate school in psychology and work toward a degree in counseling or clinical psychology. Perhaps I would continue to philosophize about psychology, but with a new inside perspective. I took the Graduate Record exam and began to decide to what schools I should apply.

In the midst of this process I received a call from the School of Psychology at Fuller Theological Seminary. Would I be interested in teaching there, focusing on the integration of psychology with Christian faith? I interviewed for and was offered the position. It seemed a delicious irony to me. I had been preparing to attend a graduate school in psychology; now I was being offered the chance to teach in one!

Much to my surprise, I eventually turned Fuller down for a number of reasons. It was yet another case in which, left to my own devices, I would have blundered into a career decision that I now see would have stifled me. However, the offer had a great impact on me even though I rejected it. I put aside my plans to leave teaching and go back to graduate school. Wheaton counteroffered by giving me a chance to teach part time in its own graduate program in psychology, while still allowing me to retain my position in philosophy. This was attractive, since one of the main negatives of the Fuller opportunity was the lack of philosophical colleagues. Despite the pull of psychology I was not really ready to cut my ties to philosophy.

Hence I returned to Wheaton after all, and my final years there turned out to be the happiest ones I had. I both taught and took courses in psychology and found myself both giving and receiving a lot. Some deep friendships were formed with new colleagues in both psychology and philosophy. Wheaton also changed a bit; a new administration brought about a somewhat freer atmosphere.

St. Olaf

Just at the time when I was most happy at Wheaton, I got an offer from St. Olaf College. Howard Hong had retired from the St. Olaf philosophy department, and they wanted me to teach philosophy and become the Curator of the Hong Kierkegaard Library. This was not an easy decision, for by this time our friendships in Wheaton were deep ones. I could see myself as the logical successor to Arthur Holmes as chair of the philosophy department at Wheaton, and the mission of this department was one I believed in deeply and had invested myself in fully. However, it was in the end impossible to turn St. Olaf down.

I had invested a lot of time professionally in the study of Kierkegaard and the Danish language. I knew the position at St. Olaf would enormously heighten my visibility and influence in the world of Kierkegaard scholarship. It seemed to me to be a strategic position for an evangelical Christian to assume, for I believed that Kierkegaard was a crucial figure for the evangelical church, and that it would be very healthy for Kierkegaard studies to have a stronger evangelical presence. My wife and I remembered our trip to St. Olaf so long ago and our musings about someday coming there. Though St. Olaf was a Lutheran college, it was quite different from Wheaton, since it did not require Christian commitments from either faculty or students. The total package was appealing to me; at St. Olaf I could maintain my identity as a Christian scholar, since I was functioning in a church college, but I could also serve as "salt" in a more pluralistic religious environment. The greater sense of personal freedom was an additional attraction. So in 1984 it was off to the frozen turf of Minnesota after a year of painful farewells in Wheaton. (I am very grateful that those farewells did not break relationships, however. After seven years at St. Olaf our closest friends are still those from Wheaton.)

One pleasant surprise I had at St. Olaf was that my work in the philosophy of psychology continued to develop. I had thought that the decision for St. Olaf was a decision to focus on Kierkegaard studies, and this would mean a corresponding lack of opportunity to continue to think about psychology. After all, I was leaving a position partly in a psychology department and taking one where part of my energy would be spent running a Kierkegaard research library. I regretted this narrowing but thought it a worthwhile sacrifice. However, soon after arriving at St. Olaf I found that my earlier work on psychology had just begun to be recognized. Speaking invitations to address psychological issues came more frequently than ever, and Fuller honored me by asking me to give the Finch lectures, which ultimately resulted in two books dealing with a Christian perspective on psychology. In fact, I found many opportunities to combine Kierkegaard, who after all had been a keen observer of the human situation, with the philosophy of psychology.

Professionally, St. Olaf has been all that I hoped. My work as a Kierkegaard scholar has become much more visible; it seems to me that articles and books that I had to struggle to get accepted earlier are now eagerly welcomed by journals and presses. As the editor of the *Kierkegaard Newsletter,* which publishes reviews and brief articles as well as news, I serve as a focal point for the Kierkegaard Society's communications. Of course I have had my share of disappointments, unfavorable reviews, and poor sales, but there have been many encouraging and satisfying responses as well. In any case, I have always believed that I am called to faithfulness, not success. In reading over some of my books, I am convinced that I have written the books I was supposed to write. Even if it were true that only a handful of readers have been helped, and this probably is true in some cases, or even if no one at all but myself has profited from the work, to me the work has been a fulfillment of my calling.

My teaching at St. Olaf has also reinforced the important truth that faithfulness is our calling. To some degree the decision to come to St. Olaf was a decision to rearrange the priorities teaching and scholarship have in my life. At St. Olaf I teach less than I did at Wheaton. At Wheaton I was a popular teacher with large (often exhaustingly large) classes. I knew clearly I had a deep impact on many lives. At St. Olaf the students are different and the numbers often fewer. Many students, rebelling against their own upbringing, react with hostility to my Christian faith. Some Christian students, much to my disappointment, seem afraid to develop their faith intellectually, preferring to divide their lives into a segment characterized by nonintellectual piety and academic study that is divorced from Christian perspectives. Nevertheless, I continue to work hard at my teaching, and I believe that my efforts are very valuable for a number of students, valuable in a number of ways. Of course I hope to accomplish what any good teacher of philosophy hopes to accomplish: to help my students to become better thinkers, appreciate the history of ideas and the value of rational argument. Nevertheless, I also hope that my teaching will benefit students spiritually, and for some I believe it does; perhaps I plant seeds that will ripen in other lives sometime later. In any case it is my task to be faithful. I do not proselytize in class; I bend over backward to be fair to non-Christian perspectives and ideas. Nevertheless, I try to add my own convictions to the conversation here, and provide a model of scholarship that takes Christian conviction as integral to the scholarly life.

Marriage and Family Life

My story has largely detailed the history of my academic life, and this might leave the impression that I am the kind of person who is obsessed with my career at the expense of other areas of my life. I do not believe this to be true; certainly I do not want it to be true, and I would be quick to sacrifice anything about my career that threatened the health of my marriage or my family. I have left out any sustained discussion of the importance of my family in my life until near the end of the story precisely because I wished to close by talking about those things that are most important to me.

I believe that my vocation is far broader than my career, though as is evident from my story, I see my career as in an important sense part of my calling. But I also see myself as called to be a husband and father, church worker, and citizen of my community, nation, and world.

I am far from believing that marriage is a universal norm for Christians; in fact, I am confident that God calls many to a life of celibacy. I am sure that I was not so called, however. Perhaps the following comment reflects a lack of faith in God's power, but I knew early on that I was not capable of such a life, nor am I today.

It is difficult for me to talk about the role my wife Jan has played in my life without resorting to conventional cliches or sounding sentimental, but I cannot tell my story without attempting to highlight it. We have lived together as husband and wife for twenty-two years. She has been everything that a man could want in a wife.

Our lives together had a rather stormy beginning. We began to date in the fall of my senior and her sophomore year at Wheaton. After a brief but intense romance we became engaged after Christmas. A few weeks later she left for South America for a semester. She broke the engagement over shortwave radio after Easter. When she returned in June we began to date again, got engaged again around July 4 and were married in early September. After a very brief, and not very thrilling honeymoon, we left Wheaton for Connecticut pulling a trailer in a VW Beetle. After car trouble and assorted perils we finally arrived at the apartment I had selected, taking in mind my meager graduate school income. After one look, Jan collapsed in tears.

Our marriage is proof that good marriages don't depend on idyllic courtships and romantic honeymoons. Rather, I would say that our somewhat rocky start has allowed us to fully appreciate the way our love has grown and our relationship gotten deeper and more satisfying over the years. I love her far more now than I did twenty-two years ago and I am confident she feels the same.

Jan has been incredibly supportive of my career. She has encouraged me when I felt inadequate, read drafts of articles and books, been understanding when I have traveled to give lectures, adventurously accepted moves and "years away." She has been a great mother. To me she has remained a lover, and has consistently been my best friend and confidante. She shares fully in my life. No joy or satisfaction to me is really complete until I have shared it with her; no vista or scene or sunset is quite what it would be if I have to observe it alone. Disappointments and sorrows are lightened by the way she shares them with me. I believe that the real purpose of marriage is quite simply communication; it is an opportunity for two people to successively reveal more and more of themselves to each other as they grow together. I think God intended marriage to be monogamous and lifelong because the human self is infinitely deep. Not even in an intimate lifetime can two people exhaust the purposes of marriage.

Marriage teaches many things, patience and tolerance among them. But it also teaches, I believe, how joyful and sweet an intimate relationship can be. The New Testament says that in the resurrected life there is no marrying; I am convinced that this means that in our resurrected state we will be able to experience the kind of intimacy that we have learned to enjoy in marriage and deep friendship with all the saints, and it is not surprising then that for such a task an infinite time, rather than a lifetime only, is necessary.

Children

Jan and I have three children. To try to describe them in their uniqueness would require far more space than this essay permits. I feel that I have learned from my children what virtually all parents learn, but I cannot resist recounting some of the more obvious lessons.

My children have taught me a lot about what it means to be "like a child," that quality that Jesus says his followers must have. They have taught me a lot about patience, and about how little of that quality I have. They have given me a profound sense of how I must make God feel at times, with my childlike desires for worldly trinkets and honors, and my stubborn repetition of certain mistakes and refusal to learn obvious lessons. I think I know more about why God's love sometimes requires him to chasten me by being "strict." I really do think God created families partly to give us some sense of what it is like to live in his family.

I am sometimes tempted by the "yuppie" or "dink" (double income no kids) life-style; certainly I had no idea before I became a parent how confining children would be, or how much frustration they would bring in their train. All things considered, however, I wouldn't have missed it for the world. Even if one discounted all of the above lessons, this alone would make parenting worthwhile: it was having children that taught me to really value and appreciate my own parents. My life might have been more "fun" without children, but I am sure I would be less of a person. But the main reason I am glad I have children is not any benefits I have gained or lessons learned. Rather it is just this: I love them and I'm glad to be their Dad.

Spiritual Growth and Struggle

My own sense of the Christian life is predominantly in tune with the biblical themes of struggle and even warfare. I believe profoundly that there are spiritual forces who war around and in my life, and that my struggles are part of a broader conflict. I can see real spiritual growth as I look back on my life, areas where I previously experienced regular defeats but now find myself vulnerable to the enemy only on rare occasions. However, even these "achievements" still retain the character of struggle. If for a minute I begin to take pride in these things as if they were my autonomous accomplishments, I find myself quickly fighting the old battles all over again. Spiritual development must constantly be renewed. I will discuss just one concrete illustration of this.

Around 1981 I developed an intense fear of flying. For a time I became incapable of traveling on an airplane, and found myself taking lengthy car and train trips to make conventions and speaking engagements. Eventually, I came to the conclusion that a major element in this fear was spiritual. Partly, it was the rather pedestrian, almost universal fear of dying. Despite my belief in the resurrection and in Jesus' victory over death, I was afraid to die. An even greater component was worry about my family. Now that I had children, I developed nightmarish scenarios of how they would suffer if I should die. I couldn't bear the thought that they would experience this kind of pain, and perhaps even become angry at God. In effect, I could not trust God to take care of my family. At the heart of the whole matter was a prideful assumption of my own irreplaceability.

Before I could get on an airplane again I had to learn to trust: to trust the pilot, the mechanics, the aircraft controllers. More important, I had to trust God to take care of me and my family. What I had to achieve was not a faith that God would never allow me to be harmed in an accident, but a faith that his hand would be with me and with my family no matter what. Coming to this realization was a struggle; I found I possessed a superstitious belief that if I truly accepted the thought of my death that this would bring it about. (Objective rational thought is not very powerful when we are dealing with our strongest and most intimate emotions and relationships.) To some degree I think God has given me this kind of trust. I don't, however, possess it as an object I own, but as a gift that must be renewed through prayer each time I fly. So I am now a frequent flier and am grateful to God for the ability to do this. However, I find that each time I fly the old temptations may confront me and some of the old lessons must be relearned. Perhaps this is in fact how God reminds me of truths I must continually keep in mind but want desperately to forget.

I am currently what I suppose one would call a "leader" in my local church. I chair the Christian Education board, serve on the Church Council, teach the high school Sunday school class, and work in the "Adventure Club" for kids. In the past I have taught adult Sunday school classes, sung in the choir, and served on various other boards. Here too I think the metaphor of struggle and warfare is appropriate. I believe firmly that the local church is the place God's work is being carried out, yet the work requires dealing with the most petty and exasperating problems. The whole experience is a perfect exemplar of faith; faith is being able to recognize the invisible in what is visible. It is a matter of believing in God's presence and discerning God at work in the midst of boring committee meetings and irksome chores, making phone calls and driving church vans, changing diapers and cutting grass.

One sign that encourages me in my own spiritual growth is that my feelings about church, particularly Sunday morning worship, have changed drastically over the years. As a young boy, I found church boring and loved any excuse to miss, though the excuses were rare. Later as a teenager, I probably went mainly because of relationships to various girlfriends. Actually, neither of the above statements is completely true. I think I also attended because I sincerely believed that this is what God expected of his followers, and that I would benefit spiritually from doing so. But I never really enjoyed church.

Now I find that I truly miss Sunday worship services if I have to be away. It helps, of course, that my church has an outstanding preacher. However, I don't go just to hear good sermons. I go because I feel I meet God there and that I worship God. I come away feeling cleansed, refreshed, and renewed.

Final Thoughts

So what have I learned from writing this essay? Primarily, I think I have had impressed upon me how grateful to God I feel for the privilege of the calling I have had. Truly, for me "the lines have fallen out in pleasant places." I have been blessed in abilities, career, family, and church experiences. None of this strikes me as deserved. I would say that I experience my life as a journey that is a calling, a *privileged* calling in the sense that the vocation I have been assigned is one that corresponds to my most cherished desires. I do not know whether this is God's normal mode of operation, or whether he sometimes calls us to go against all our fondest hopes and desires. I suspect that he sometimes does do this, and that it is a mark of spiritual maturity to be able to do this. I know others have walked more difficult roads, and of course I do not know where my own road will take me in the future. Still, up till now, my own paths have generally been level and straight. Perhaps the gratifying character of my own life is a kind of concession to my weakness, a sign that I was not up to sterner, more challenging tasks. But I cannot in my humanness refrain from thanking God for what he has given me, even if this is so.

The other note I wish to sound is how God has guided my life. Perhaps that sounds arrogant, but I mean it as humility. As I look back on my life, I see many points where God has given me what I consider clear guidance. I also see many points where God prevented me from disaster, places where if I had done what I thought I should do everything would have gone wrong. As I think about some of the wrong decisions I almost made, I feel as a man would who has traversed a path in a dark fog and the next day discovers there was a cliff next to the path that he was completely unaware of the night before. The truth is that I am not nearly clever enough to have made wise decisions; in most cases where I went down the right path, it was because God pushed me very strongly or simply blocked every other path.

My final thought is a word to anyone who might be reading this story to learn something about his or her own life, particularly a younger person setting out on life's quest. What I would beg you to see in my life story is not what is unique but what is universal. That is, do not think, "Evans has written all those books, and held all those posts and honors; I want to be like him." The achievements in my life are in one sense temptations, for me as well as for others. Even books written for Christian audiences can be "worldly distinctions." The important thing is not what I have accomplished, but what I intended, and even more significantly, my motivation for so doing. If there is anything admirable in my life to be emulated, it lies in this: I have tried faithfully to fulfill the calling God has given me. That task is a universal one, and I think my life would have the same significance in God's eyes if I had been called to be a handyman, bus driver like my father, or custodian. For that matter, the life and death of a celibate carpenter in first century Palestine dwarfs in significance that of any other.

Of course a person's calling must be concrete and specific. Perhaps someone reading this has indeed been called by God to a life of Christian scholarship. If so, I will rejoice if my example is helpful to such a person in any way. I certainly remain convinced of the need for Christians to be present in the academy. However, in the end, we must not be self-important by measuring the significance of our lives in terms of our accomplishments. In the end God is sovereign; if he chooses to use us it is not because we are so admirable. God is capable of accomplishing his purposes in myriad ways. Rather, we must all measure our lives by thinking about whether we will someday hear these words: "Well done, thou good and faithful servant." Whether our service be about things considered great in the world's eyes matters not at all.

Providence and Choices: The Ingredients of a Life Story

David G. Benner

In his autobiographical volume, *Memories, Dreams, Reflections,* Carl Jung states that "my life is what I have done, my scientific work; the one is inseparable from the other."[1] Perhaps it is because I am only just slightly more than half the age of Jung at the point at which he took pen to hand and attempted to tell his story, but I do not feel as ready as he to allow my work to be equated with my life. My work is a part of my life, but there is much more to me than is expressed in my writing or professional accomplishments. My story cannot be told without reference to my work, but the context for understanding my work is my life, and this is much more true than the reverse.

Supplementing Jung's understanding of the relationship between one's work and life story, Canadian literary critic Northrop Frye has suggested that an adequate understanding of a person's story is obtained only by considering both the objective record of what the

1. Jung, C. 1963. *Memories, dreams, reflections,* ed. Aniela Jaffe, trans. Richard and Clara Winston, 222. New York: Pantheon Books.

person has done, as well as the more subjective record of what the person has tried to do.[2] In particular, Frye feels that one cannot understand a person's life without considering what that person has tried to make of himself. In such a view, I am my work, but I am also the intentions behind my work. While this helps flesh out and interpret the objective record of accomplishments, it also introduces the question of our ability to accurately know and report our intentions. Depth psychologists have, of course, generally been rather pessimistic about this ability, suggesting that our real motivations are much more complex than the conscious reasons we associate with our behavior. However, conscious intentions do provide a starting point in understanding a person's life, even if no more than a way of understanding how the person understands himself. They seem, therefore, to be an important part of one's story.

This is a book of stories of Christians in psychology. I am a Christian psychologist. However, many aspects of my identity are more fundamental than that of my work as a psychologist, and so I start my story with these more fundamental matters. Long before I was a psychologist I was a Christian, and the context of my Christian faith is my family. So it is here, with my family, that my story begins.

Family Roots and Expectations

To be born as David Gordon Benner, first son of Margaret and Gordon Benner, was to be born into a family with a keen sense of its history, and full of expectations for its progeny. It was, first of all, to be a sixth generation Canadian with known roots going back two generations before that to Ireland, and then to England and Germany. Throughout my life, several members of our extended family have been continuously at work on further genealogical studies. Regular family reunions always provide a forum for updates on this research. To be born as a Benner in southern Ontario was to grow up with a deep sense of legacy; this was very clearly my experience.

My eight generations of known personal genealogy begin with Henry Benner, who, with thousands of other Protestant families seeking to escape the religious persecution experienced at the hands of the armies of Louis XIV of France, left Germany in 1709 and moved first to London, and then to Ireland. The Benners remained in Ireland until 1822 when his grandson, my great great great grandfather (also named Henry Benner) left Bennersville, County Kerry, North

2. Frye, N. 1982. *The great code,* 49. Toronto: Academic Press Canada.

Ireland with his family of nine children and moved to Canada. They settled in Binbrook, Ontario, just fifteen kilometers from our present home in Ancaster. The second youngest of his sons, Samuel Steven Benner (my great great grandfather), married and traveled by covered wagon with thirteen other families to Alberta where they set up homestead. His twelve sons made their own homesteads throughout Western Canada, many of them eventually returning to Ontario where I was to be born.

In addition to Canadian roots that precede confederation by forty-five years, to be born David Gordon Benner was also to be born into a family with a long history of deep spirituality and notable religious service: this on both my father and mother's side. I was named after my mother's only brother, David Boyd Long, a man I did not meet until my teens, but with whom I grew up by means of the stories about him that circulated within our family and wider religious community. David left Ireland as a young man of twenty to travel to Africa as a missionary. He remained there for thirty-four years, single-handedly translating the entire Old and New Testaments into the language of the tribe he was working with in Angola. To be named after him was no mere exercise of sentimentalism: it was a communication of a destiny, an expectation of significant Kingdom service. My great grandfather on my father's side, Samuel William Benner, was also a missionary, spending a number of years in Trinidad. Benners who were not missionaries or ministers were usually active as lay preachers. I grew up with a keen sense of being surrounded by a cloud of witnesses, a great many of whom were relatives.

As would be expected, my parents were the primary conduit of these expectations. But to their credit, while I was aware of the magnitude of their hopes for me, never once did I consciously experience pressure to perform. Rather, my experience of these expectations was one of affirmation and honor. Similar expectations were often communicated by others in our extended family, and even from nonrelatives in our church. I well remember a lady approaching me at church one Sunday morning when I was seven or eight and telling me that she had prayed for me every day since I was born and would continue to do so until she died, this out of the conviction that God had something very special planned for my life. This, coming from a relative stranger, could not but help to have a significant impact on a young boy. And it did on me.

Nuclear Family and Religious Community

I recently saw a cartoon depicting a meeting of an association called "Adult Children of Normal Parents and a Happy Childhood." One person sat alone in a large hall. I might not have attended this meeting, but I would have been eligible. My childhood was a distinctly happy one and I have few memories of unpleasant experiences.

My earliest memory is of my only sibling, a brother younger than me by four years. Not surprising for a first born, the content of that memory is of my mother arriving home from the hospital with him. A four year gap meant that sibling rivalry could be minimized by ignoring the intruder, and this must have been my strategy since we were never particularly close. Most of my early memories of my brother involve activities with either the whole family (car rides on Sunday afternoons, family meals) or, at a slightly older age, activities involving us with our father. Often this involved fishing outings, something I never enjoyed as much as either my father or brother.

My father is probably the most gregarious person I have ever known. Seriously miscast vocationally as a technician in the telephone industry, he spent his working years dealing with things, while his passion was for people. From my earliest years he has been continuously involved in organizing and running various boys clubs, directing harmonica bands for anyone whom he can talk into giving the instrument and experience a try, visiting the sick and shut-ins from his circle of acquaintances, serving as a volunteer in such capacities as probation officer and telephone distress line counsellor, and generally looking for whatever excuse he could find to go through the neighborhood, knocking on doors and talking with people. For years this took the form of raising bees so that he could have honey to carry with him as he walked from door to door chatting with people. A rather poor businessman, he often gave away more honey than he sold. However, the honey did legitimize the visitation, and his infectious interest in and love of people was so obvious that he was always able to find people who were delighted to have someone sit and chat with them for a while.

As long ago as I remember, my father has always had an interest in the print media. He produced and distributed (mostly door to door) numerous papers of Christian witness. I began writing articles for these during my high school years. He also serves as a distributor for any good Christian books that he discovers, usually doing this simply by buying a number of copies at retail and then reselling them whenever he is able to do so. His heart desire in all of these activities is Kingdom service, and he is relentless in exploring new avenues to reach people with the gospel.

My mother is equally genial, although much more a product of British socialization. Always warm and affable, she is, nonetheless, somewhat restrained and proper. Very much in control of herself and whatever situation she finds herself in, my mother provides balance and form to my father's passion and vitality.

Although it is not something that anyone who knows her would be likely to do, it would be a serious mistake to confuse my mother's gentleness with weakness. Never quite reaching five feet at her tallest, she has nonetheless always been a tower of strength and determination. She faced a number of serious medical problems during most of her sixth decade of life but each time fought her way again to health and strength. Her physicians could only speak of an unusual capacity for healing, this being invoked to explain her recovery after illnesses from which they thought she would not recover. But this language of "capacity for healing" is too passive to describe the source of my mother's present health. It lies much more in her love of life and a fighting spirit that makes her a formidable scrabble player and a dauntingly aggressive hiker for her age.

It is really quite difficult to talk about my family without talking about our church. For three generations both sides of my family had been closely identified with the Plymouth Brethren and the Gospel Hall in Orillia, Ontario. It was without question the center of our family's life in my early years. Orillia, situated one hundred kilometers north of Toronto at the edge of a vacation region of the province, was a town of about 30,000 people and two Brethren churches. The one our family was associated with was identified as the "open" one; that is, the less legalistic and separatistic of the two.

As with any religious tradition, being raised in the Brethren held both advantages and disadvantages. To be a young man in a Brethren church was to be raised with the expectation that ongoing personal Bible study would be undertaken with sufficient diligence so as to prepare you to step into the role of a spiritually mature male; that is, one who contributes to the leadership of the church and who regularly speaks in services. I took my first steps toward this by about age ten, when I made a personal confession of faith and began a serious commitment to systematic personal Bible study. Through my teen years I undertook this with more diligence than I have at any point since then, spending hours each week reading my Bible, studying commentaries, and taking copious notes on my research. While this would eventually lead me to theological understandings that would result in my leaving this denomination, it did prepare me to offer short devotional thoughts, sermons, and even evangelistic messages to our congregation and others by my early teen years. I continue to be most thankful for the grounding in Bible study and training in public speaking that these experiences provided.

The major disadvantage that I experienced from my early years in the Brethren church was the sense of being cut off from the rest of the world. While I responded to the warmth and support of our relatively closed religious community with a sense of security, its separatistic and isolationist tendencies left me with a sense of being on the outside of life looking in. As a young child I had a sense of being unlike everyone else in town other than those who went to our church, and I didn't like this feeling. Deep down I felt sure that I was more like those other people in my world than Brethren theology seemed to suggest, and more and more my church world began to feel too small.

It was in high school that I first discovered that there were other Christians in the world beyond those in our church. This discovery took me greatly by surprise. But it was a liberating insight that would leave me forever changed. The context of this discovery was Inter-Varsity Christian Fellowship, a school club with which I became involved from my first days in high school. My parents' reaction to my involvement with this group, and to my discoveries within it, was one of unqualified support. Even though they knew my pilgrimage was taking me to places other than where they had made their home, they were then, and have always been since, nothing less than consistently affirming and supportive of me and my quest.

They were also supportive when I began attending an Anglican church for the special services of the Christian calendar. This began when I was invited to play my trumpet at an Easter service at the Anglican cathedral. This was my first experience of Christian worship as celebration, worship services in the Brethren being built entirely around Communion and taking the form of the remembrance of the death of Christ. I was immediately struck by the richness of the liturgy and the power of the symbols. But even more powerful was my experience of solidarity with the broader Church of Christ. This was my answer to the feeling of being on the outside looking in. My insularity within the Brethren had given rise to what I now understand to be one of the deepest themes in my spiritual quest: that is, my ecumenism. Since this period of my life I have longed to see the

Church as a whole rather than in its fragmented parts, and my quest has been to experience myself and live my life as an integral member of this historic worldwide catholic Church.

School Days

Elementary and secondary school years were for me years of initiative, industry, and identity formation as described by Erikson. My earliest extrafamilial/ecclesiastical initiatives took the form of part-time jobs, which I began by about age twelve. At first this involved a paper route, although by age fourteen I was also engaged in door-to-door sales of a line of health care products and working in a grocery store. Part-time work would continue from then to the present, providing me with a significant degree of financial independence by my teens and serving as the soil for what has clearly turned out to be a rather well-developed case of workaholism.

Achievement has always been a rather exhilarating experience for me. I have never been particularly competitive in relationship to others. When combined with rather mediocre athletic skill, this was one of the reasons why I never participated much in sports. However, my competition with myself has always been fierce. I have always pushed myself harder than anyone else would ever dare to push. My pattern has been to either ignore or internalize the expectations others held of me, and if the latter, to then set out to exceed this expectation. With the wisdom of midlife I am beginning to now realize the treadmill I have built for myself with this agenda. But, I must admit, I give it up only with reluctance and difficulty. For the most part it has served me well and I continue to enjoy both the experience and fruits of overachievement.

My achievements during school years were primarily academic and musical. I excelled in my performance on the piano and the trumpet as I did in my studies. Learning some of my mother's correct speech and self-presentation, I also excelled in public speaking, winning for these activities a trip to the United Nations in my fourteenth year. My one area of significant physical achievement involved lifesaving and swimming awards earned during the many summers I spent at Christian camps, first as a camper and later as a counsellor. These were tremendously good experiences for me. I learned to enjoy leisurely walks in the woods, quiet times of reflection, and the stimulation of wilderness challenges. Most commonly these took the form of extended canoe trips where I thrilled at the opportunity to push myself to my physical limits and test myself against the forces of nature. These experiences were unquestionably among the highlights of my youth.

It was at one of these summer camps as a counsellor that I first remember experiencing ambivalence about leadership. I clearly recall one of my fellow counsellors saying to me one summer that he had mixed feelings about the leadership opportunities he saw increasingly opening up for him as he returned from camp each year. This comment struck me as completely unintelligible. I was aware only of enjoying those same leadership experiences, for by then I was President of both the Student's Council and the InterVarsity Christian Fellowship of our high school and deeply involved in the leadership of our church youth group. However, the comment stayed with me over the next year while I, too, became aware of some mixed feelings about these roles. I became aware that, while I liked to be in charge of groups of which I was a part, I also missed being an ordinary group member. In fact, over time I came to resent what seemed to be my automatic rise to leadership in new group situations and began to purposely minimize my contribution so as to limit expectations of me. I was becoming aware that it was harder to retain ownership of and control over expectations others had of me when I was in a role of leadership, and this I did not like. I then began to realize what I now see much more clearly: that leadership is a gift of oneself and that all meaningful leadership is by necessity offered at personal cost.

However, in the midst of these questions I had an increasingly clear sense that my calling related to work with people. It had not yet entered my mind that psychology might be the professional packaging this would involve. In fact, I gave almost no thought as to what I would do vocationally until after my first year of university. But in spite of an absence of vocational dreams or even reflections, I did think a good deal about leadership and felt increasingly certain that my gifts and interests were leading me to some form of service for and work with other people.

Intellectual Awakening

My years as a university student were among the best of my life. High school had been enjoyable and even at points challenging. However, it had never really been intellectually stimulating and this was what I discovered from my first days as an undergraduate at McMaster University in 1966.

The mid 1960s were of course a heady time to be on university campuses anywhere in North America. This was the peak of America's involvement in the Vietnam war and political sensitivities had not been higher for decades. The presence of large numbers of draft dodgers and deserters on Canadian campuses kept these issues at a continuous boil. With debate on these and other important social issues often beginning in the universities and then spilling over into the media and legislatures, the universities were definitely the place to be.

But it was much more than political sensitivity that was forming in me during those days: it was a love of ideas. I was infatuated with ideas. Theories of all sorts captured my imagination, presenting themselves to me as grand ways of viewing reality. My first year studies were, with the exception of one course in psychology, all in mathematics and the natural sciences. These subjects had always been of interest to me but had never before awoken my passions. Now I was energized by their models of reality. Creation was so much more interesting with the new theoretical tools I now had for looking at it. And the tools themselves were of interest to me, not just what they showed me of reality. My studies in cosmology were of particular interest and my tentative plans from early on in that year were for a major in theoretical physics.

My course in psychology that first year was the least interesting of all my courses and my grade in it was by far the lowest. I took this class along with 2500 other students in one of several large auditoriums scattered across campus, where we watched a forty-foot-high video image of our professor. But something caught my attention in that class. Responding to a cavalier, one-lecture dismissal of Freud, something that is quite common in Introductory Psychology courses, I decided to buy a used copy of his *Interpretation of Dreams.* Little did I know the magnitude of the change that that book was to introduce into my life. For in it, I discovered an approach to psychology that captured my mind and stirred my imagination. While psychoanalysis has serious limitations as either a comprehensive psychology or a theory of personality (limitations that are even more clear to me now after twenty-five years of study), its theoretical power has continued to impress me and I still recall the way in which it did so in that first exposure in the fall of 1966.

The consequence of this was that I decided, upon the completion of my first year of studies, to declare psychology as my major. This was somewhat of a step of faith as I recognized that it involved a commitment to three more years of study of courses in biological and experimental psychology before I could pursue graduate work in clinical psychology. While I had only occasional periods of excitement in my work in general psychology over those next years, my reading in Freud and other depth psychologists provided continuing affirmation of the correctness of my decision to pursue a Ph.D. in clinical psychology and helped to sustain me during the period of waiting for these more specialized studies.

At the end of my first year at McMaster I also decided to accept a summer job in a psychology department of a residential facility for retarded adults. This too turned out to be quite a formative experience. While I accepted this position with the expectation that it would give me exposure to clinical psychology, in reality what it presented was an introduction to organizational psychology. Here I joined a team of other psychology graduate and undergraduate students who were charged with the task of developing a comprehensive information system for the institution. This was to be built around the clinical goals for the residents but was to also serve as a tool for management in their evaluation of staff and institutional effectiveness. This project was to last for the next four summers and served to awaken my interest in organizational and management psychology, an interest that was to take more clear expression after the completion of my Ph.D.

While the bulk of my undergraduate psychology courses failed to engage me the way my continuing Freud studies did, my more liberal arts studies did. This was particularly true of my courses in religious studies. I had always read and enjoyed theology but had been rather limited in my exposure, reading mostly safe theologians with whom I tended to agree. This was not to be my lot in coursework in the Department of Religious Studies. The courses on Christianity contained little that was familiar and much that felt distinctly unsafe. However, this was a tremendously stimulating experience for me both spiritually and intellectually. It was here that I discovered the great advantage of reading, not just those with whom I was most likely to agree, but rather, those by whom I was most likely to be stimulated to think.

My involvement with InterVarsity Christian Fellowship at McMaster University was also a tremendous growth-producing experience. During these years, this campus Christian organization had a distinctly intellectual character, and it was here that I first began to think through my faith in a systematic way. Through InterVarsity I was introduced to C. S. Lewis and Francis Schaeffer, both authors who had a great influence on me over the next decade. Through InterVarsity I also had my first opportunity of coming to know and respect

Christians who did not share either my evangelical heritage or conservative theological perspective. I am deeply thankful that I did not have to wait any longer for this experience of learning that liberals could be good Christians. It taught me that Christianity did not have so much to do with theology as with following Jesus Christ. This experience further fed my developing ecumenicity and was a great help in showing me that the relevant antithesis in the world is the contrast between the Kingdom of God and the kingdom of this world, not that associated with the relatively minor differences between Christian subgroups.

I am happy to note that my years as an undergraduate were not entirely filled with these intellectual and spiritual discoveries. Through InterVarsity Christian Fellowship I also met my wife. An East Indian from Trinidad, we met one week after she arrived on campus and six weeks later we were committed to marry each other. While our marriage was not to take place for two additional years, the soul companionship was already developing and has been, without question, the most significant I have had in my life.

Years of Professional Preparation

Completing my B.A. (Honours) at McMasters University in 1970, I entered the graduate program in clinical psychology at York University in Toronto. Here I had the good fortune of being accepted for work with an extremely gifted researcher and clinician, Dr. Robert Sanderson. When completing his own Ph.D. program, his dissertation received the distinction of being named one of the three most important dissertations completed that year in North America. A man of unusual creativity and seemingly inexhaustible energy, he was the hub of a whirlwind of activities that emanated from the group of postdocs and graduate students working with him.

I began meeting with this research group the summer prior to the formal commencement of my graduate program, and by the end of that summer, I had my M.A. thesis topic approved and was well underway collecting my data. The consequence of this head start on my master's program was that I was able to complete my master's thesis well before the corresponding course work, and by the second summer of my program, I was working on my doctoral dissertation. This good fortune in my research resulted in my completion of all academic and clinical requirements for both my M.A. and Ph.D. within two years; this a full two years under the minimum residency requirement of the University. Almost forced to wait and pay tuition for two additional years prior to being allowed to graduate, a successful appeal to the Faculty of Graduate Studies of the University resulted in my being granted an exception to this four year minimum residency. I was awarded my Ph.D. in 1972.

One consequence of this very accelerated graduate program was that at the point of graduation I felt that I still had a good deal to learn. Although I had completed all the normal internship and residency hours for the Ph.D. program (taking these concurrent with coursework rather than sequentially), I felt better prepared as a researcher than as a clinician. However, my primary interests at this point were in clinical work, and so I accepted as my first postdoctoral job a staff psychologist position in a children's psychiatric hospital in Toronto. This turned out to be an excellent place to develop a base of good clinical skills, and I immersed myself in my clinical work during the next several years in the same way as I had done with my research in the previous ones.

During this and my next job as Senior Psychologist on an adolescent ward of another psychiatric hospital, my psychological and spiritual interests remained relatively divorced. In fact, looking back I see that this fragmentation really began in graduate school. Here my preoccupation had been one of meeting formal degree requirements, and now it was that of acquiring as much clinical skill as I possibly could. I remained active in my Christian life, but these activities and commitments seemed strangely unrelated to my psychological pursuits and activities. From time to time I reflected on this peculiar bifurcation that seemed to exist within me, but felt at a loss to know how to do anything about it. I rationalized that, with regard to my professional responsibilities, being a good Christian meant simply being a good psychologist, but somewhere deep within I was dissatisfied with this answer.

Over the next several years I became increasingly concerned about the need to mend this split between my psychological self and my spiritual self. But I could find little help for this task. Most Christians with whom I discussed these matters tended to relate to psychology more emotionally than intellectually, viewing it as either the enemy of Church or the great hope for the survival of the same. Both postures seemed to me to be quite unsatisfactory. The few Christian mental health professionals whom I knew tended to be primarily interested in practical clinical questions such as the place of evangelism in therapy or whether or not a psychotherapist should pray with a patient. These questions seemed to me to be somewhat trivial and relatively uninteresting. The more basic question seemed to be a theoretical one; that is, the relationship of spiritual and psychological dynamics of personality. However, I found little to help me in knowing how to pursue these theoretical issues.

I find it interesting to note that my first piece of integrative scholarship was a publication based on an address I gave to the Christian Association of Psychological Studies (CAPS) in 1976 on what I called the "psychospiritual unity of personality." At the time of this present writing, fifteen years later, the relationship of psychological and spiritual dynamics in personality remains a primary matter of theoretical interest for me. This continuing interest quite transparently reflects my own struggle to overcome the psychospiritual disunity that was such a part of my early years of professional development. It also reflects my response to what I perceive to be the psychospiritual dualism that exists in much of the so-called integration literature relating psychology and Christianity. This literature frequently sets psychology and Christianity on opposite sides of a nonpermeable barrier. Each is viewed in relationship to the other, but each is relegated to separate nonintersecting domains. This is the sort of dualism and compartmentalization that was reflected in my early years of professional development, and which, as a consequence, I have since been concerned to address.

This period of isolating my faith and psychology lasted for about the first five years after the completion of my Ph.D. Probably not coincidentally, my dissatisfaction with this posture was reaching its zenith just at the time that my wife and I entered parenthood, our first and only child being born in 1975. Part of my own psychological and spiritual preparation for fatherhood involved reflecting on my life. This was an important context for my strivings for more wholeness in both my personal and professional life. As occurs with any parent who is open to learning, our son has taught me many things in the ensuing years. However, the continuing challenge that he presents to me: to be authentic, presented by the engagement that is a normal part of any intimate relationship, has been a most significant catalyst pressing me to continue toward this wholeness.

While my primary professional interests and activities during these early years were clinical (including a private practice and ongoing consulting relationships with several treatment centers and group homes), an area of continuing secondary professional interest was organizational psychology. My work as an undergraduate in management by objectives in mental retardation services had led to an appointment as a consultant to the Ontario Ministry of Health, working toward the implementation of similar management information systems in a number of psychiatric hospitals in the province. This in turn led to contracts with the Canadian Department of National Defense, the University of Pennsylvania Medical School, and a number of other business and government agencies. These responsibilities increasingly involved more general management consultation.

Colleagues frequently chided me during this period of time and later for spreading myself too thin. I was advised by them that if I was to make a serious contribution to and through the field of psychology that I needed to focus my efforts more clearly on either clinical or organizational psychology. Further, they advised, I needed to focus on certain clinical and research areas within this chosen field of specialization and not continue to allow my interests to drift in what was perceived to be a rather undisciplined manner. But I have always resisted this specialization. While I recognize that my eclectic interests have cost me something in terms of the contribution that I could have made with a more focused research program, I would not change a thing in this regard if I had it to do again. The combination of clinical and organizational psychology has allowed me to function within both investigative and remedial/facilitative roles in clinical, educational, corporate, and government settings, and I cannot imagine another vocation that could provide this sort of breadth of professional activity. This continues to be one of the most rewarding aspects of my professional life.

First Steps Toward a Christian Psychology

In 1976, as a response to my growing dissatisfaction with the compartmentalization of my faith and professional life, I made a major move. I left my secure and professionally prestigious position in a major psychiatric hospital for a seemingly rather insignificant position in a Bible college and theological seminary. The reason for this move was that I anticipated that this context would support the sort of theological reflection that I wanted to do with my work in psychology. The questions I was asking about the relationship between psychological and spiritual dynamics in personality were questions that I knew were not going to be simply answerable by either psychology or theology. However, while I knew the psychological literature of personality theory reasonably well, I was much less conversant with theological literature, and I hoped that a sojourn in a school of theology would help me develop some competence in theology—

this as a foundation to further work on the questions that were becoming increasingly pressing for me.

Ontario Theological Seminary and Bible College turned out to be an excellent setting for these pursuits. While my responsibility was for teaching in the areas of pastoral psychology and counselling, my research and study was primarily in biblical and theological anthropology. I audited theology courses, picked the brains of the theologians, and devoured everything relevant that I could find in the library. While the two years that I spent here did not answer all my theological questions, they did give me a good foundation for my work on strategies for relating faith and psychology. However, they made it clear that this work could better be conducted within the context of a Christian liberal arts college or university. The training of clergy was of interest to me but was not what I perceived to be my primary calling. When, therefore, I was approached by Wheaton College in 1978 about the possibility of helping them establish a graduate department of psychology, I was easily convinced to make the move, this being where I was to spend the next ten years.

My years at Wheaton College were deeply rewarding both personally and professionally. While my wife and I had moved among a number of denominational and theological traditions over the previous years of our marriage, this was the period within which we found our way into the reformed theological tradition and the Presbyterian Church has been our home since then. This was also the period of six years of service on the Board of Directors of the Christian Association for Psychological Studies; this providing me with a network of support, not only for my efforts to work out the relationship between psychology and faith, but also with what have been some of my most important adult extrafamilial relationships. This was a period of significant professional accomplishments and satisfactions, both in terms of the work I and my colleagues were able to do in establishing and developing the graduate department in psychology at Wheaton, as well as in my own work as a psychologist-Christian who was trying to become a Christian psychologist.

Wheaton College was a most supportive context for my work on the integration of Christianity and psychology. The Graduate School had several very capable theologians who were quite interested in theological/psychological anthropology and my colleagues in psychology were each actively pursuing some aspect of the interface between psychology and faith. But by far the greatest support for and stimulation in pursuing these interests came from the students. Selecting Wheaton College as the place to pursue their graduate training in clinical psychology, the vast majority of these students had a deep commitment to developing approaches to their research and professional practice that were distinctively Christian. These commitments helped us, the faculty, to keep pushing ahead with fresh understandings and approaches to this task. The classroom became the laboratory for my ideas and, once tested by fire in this setting, many of the approaches to thinking about the relationship of faith and psychology that I now hold were first committed to paper during these years. While my writing during this time was to range across topics in psychopathology, psychotherapy, psychoanalytic theory, and neuropsychology, in retrospect I am now able to see that all of this work reflected in one way or another my primary interest in questions of the unity of personality and the foundational role of our spirituality in structuring this unity.

Because my primary teaching responsibilities at Wheaton were in the area of psychoanalytic psychology and psychotherapy, in 1980 I enrolled in a one-year postdoctoral training program at the Chicago Institute for Psychoanalysis. This provided me with both supervision in the practice of psychoanalytic psychotherapy and a chance for further study in object relations theory, that branch of contemporary psychoanalytic theory that had become something of a theoretical home base for me by this point in time. Psychoanalytic psychology seemed to me to preserve something of the depth and mystery of human personhood that is lost in the other major systems of psychology. In addition, it seemed to me to provide a way of understanding aspects of what Christians mean by the concepts of sin, particularly the bondage of the will through self-deception. However, in its classical drive-theory expressions it is much less adequate in helping us understand the uniquely personal aspects of human experience, and because of this, the less reductionistic work of the British object relations theorists (particularly Fairbairn and Guntrip) caught my attention and became my working theoretical framework.

From 1976 to 1982 most of my psychotherapy was conducted within the context of a part-time private practice. During these years I accepted only cases that would be good candidates for psychoanalytic psychotherapy and my work almost entirely involved long-term intensive treatment. This I found uniquely rewarding, and the cross-fertilization of teaching, clinical practice, and research in psychoanalysis was quite stimulating. However, in 1982 I became involved in establishing a hospital-based eating disorders program and in my work as Clinical Director of this program over the next five years I found myself moving rapidly from my position of something of a psychoanalytic purist. Starting with a clinical population and working toward the development of a programmatic approach to treatment left little room for pursuing a specialization in psychoanalytic psychotherapy; consequently, this period of highly focused work in psychoanalysis came to a close.

While I was to miss my work in intensive long-term psychotherapy, this new clinical opportunity had its own benefits. The first of these was that I came to learn a good deal about eating disorders. My responsibility over these years for the treatment of over 500 people suffering from anorexia, bulimia, or compulsive overeating provided opportunity for the development of a good deal of specialized skill in this area. But even more important was the opportunity this program provided for further work on the relationship of psychological and spiritual dynamics. Our inpatient program was offered within the context of a twelve-step program that combined elements of Overeaters Anonymous and Emotions Anonymous. Because we marketed this program as being spiritually based, patients came expecting to address spiritual issues in therapy. While this meant quite different things to each person, it did give us a unique opportunity to therapeutically explore the interplay of each person's spiritual and psychological functioning, and this was the primary context out of which my book *Psychotherapy and the Spiritual Quest* arose.

During these years I also stumbled into another area of clinical specialization. In 1981 I began treating a woman whom I diagnosed as multiple personality disorder. A publication based on this work led to my being invited to join the steering committee of an international group of psychiatrists and psychologists who were developing a professional association for the study of this disorder. This group came into being in 1985 as *The International Society for the Study of Multiple Personality and Dissociative Disorders,* and although I was to retire from the leadership of this group soon after that point, the visibility it afforded me suddenly resulted in my receiving more treatment and consultation referrals than I could manage with my part-time practice. Lacking other appropriate referral outlets, I offered my referrals and supervision to several of my former graduate students who established a clinic and quickly acquired considerable recognition for their work with multiples. By means of this arrangement, I was able to ensure appropriate service for those who sought my help while maintaining my primary focus as an academic psychologist. I was also able to continue some involvement with multiple personality disorder patients without having to carry the immense clinical responsibility that is associated with their treatment and that is so potentially overwhelming for anyone in a part-time practice.

Once again I found that this setting provided wonderful experience in my continuing interest in understanding religious and spiritual dynamics in personality. Multiple personality disorder provides a window into the mind affording a point of observation of mental operations and dynamics that are often otherwise quite obscure. Religious psychodynamics are, thus, quite accessible for study in these individuals, and my work toward an understanding of these dynamics in the individuals I treated during this period continued long after I left this area of major clinical responsibility.

In 1988, ten years after moving to the U.S. to take the position at Wheaton College, I received an offer from Redeemer College, a Christian university in Ancaster, Ontario, in its early states of development. I was both ready for a change and attracted by the opportunity to contribute to Christian higher education in Canada. The only Protestant Christian university in the province of Ontario, and one of only three in the entire country, Redeemer College seemed to me to be a strategic frontier, and I found myself attracted by the challenge of being a part of its development. I was also most attracted by its commitment to research. Redeemer saw its mandate as not merely the dissemination of knowledge through teaching but also the development of knowledge through research. I was, at this point, ready to spend less time in teaching and more in research and writing, and the move held out the promise of doing this.

Returning to Canada has proven to be a rewarding experience for a number of reasons. Redeemer has lived up to its promise as a setting that is unusually supportive of the sort of research and scholarship to which I have been committed. A cross appointment at the University of Toronto has kept me in contact with the mainstream of Canadian university life and has afforded a strategic opportunity for teaching in the Christianity and Culture Program of the University of St. Michael's College, a Roman Catholic affiliate of the University of Toronto. The opportunity to explore the relationship of psychology to Christianity, both within a Reformed Protestant context (Redeemer College) and a Roman Catholic one (St. Michael's College), has been enriching and has helped broaden my understanding of the Christian perspective that I wish to develop in my work and in my life.

Beyond Psychology

Although I began by stating that my life is more than my work, I have talked primarily about the vocational and professional aspects of my story. Let me now turn to several other important aspects of my life, which may be hinted at, but are certainly not revealed very clearly by my professional activities.

The first of these is my interest in business. This began to develop during my years in graduate school when I first became involved in management consulting. What I discovered, through the opportunity of the consultant to peek into a number of different institutions and corporations, was that the challenges of business differ substantially from those encountered in the educational and health care sectors. People are, of course, basically the same in each of these contexts. However, the purposes for which the institutions are structured make enormous differences in the ways in which they function.

This became very clear to me in my earliest consulting work in the corporate sector and even more clear when I began my first business, a psychological services clinic. This venture, representing a marriage of business and clinical services, was a good introduction to business. However, while many psychologists experience the business side of such a clinic to be an unavoidable and somewhat unsatisfying aspect of their work, my experience was one of appreciation of the unique challenges that were represented in both the clinical and business sides of the enterprise. Valuable lessons learned in this first experience were to provide a good foundation for later business experiences. The most recent of these began as a partnership of myself and several others who wanted to help people employed by churches and Christian charitable organizations get home mortgages at a discounted rate. Two years later, this company has evolved into a full-fledged financial services corporation for which I serve as president. The challenges that I have faced in the development of this business are unlike those that I have ever faced in either providing clinical services or working as an employee in universities or colleges. I am thankful that I have had the opportunity to experience both worlds.

People in the academic world often tend to neither trust nor understand those in business, and the reverse is often equally true. Part of the reason for this is that so few people live in both worlds. This is unfortunate, as each of these two worlds has much to offer the other. I appreciate the fact that I came to business from the helping professions and have come to recognize that good business starts with, and builds on, service. Business that is primarily about making money is neither good business nor, in my view, Christian business. But I have discovered that a business built on a desire to serve others can be both deeply rewarding and of significant Kingdom service.

A second important aspect of my life that goes beyond my work in psychology is my love of cooking. Taking cooking classes in my midthirties was something of an experiment. To that point, I had done little more than basic backyard grilling and the most rudimentary kitchen preparations. Nor was I aware of any particular interest in cooking. However, I did observe that whenever I thought about retirement, one of the central features of that fantasy was that I saw myself taking cooking classes and making gourmet meals for my wife and friends. My father taught me that dreams are meant to be pursued, not merely held as objects of fantasy. On this basis he had encouraged me to get a motorcycle a few years before this, when, after reading *Zen and the Art of Motorcycle Maintenance,* I had shared with him my dream of touring cross-country on a motorcycle with my son. I had followed this dream and, at that point, my son and I had had five or six years of wonderful summer touring experiences. I, therefore, responded to this newly emerging dream by launching into cooking classes, deciding that if it was worth doing when I was retired, there was no good reason to wait until that time to start.

What I discovered as I began to learn to cook was the wonderful marriage of creativity and service that is a part of a well-conceived and prepared meal. Cooking is not an event complete within itself. Cooking is preparation for eating, and a specially prepared meal is best prepared not simply for one's self, but for others. The joy of cooking is, therefore, the joy of preparing an experience for one's family or friends. Special gourmet meals, as well as a measure of regular domestic food preparation, provide me with significant satisfaction and have come to be one of life's rich pleasures.

Another important aspect of my story that is not contained in the record of my professional activities is my love of a physical challenge. While pushing myself to my limits in any aspect of life has always been exhilarating, pitting my skill and endurance against a mountain or a wilderness has long been an especially satisfying activity. While I love to hike or climb with others, my reputation of ruthlessly pushing myself onward farther, or higher, has often marked me as an undesirable companion in these pursuits. Over the years my sixteen-year-old son has been my best colleague in these activities, at first being the object of my patience as we climbed mountains and hiked backwoods trails, and now having the opportunity to demonstrate the same patience to me.

Such physical activity is, for me, much more than a form of exercise or a simple leisure pursuit. It is both therapeutic and spiritually renewing. Setting myself against some form of physical challenge (even hard physical work) is a way of putting my life into perspective. It is, in some ways, an experience of self-transcendence. In such experiences I am able to lose myself, to transcend my normal ways of experiencing myself and my world. It is, therefore, often accompanied by what contemplatives and mystics describe as a unitive experience: the sense of being-at-one, often accompanied by the experience of being caught up in a state of awe and wonder or possibly even fear or anxiety.

Part of what gives these physical experiences a spiritual character is the fact that I find prayer to be most natural when I am physically active, particularly when I am walking. While I have experimented with and regularly practice other patterns and postures of prayer, none provide me with the ability to lose myself in my relationship to God quite like prayer offered when walking. I first became conscious of this when I decided to formally use my early morning walks as a time of prayer. To my great surprise, I immediately discovered that this was something I was already doing. Not always does this involve well-formed prayers. More often it involves thought conversations, possibly fragmented and disjointed, but always a form of communication. Other times I repeat the Jesus Prayer ("Lord Jesus Christ, Son of God, have mercy upon me, the sinner"), make intercessions for others, or present my own petitions. But the rhythmic nature of walking and the groundedness of being that I experience as I walk both serve to facilitate my communion with God and make the experience of walking one of the ways that I am best able to restore order to my soul.

In Retrospect

I suppose that with the exception of a person on their deathbed, anyone writing their story must, like me, have the sense of that story still being quite incomplete. In fact, the process of writing my story in midlife has felt somewhat strange. It seems to be too early to tell the story of David Benner. There is still so much more that will hopefully develop in this story. It is too early to pull the plot lines together and give the story closure.

And yet writing my story at this point in my life has helped me appreciate that I am not only writing this story when I sit down now at the computer: I am writing it every day with the choices I make. While I believe my life to be under the hand of God and take much comfort in the doctrine of Providence, writing this account of my life to this point has made me much more clear of myself as the author of my story. I obviously did not create any of the basic ingredients of my life. Both my physical and spiritual life, my family, my body, the country and epoch of my birth, much of my personality—all these and much more were given to me by God. But as Alfred Adler points out, these givens of my life are only the raw materials. I am the architect; I choose how to employ the raw materials. The way in which I have arranged these basic building blocks of my life, what I have done to and with them, this is how I have shaped and written my story.

And this is how I continue to do so. I am becoming more and more aware of the fact that my choices make me who I am and who I am becoming. But my choices are made within the context of my beliefs and desires. I choose one thing over another because of what I believe to be true and what I desire to achieve. Thus, I would suggest that I chose to move to the United States and take a position at Wheaton College in 1978 because, among other things, I believed that it would offer me better support for my desire to further explore the interface of psychology and Christianity. Related to this was a belief that this move would make available further professional opportunities, and this was also something that I desired. Reframing this in the language of intentions offered earlier by Northrop Frye, we might say that among the reasons motivating my move to the United States was my intention to work on the relationship of psychology and Christianity and my intention to acquire further professional experience and distinction. Employing this notion of intentions as the context for choices, what can I offer by way of a beginning understanding of the major intentions that have directed my life?

One overriding conscious intention has clearly been to master whatever I undertake. Minimal competence has never been adequate for me. This is not to suggest that I have not at times confused minimal competence with mastery or that at other times I have not knowingly accepted the former as a substitute for the latter. However, in general, I have desired to achieve mastery of those things to which I have committed myself and have pushed myself until I either achieved this or gave up the pursuit. Although related to perfectionism, this pursuit of mastery seems to me to be slightly different from it. Both have their roots in the soil of an obsessive compulsive personality style and this I acknowledge to be a dominant part of my character structure. However, I experience my perfectionism to be more selective than my pursuit of mastery. While I can be quite perfectionistic about some matters, I am quite capable of living with much less than perfection in many areas of my life. However, my more basic need is that I must be able to perform with excellence those activities to which I set my hand. Once I have mastered something, I am quite willing to no longer have to perform it either with excellence or to do it myself. However, I now know how to do it and to do it correctly and this has always felt very important to me.

While I experience myself as pursuing this agenda for myself rather than others, I am also aware of the way in which it relates to a second rather basic desire or intention; that is, my desire for respect. I have at times deceived myself about how important this is to me. I often feel able to operate relatively well outside the expectations or opinions of others. But I know that this is only partially true. What I desire from others is respect. I need this even more than liking. I can tolerate someone not liking me without too much difficulty. Of more importance to me is that they respect me.

Taken together, these two desires suggest to me that my need for achievement is not as internally motivated as I like to think. It appears to me that I have somehow come to believe that achievement is the route to respect. This insight I note for further reflection.

Two final overriding desires are closely related to each other, namely my desire to be in the mainstream of life, rooted in traditions rather than flirting with innovation, and my desire to be different from others. My desire to be in the mainstream seems to transparently reflect my childhood experience of being in a fringe religious community. Consequently, I now choose to live out my faith life in a mainline denomination. Not content to merely be associated with the Presbyterian/reformed tradition (the oldest Protestant tradition), I was attracted to and worship in the oldest and most traditional of the Presbyterian churches in our city, Central Presbyterian Church. While my ecclesiastical and theological roots are thus firmly grounded in the reformation, my spiritual roots extend well back into prereformational Christendom (particularly the medieval Catholic mystics), and also include much from the Eastern Orthodox Church. Although these have never been my formal religious traditions, I feel deeply connected to them spiritually and my Christian experience cannot be understood apart from some reference to these Christian traditions.

I experienced the same desire to be connected to the great traditions in psychology. My early clinical training was all in behavioral and humanistic psychology. That others had made the pilgrimage from psychoanalysis to these second and third forces of psychology was not good enough for me. I had to go back to the beginning myself. Thus, when I found myself in an internship in 1970 that was offering training in some highly innovative work in intensive residential family therapy, I found myself wishing instead that I could be receiving exposure to traditional individual psychotherapy. Similarly, when others were abandoning the use of projective tests in psychological assessment, I felt a strong need to learn and master these tools that had served others so well for so long. Thus I accepted an internship that offered specialized treatment in the Rorschach and psychoanalytic psychotherapy while my peers were rushing to catch the latest fads in community psychology, biofeedback, and family therapy. My interests have always been in the most traditional expressions of clinical psychology and it seemed that I could only move forward and beyond these after I had moved back to them and experienced them for myself.

But while I desire to be connected to the great traditions of my culture, I also have always desired to be different. If everyone else gets interested in whatever I am interested in, the chances are very good I will lose interest in it. This happened with my work with both eating disorders and multiple personality disorder. My period of major involvement with both these disorders preceded the period of most pronounced public and professional interest in them. At the point of this increased interest in these topics I found myself shifting to other areas of work. I suppose the same might have happened if there had been a significant swing back to psychoanalysis. In fact, it is certainly possible that traditions attract me precisely because they are so quickly abandoned by others.

My story is, I hope, not yet over. However, my account of my life to the point of the summer of 1991 is now complete. To what do I look forward and what do I intend for the future?

Briefly, I first intend to achieve a better balance between work and rest. This has been my pursuit for the past five or six years and, in general, I am making good progress in the matter. My goal is to spend less time on professional and business pursuits and more on familial and personal recreational ones. Specifically, I hope to spend more time cooking, sailing, reading, and enjoying my family and friends. Second, I intend to continue my shift from teaching to research and writing. While I still find engagement with students richly rewarding, I increasingly experience my calling to be to speak to larger audiences than I can fit into my classrooms. These audiences I can address through my writing, and I intend to continue to give this, and the related research, increasingly high priority. Finally, I intend to continue to pursue professional interests as they open themselves to me, rather than follow a predeveloped plan. My interests evolve and change continuously, in part as a function of opportunities, and in part as a result of my own development. After being away from experimental research for twenty years, I have just recently returned to such work after stumbling on some interesting clinical data at a clinic where I consult. This was not a part of any plan of mine and, in fact, pursuing this research takes me away from other things I had anticipated doing. However, the most exciting things that have come into my life have all emerged in this sort of manner, and I anticipate continuing to pursue my life in what Gerald May calls a willing manner, as opposed to a willful one.[3]

Metanarration: On Writing My Story

Writing has always been a form of discovery for me. I do not write because of what I know or think. I write to *discover* what I know or what I think. And once again, this present piece of writing has involved significant discovery.

The discovery this time has not been just that some ideas, once written, are now more clearly understood. Rather, my discovery in writing this autobiographical essay is a discovery of my story. While this may sound rather trite, in actuality, the experience has been quite a significant one. It is not the first time that I have thought through much of the material presented in this essay. Experiences in psychotherapy have at several points afforded me the opportunity to reflect on my life. However, never before have I set myself the task of examining my whole story, of identifying and writing out what I judged to be the most significant aspects of my experiences to this point in my life. I had known the potential benefits of such an exercise and had often recommended it to others, particularly people seeing me in psychotherapy. However, I had never taken my own advice.

As I commented in the closing paragraphs of the essay, the strongest impression that I am left with on completing this assign-

3. May, G. 1982. *Will and spirit: A contemplative psychology.* San Francisco: Harper & Row.

ment is that of my own responsibility in shaping my story. This is a very important awareness for me, since I find it easy to live my life feeling that I am reacting to events and influences around me, not always (or even often) in control of these events. But as I reflect on the big picture of my life I become very aware of the fact that my life is not merely the result of forces acting upon it. It is a creation. It has coherence and direction and I feel very good about claiming ownership of it. This should be understood in any way that minimizes the influences that are beyond my control, particularly, the influences that I invoke and the controls that I have relinquished in my commitment to the Lordship of Jesus Christ in my life. But my experience of writing this essay makes me aware of myself as being the author of my story and, at the same time, makes me aware of some of the big themes of that story. This is an experience of real value and I am thankful for it.

My Many Selves

Al Dueck

In the summer of 1983 I participated in a postgraduate seminar at Yale University in psychology of religion. We were asked to introduce ourselves at length. One person mentioned where studies and degrees were completed and talked of research interests. Others mentioned reasons for participating in the seminar and their personal hopes for our summer together. I did something I had not done before: I told my Mennonite story.

During my graduate training, I had been reticent about my Mennonite faith heritage and its connection to the research I was conducting. I grew up in an ethnic Mennonite home. I sensed as an ethnoreligious group that we had never really made it into contemporary society, given our ethnic foods, use of the German language, and isolated ethnic enclaves. That sense of ethnic embarrassment followed me through college and graduate school. That summer at Yale I decided to risk it.

My story, I began, is one that has its roots in the left wing of the Reformation, develops in the Netherlands in the seventeenth century, winds through Poland and South Russia in the eighteenth and nineteenth centuries, and continues through Canada and the United States into the present century. As I wandered through the eras I mentioned events that shaped my self-perceptions: the importance of the call to follow Christ; persecution by the magisterial reformers for refusing to baptize infants; small house churches that called individual Christians into communal accountability; long migrations replete with illness, privation, and death; my own growing up in an ethnic Mennonite community in Canada; and some of my experiences in the church.

In their desire to follow Christ in obedience, the sixteenth century Anabaptists gave public expression to that commitment in adult baptism. The state should not dictate to the church on matters that were her concern. The state however, found such actions a threat and so the Anabaptists (rebaptizers) were drowned, burned, or killed. That story I have heard told and retold. The implicit message was always that being a disciple of Christ (Nachfolge Christi) affects all of life. We are to live a life of quiet resignation to God's will (Gelassenheit). My story invites me not to coerce, choices are to be voluntary (contra Constantinianism). It reinforced the fact that the freedom to express my faith requires that I grant others their freedom as well. The Christian life is communal (Gemeinschaft).

What happened thereafter in that summer seminar I had never experienced before. During a discussion of Freud, Jung, or William James, one of the participants in the seminar would turn to me and ask how I viewed the issue given my Mennonite story. They helped me to flesh out the implications of my own particular understanding of the Christian story for how one constructs a psychology of religion.

I have come to the point where I am not embarrassed about my ethno-religious story. In fact, I see it as a gift. It is my story, and in ways I sometimes hardly realize, it shapes my theory, research, and therapy. I did not create it. My Mennonite story does not begin with my birth. I am a part of a particular people and a global community, the Mennonite community and the worldwide Christian and human community. My ethno-religious story is not just my own personal conscious history, it has increasingly larger contexts: the German-speaking (several decades ago) Mennonite community, North American culture, migrations from the "old world," the left wing of the Protestant Reformation, the Constantinian and medieval Catholic church, and before that the Greco-Roman and Judeo-Christian heritage. I realize my story is, of course, only one version of that larger particular story of the Reign of God, one instrument in that grander orchestra. On the other hand, being ethnic is a particularity that is affirmed by the fact that God came to a Middle Eastern tribe through whom to speak to the world.

On Developing a Masculine Self

My maternal and paternal grandparents lived in the Ukraine. But with the Russian revolution and turmoil of the 1920s they emigrated to Canada. Not surprisingly, I still have dreams with a cast of Russian revolutionaries!

I come from two generations of widows: first my maternal grandmother and then my mother. Grandfather died shortly after arriving in Canada. My father drowned in the Pacific Ocean in a fishing accident when I was two; my mother was pregnant with my brother.

It has been interesting to learn of my own father. In his youth he was a creative storyteller for his younger brothers, weaving tales of mystery and intrigue. He was a risk taker. He swam the Dnieper River with inflated wet pillow cases as ballast. When the sun dried them and the air escaped, he swam back to shore. When the Dueck family came to Canada in the 1920s and lived in a small Mennonite town, my father found both his father and the community too restrictive. Apparently there was a long history of conflict with Grandpa Dueck. And so my father traveled the country in railway cars and played fiddle at hoedowns in order to stay alive. In his late twenties, father had a significant religious awakening and then attended a Bible school. He later worked in an auto paint shop but for health reasons a doctor recommended he not continue. To make extra money he fished. My parents had been living cozily in a houseboat under Second Narrows Bridge in Vancouver, British Columbia. One July day in 1945, he went fishing with another man and they never returned. Two weeks later my father's body washed up on the shore of Vancouver Island.

I have had to learn how to deal with the aftereffects of growing up in a single parent family and living without a father figure. I have had a number of individuals who were male models for me. My father's youngest brother symbolized spontaneity and intellectual curiosity. He was inventive and creative. Though the youngest of the siblings he was quite willing to disagree with the others and chart his own course. He was the first to leave the home town of Winnipeg and become active in the Charismatic movement.

The absence of a father in my childhood created a void. I have never thought of my father's absence as a wound. I do now. I see now what I have missed. Mother tried to model strength and gentleness but I needed to see it in men. A friend once told me that it was a wound that would never go away. When I protested he said that though a tree is wounded, the wound remains and the bark grows around the wound. The wound is also a gift when it doesn't determine my responses. It may in fact be connected to what gifts I possess. I think it has kept alive in me the importance of tenderness, a tenderness that has also been the reason for a lack, at times, of confidence.

With many of my contemporaries, I wrestle with what it means to be male. I have had to deal with patriarchal institutions, dogmatic theologies, and ideological psychologies. The metaphor of God as father has been helpful. It has relativized the power of institutions, theologies, and ideologies on the one hand, and pointed to the gentleness of a father on the other. I understand that God as father is more meaningful to me than for someone whose father has been abusive. I pray "Abba Father" with joy.

My Pastoral Self

Since mother was without resources after my father died, she moved with her young family back to the prairies where all the relatives resided, her biological community. We lived in a small 800-square-foot house with three rooms, a crab apple tree, a plum tree, a gooseberry bush, three elms, and a lilac bush. But our community was as large as the Mennonite neighborhood in North Kildonan, Winnipeg. There was Mr. Dyck who took me fishing. Mr. Jantzen encouraged me to obey my mother, and Mr. Unruh gave me a job mowing his lawn. There was Uncle Abe who taught me to drive a car, shoot a rifle, and took me to the Shrine Circus.

My widowed grandmother was my constant companion the first three years in Winnipeg. While my mother raised two very lively, cantankerous boys, she never did so alone. Mother was never so possessive that others could not correct and love her children. We lived on welfare for several years but had the riches of family and congregation. I remember grocery bags at Christmas from the women's sewing circle, and Mr. Suderman who took us out for a special dinner on Father's day. These were my mother's friends. They were faithful to a widow.

My personal development very much depended on that community. The church and ethnic Mennonite neighborhood gave me many of the qualities of a healing community: good memories that shape me even today. The church and neighborhood gave me male models to serve in my father's place, a sense of belonging to community, a regular rhythm of rituals (Thanksgiving, Christmas, baptism, Easter, foot washing, communion, and of course, the Sunday school picnics), a network of friends that stimulated me to growth, a story powerful enough to create a community and capable of healing, a community that had clear limits and let you know the consequences when you failed. It could say "no." It was also a community that could say "yes." This was a community that allowed me to exercise my gifts. I preached my first sermon at the age of eighteen. I remember wondering aloud in the sermon why our lily-white congregation was not more multicultural. The pastor, who followed my sermon, tried to contain the fallout.

I remember most clearly my mother's love for the church. Once as an idealistic adolescent I was severely criticizing the church, Mother said to me, "Alvin (it was always Alvin when the topic was serious), I happen to love the church." I have learned to love God's people, but a critical perspective is at times needed.

During the 1950s a family moved to Winnipeg from Germany. They lived nearby and my mother cared for them. Being very practical, my mother would send for a repairman if they had problems with the washing machine. When their children ran over to say their mother was crying again, my mother would go over to comfort her. Maybe that is why I have been both a pastor and psychologist over the years.

The biblical theme of God's people is a most meaningful one for me. That it has become so I attribute in part to the experience of peoplehood as a child. When Jesus invites Peter to "Feed my sheep," I understand.

An Adventurous Self

I attended a small rural Bible school after high school and I was confident the school would make a preacher out of me. But the two years away from home gave me the opportunity for the individuation I needed and I charted my own direction. It was here that my interest in psychology was kindled. The instructor was a pastor, not a psychologist, and the text he used in 1961 was already quite outdated (1938). But it was clear that psychology could be a servant of the church and my appetite was whetted. It wasn't long before I wondered, "What has Jesus to do with Freud?"

It was here in Bible school that I first met Anne. Anne had a zest for life, self-confidence, and a commitment to the life of the church.

We were married in 1965 and my love for the discipline of psychology has never matched the passion and romanticism of our relationship.

Dr. Robson, my next psychology instructor at the University of Winnipeg, modeled for me gentleness and scholarship. My world was opened to the insights of Rogers and Skinner, learning theory, and existentialism. I took enough courses in philosophy to constitute a minor concentration. By the third year I felt I needed to be back in theology: this time at the Mennonite Brethren Bible College in Winnipeg. The next two years I attended both the Bible college and the university at the same time, a pattern of tacking back and forth that has followed me through the years. I must confess, I didn't know how to put it together: 1 Corinthians and Oedipal conflict, Old Testament theology and norepinephrine. At that point they simply coexisted without animosity. At times I assumed that being a psychologist was really no different than being a pastor. At other times, I felt pastors would do well to converse with psychologists. At yet other times, the enterprise of therapy seemed little more than a business that reflected American capitalism.

My convictions have changed over the years, largely because of experiences and relationships that have forced reassessment. A most significant event occurred the summer before entering graduate school. I had been accepted into the graduate psychology program at the University of Manitoba and would be conducting research in learning with the proverbial white rat as subject. But Anne and I received an invitation to assist a group of Mennonite churches in North Carolina. The conference numbered 200 members in seven small churches and were spread across 200 square miles. We accepted.

It was all new: our first extended trip into the United States; the first time we crossed the Mason-Dixon line into the American south; the first thirty-six hour bus ride anywhere; the first encounter with red clay that wouldn't wash out; our first experience with African-American Mennonites.

What happened was entirely unexpected. We helped out with camp work and at the end of the summer the church leaders invited us to return. That an African-American community would invite us to live with them was overwhelming. We were honored. I quickly applied to the counseling program at Appalachian State University in Boone and was accepted with a teaching assistantship position as a bonus. The church leadership asked us to work with the young people and assist in pastoring the churches. We were excited.

April, 1968. The wooden casket carrying Martin Luther King moved slowly across the screen of our little black and white TV. Rev. Rhondo Horton, the conference leader, and his wife, "Miz" Ruth, were with us. There couldn't have been a starker contrast. They were dark skinned, we were white. They had sharecropped with their parents at the turn of the century. We grew up in the fifties in Mennonite homes. For years Rev. Rhondo had hauled coal from the Virginia mines. We had attended college. They knew unconsciously where the color boundary was in every public place, whether restroom or restaurant. We barely knew where the Mason-Dixon line was. "Miz" Ruth sat there dabbing at her eyes with her white handkerchief. Rev. Rhondo cried openly. We sat quietly. For both of them Martin Luther King had been a modern Moses.

In Boone, North Carolina, where we lived those two years, the African-American neighborhood was small and conspicuous in a predominantly white county. When we arrived in the late 1960s, the young people in our church had never bowled in the local bowling alley. They had eaten in the local restaurant only a year earlier. They had never seen a movie in the local theater. Such blatant prejudice was simply not part of our repertoire of experience. Or perhaps we had been blind to it in Winnipeg.

There was the time we went swimming at an all white beach. When we arrived some thirty strong, the beach was sprinkled with whites. Half an hour later, we were alone. I had naively assumed that beaches were for swimming regardless of skin color. I had just completed my undergraduate work in psychology and philosophy and was committed in an abstract way to respecting the African-American culture. This was different. This was not theoretical. These people were our primary friends. We played baseball, told stories, and laughed together. Our landlord was the conference moderator. We lived in the African-American community by their invitation, something my faculty at the University where I was completing a masters program in counseling could never understand.

I learned about the experience of the Mennonite church in the south through their eyes. Missionaries had arrived in North Carolina in the late 1890s from the midwest and with wonderful naivete assumed that if one creates an orphanage it should be available regardless of skin color. Not so, said the town, with rocks through the windows, late night warnings by vigilantes, and cross burnings. So this white couple made it an orphanage for African-Americans from which emerged some of the leadership of the Mennonite churches in the area.

The impact of these experiences on my view of the discipline of psychology and psychotherapy has been considerable. Even then I studied therapy in the context of a marginal community. My masters thesis[1] examined self-perceptions among African-American and Caucasian adolescents controlling for social class. Not surprisingly, the scores on self-esteem for the Caucasians were higher. The research and experience impressed indelibly on me the connection between social and personal issues. Psychology must deal with issues of liberation and freedom. Therapy must have something to do with freeing people to experience the new. The biblical narrative describes God as one who frees the oppressed, gives sight to the blind, who creates a liberated people. Given the plight of African-American peoples, it is obvious that the reign of God has not come in fullness in this nation.

Becoming a Psychologist

I knew I would eventually complete doctoral studies but did not know when. After two years of teaching undergraduate psychology at Tabor College (1969–71), I took a three year leave of absence (1971–74). I applied, was accepted at Stanford University, and received a Canada Council Grant to pay expenses. I was elated (or was it inflated). Stanford with its ivy-covered walls, tile-covered roofs, arched walkways, Memorial Chapel, and Hoover tower gave the impression of academia at its best. The faculty were world renowned, served on Senate subcommittees, were forever publishing books, and seemed to have an unlimited supply of money available to do research. And I was to be one of their students (more hubris).

Many of the departments ranked highest in the nation. The university research library boasted a million holdings, and its football team (at that time) went to the Rosebowl for the second time with Jim Plunkett as quarterback. And I was going to be a graduate of Stanford University, I hoped. I arrived starry eyed and suffering from a colossal inferiority complex. Starry eyed because this upstart from North Kildonan had made it to graduate school, and depressed because he thought he would never make it through. My fellow students came from Harvard, Princeton, and Yale, while my faculty advisor could

1. Dueck, Alvin. 1968. The relationship of self-esteem in negro and white adolescents to perception of others. Unpublished Masters Thesis.

never remember where I had completed my masters work. Appropriate deflation!

Of course I do not know, but I do not think I would have considered ten years of teaching in Christian higher education (Tabor College, Goshen College, and Fresno Pacific College) after Stanford if it had not been for the life of a small Mennonite Brethren congregation in Santa Clara, some fifteen miles from Stanford. Its membership numbered less than a hundred and was not growing very quickly. It was not well known and hardly respected by the large and growing evangelical churches in the Santa Clara valley. It faithfully preached the gospel, sensitively cared for its members, tentatively reached out into the community with a day-care center, and joyfully ate together.

My world was split. Systematic research on cognition and memory on the one hand,[2] and being associate pastor at El Camino Bible Church. It was the church experience that kept my faith alive. Stanford developed the research skills I have used to help my own denomination reflect on itself, using surveys and analysis.[3] But Stanford was and is an institution deeply immersed in the modern world where knowledge is power. There is no question that in the modern world knowledge enables one to predict and control. When I reflect on my spirituality, as it was while attending Stanford, it is clear that my professional growth was as much a consequence of my church experience during those years as it was of graduate school. The church relativized the power of the academic community. Essentially, the discipline of psychology and Christianity remained separate the three years at Stanford. Research and reading psychology on the one hand and pastoral work on the other.

It was not until I returned to Tabor in 1974 that I began serious work at integrative dialogue. I discovered at a much more existential level the Anabaptist heritage I had learned about in Sunday school and Bible College. I began to see its relevance to the professional world.[4] That heritage focused on a radical discipleship ethic, a commitment to accountable Christian community, and a critique of soci-

2. Bower, Gordon, Marty Karlin, and Alvin Dueck. 1975. Comprehension and memory for pictures. *Memory and Cognition* 3:216–20; Dueck, Alvin. 1979. Perception of order in scrambled text. Unpublished Doctoral Thesis, Stanford University.

3. Toews, John B., Abram Konrad, and Alvin Dueck. 1986. Mennonite brethren church membership profile: 1972–1982. *Direction* 14:1–89; Enns, Robert, and Alvin Dueck. 1988. Mennonite brethren in three countries: Comparative profiles of an ethnoreligious tradition. *Direction* 17:30–59.

4. Dueck, Alvin. 1982. Prolegomena to Mennonite approaches in mental health services. *Mennonite Quarterly Review* 56:45–65.

ety. I spent considerable time thinking about the connection between my Anabaptist heritage and my psychological interests.[5]

But instead of integration, segregation set in. I was increasingly aware of the larger social world I was living in. I read the literature on technological advances. Civil religion, nuclearism, individualism, sexism were part of North American society. How could the discipline of psychology or mental health professionals avoid the influence of Western culture? How does one deal with issues of justice?[6]

I became increasingly aware of how religious mental health professionals seemed to outgrow the church.[7] Church was what one did on Sunday. It felt like what is sometimes referred to as being a "Saturday night ethnic": an occasional nostalgia for tradition. The rest of the time the standards, customs, and community of the profession prevailed. The individualism of the profession didn't seem to bother them.[8] That behaviorism might be the incarnation of a technological society, went unnoticed. To be a Christian professional meant doing what every other member of the profession was doing, only doing it better or with a fish sign on the Volvo bumper or Choice books in the waiting room. The fees were the same. The clients were the same: middle class, the ones who could pay and whose problems were amenable to a middle class therapy. The church it seemed was irrelevant relative to the profession. Yes, I probably romanticized the church in those days in my reaction to professionalism. But at the same time the church's vision for a new society and a new person was not getting its due.

In 1984, after teaching in undergraduate departments of psychology for twelve years, our denominational seminary invited me to develop a counseling program. To prepare pastors and counselors to

5. Klassen, Michael, and Alvin Dueck. 1976. Moral development: Issues and perspectives. In *Research in mental health and religious behavior,* ed. William J. Donaldson, Jr. Atlanta; Dueck, Alvin, and Gordon Zerbe. 1976. Interpretations of Christ and culture: The church, the world and the profession. A paper presented to the Christian association of psychological studies (CAPS), Santa Barbara, Calif.; Dueck, Alvin, and Mike Regier. 1978. The Christian as professional psychologist? Paper presented at CAPS; Dueck, Alvin, and Kevin Genich. 1978. Integration of Christianity and psychology: A critique of Jeeves and Collins. Paper presented at CAPS.

6. Dueck, Alvin. 1976. Education for justice. *Direction* 5:14–22; Dueck, Alvin. 1979. Religion and morality: An evaluation of Kohlberg's theory of moral development. Paper presented at CAPS.

7. Dueck, Alvin. 1982. Contexts of professionalism. Paper presented at the annual Mennonite graduate seminar, Manhattan, Kansas; Dueck, Alvin. 1988. Psychology and Mennonite self-understanding. In *Mennonite Identity,* ed. Calvin Redekop and Sam Steiner. University of America Press.

8. Dueck, Alvin. 1980. Individualism. Paper presented at CAPS; Dueck, Alvin. 1980. Contexts of conversion. *Direction* 9:10–15.

work in the church and society was a challenge I could not pass by. At first I focused on teaching classes related to pastoral counseling. My thinking and writing largely focused on issues of ethics and therapy.[9] That culminated in the presentation of the Integration Lectures at the Fuller School of Psychology in January, 1986. The metaphors that shaped the lectures were the ethical implications of the Reign of God, the responsibility of the church in assisting the professional therapist in ethical issues, and the transformation of the character of the therapist as ethical agent by the larger story of the Reign of God and the involvement in the community of faith.[10]

Eventually, I realized I needed to be actively engaged in therapy to serve as support for my teaching and reflecting. And so began the process of moving toward licensure. Could I really immerse myself in a process of professionalization given all the misgivings I had had? At the encouragement of the seminary and friends, I went with it. I needed 3000 hours of supervised counseling and to pass the state licensing exams. I began the process in 1987 and completed it in 1990.

From 1984 to 1991 I directed the Marriage and Family Counseling program at the Mennonite Brethren Biblical seminary. Students went from our program to Christian counseling centers, pastoral positions, and graduate school. My thinking increasingly moved toward the issues of the family in the modern world.[11] I taught a course in ethics and family therapy and wondered again how Judeo-Christian ethics intersected with the various approaches to family therapy.[12]

Today, in addition to my teaching and writing, I see some five clients and supervise another five students. Our clients are largely poor. The clientele reflects Fresno's multicultural diversity. The counseling is very difficult.

9. Dueck, Alvin, and Will Friesen. 1988. Whatever happened to law? *Journal of Psychology and Christianity* 7:13–22; Dueck, Alvin. 1989. Story, community and ritual: Anabaptist themes and mental health. *Mennonite Quarterly Review* 63:77–91.

10. Dueck, Alvin. 1987. Ethical contexts of healing: Peoplehood and righteousness. *Pastoral Psychology* 35:239–53; Dueck, Alvin. 1987. Ethical contexts of healing: Ecclesia and praxis. *Pastoral Psychology* 36:49–60; Dueck, Alvin. 1988. Ethical contexts of healing: Character and ritual. *Pastoral Psychology* 36:69–83; Dueck, Alvin. 1986. Sectarian pastoral care. In *Dictionary of pastoral care and pastoral counseling,* ed. Rodney J. Hunter. Nashville: Abingdon.

11. Friesen, Delores, and Alvin Dueck. 1990. The changing family in today's world. *Direction* 19:12–28.

12. Dueck, Alvin. 1989. On living in Athens: Models of relating psychology, church and culture. *Journal of Psychology and Christianity* 8:5–18; Dueck, Alvin. 1992. Metaphors, models, paradigms and stories in family therapy. In *Family therapy: Christian perspectives,* ed. Hendrika Vande Kemp. Baker Book House.

My close friends have commented on the change. Critique of the profession in the 1970s; immersion in the 1990s. Somewhere in the eighties I had begun to change. I began to see the discipline from a more pragmatic point of view. What's useful, use; what's consistent, apply. Avoid the ideology.

I am grateful for the many models of professionalism that I have encountered over the years. I remember a medical doctor who was not so tied to the profession so as to be unable to leave his practice and serve in Cambodia, and whose relationship to patients involved an attempt to treat the whole person, not simply a body or one of its parts. I have business acquaintances who consider profit sharing as a way of creating a sense of community between employees and employers. There is the architect I know who is committed to designing buildings or homes that reflect a concern about energy usage and land consumption. I remember a lawyer who, because of God's particular love for the oppressed, chose to work with the weak and helpless in tenant-landlord disputes. I personally know a number of teachers who teach with low pay in difficult ethnic minority schools.

Then there are the psychologists who have significantly impacted me. I think of Kirk Farnsworth and how his commitment to live a simple life-style has enabled him to see many clients *pro bono.* I think of Irene Loewen who combines competency as a clinician with a Christian spirit of graciousness. They are an inspiration for me to do and be the same.

In the Spring of 1992 I was granted a sabbatical. Three of the months were spent at Heidelberg University in Germany with Dr. Helm Stierlin's team of family therapists. What an experience! I was included in a team that worked with families. I could view any of 2000 videotapes of their work over the past fifteen years. I attended classes, read the family journals in their library, and attended an international conference hosted by Stierlin's group. Perhaps the best surprise was to discover that Stierlin has written a pamphlet (in German) entitled, "The Christians in the World Family" in which he shares his own personal faith. The book uses material from the field of family research and from the Sermon on the Mount to talk about peace in the family and in society.

The Heidelberg experience was incredible. Helm's warm invitation to come, the generous invitation to use whatever materials were at hand (books, tapes, files, and actual sessions) was more than I expected. Joachen Schweitzer's warm embrace and offer to work with him as a therapeutic team member was unforgettable. During each counseling session the therapists would take a break to plan with us the direction of the remaining time with the family. The fact that this group read widely in linguistics, sociology, and philosophy and integrated it into therapy was refreshing. Their awareness of the discussions of post-modernity was encouraging. I found myself both intrigued by their approach to circular questioning, use of pauses for planning interventions, and their use of metaphor and narrative in therapy.

We lived a half-hour drive away in a small hamlet, Frankenthal. Here a congregation of Russian-Mennonite emigres lived and worshipped. We lived in the home of one of the immigrant families. Their congregational Bible study was most interesting. They selected a text in advance and thus everyone would know which text would be discussed. Young and old attended. The church opened the meeting for everyone to participate. Some had prepared a mini exegesis and shared it. Others responded spontaneously. A variety of perspectives were presented. Young people felt free to present. The church was otherwise rather hierarchical, but in this respect they were very communal. It was a wonderful moment when the moderator said: "Let the church speak," and then sat down and did not say another word until the closing.

What a contrast between Frankenthal and Heidelberg. Frankenthal represented for me all that is old world, conservative faith. The German spoken was not as elegant, the faith was very simple and somewhat ethnocentric. Heidelberg was cosmopolitan, secular, sophisticated, and complex. Every day I moved between these two worlds. I actually did not mind it. I was clearly at home and loved in the Frankenthal community. In the Heidelberg community I was appreciated for my analysis of family therapy.

This is my more professional self. I see my work as part of a calling, a vocation. It has a context. That context I want to be the Reign of God. What has changed over the years is my awareness of when my work is more a reflection of modernity and less a reflection of the Reign of God.

On Being Communal

After four years of undergraduate teaching (1974–78), I was burned out. We had an invitation to teach at Fresno Pacific College, had accepted, but were not ready. So, in the year between teaching in Kansas and moving to the west coast where I would spend five (1979–84) wonderful years teaching at Fresno Pacific College, our family spent a self-supported sabbatical in Elkhart, Indiana. I taught part time at Goshen College and attended theology classes at the Associated Mennonite Biblical Seminaries and the University of Notre Dame. These were formative years in shaping my theology. At the level of the heart, however, it was while living with the Fellowship of Hope that personal renewal occurred. I had also wondered what healing would be like in a communal context. We had begun to wonder what the church would look like if it took accountability and body life more seriously. The Fellowship of Hope is an intentional Christian community. It was begun by four seminary families in the early 1970s. They were committed to a vision of the church as a community. They were willing to assume liability for each other. This meant emotional, spiritual, and financial support. They chose to live together in a large frame house in one of Elkhart's transitional neighborhoods. Living arrangements included single family dwellings and households of singles and couples. Economic arrangements then included a common fund and independent family accounts.

Of particular interest to me was their common life. Every Thursday supper was eaten together, a common meal. Often the meal was followed with games, storytelling, and singing. The meals were very simple and nutritious. Sunday evening the community broke into smaller groups of ten or so for discernment and accountability: a courtship was discussed, a new business venture was considered, parents were supported, personal difficulties or conflicts with others in the community were worked on.

The community attracted profoundly broken people. A family of eight came to the community in need of help. The father was unable to support the entire family. Family life was absolutely chaotic. One of the elders spent significant time with the parents teaching a system of budgeting. In the small groups we discussed parenting styles. Other individuals assisted in the parenting process by taking the children separately on excursions. When we left they had been there six years, father had deserted the family but mother was developing a sense of responsibility.

A pregnant fifteen-year-old prostitute came for help. She had no medical insurance. The community paid for it even though they themselves had no medical insurance. After giving up the baby for adoption, she left. A year later she came back, again pregnant. The community helped her once more. Again she gave up the child for adoption and left. The fall we arrived she again arrived pregnant. This time she stayed. She lived with one of the church families. She was unable to cook for herself. They taught her. She became angry when the child cried. The family taught her how to care for the child and to respond with patience. She began attending church services and common meal. The child was slowly becoming her own. It was a moment of incredible rejoicing for the entire community when she became a Christian and was baptized. But it was equally sad when several months later she again left.

For several years I had wondered what a healing community would look like. It was clear that individual families would not have been able to respond to the young woman's needs had not the community supported them with financial and emotional relief. As I have reflected on this experience, it has become clearer to me that healing always has a communal context and that the quality of my work as a therapist is in part dependent on the quality of the community I or my counselees share. It was Bonhoeffer's book *Life Together* that deeply moved me during these days. The Fellowship of Hope was making an attempt to live out their spirituality with clear corporate commitments. This is not the only model of corporate Christianity but it does set a contrast to rampant privatistic Christianity. The modern world—and particularly Western culture—values independence, individual uniqueness, and personal actualization. But it is the particularly middle-class male who sees accountability as meddling and community as oppressive. Christians live in this same world, only they often tend to bless their individualism with the label of spirituality. In individualistic societies, spirituality is private and personal. How I live my life is between God and me. Spirituality has then little to do with accountability.

It was refreshing to be with people who emphasized interdependence, community witness, and personal sacrifice. It should come as no surprise that over the years I have been fascinated with social and community psychology, network therapy, and systems theory. I have taught ethics and personality from a social-psychological perspective, recognizing the importance of symbolic interactionism and object-relations theory. Teaching counseling in a seminary is one way I feel I still encourage the development of a healing context, the church community, for therapy. The experience at the Fellowship of Hope raised for me the fundamental question: "Who are my people?"[13] The

13. Dueck, Alvin. 1981. Who are my people? In *Perils of professionalism,* ed. Don Kraybill and Phyllis Good. Scottdale.

fact that I have chosen to teach in a seminary context is clearly influenced by my experience at the Fellowship of Hope.[14]

An International Identity

While teaching at Tabor College and again at Fresno Pacific College, I took a group of students to Guadalajara and Mexico City. Both were life-changing experiences as we struggled to learn the language and the culture. The Orozco and Rivera paintings integrated art and politics. The evangelical missionaries taking language study with us were so dogmatic and ethnocentric, I was embarrassed for the witness of the church.

While in Mexico City I visited the national university. I was awed with its imposing architecture, size (200,000 students), and advanced psychology department. While browsing in the bookstore, I noticed that psychology books consumed more than a quarter of the space for student texts. I was intrigued. Why such interest in psychology? I began examining the textbooks. It appeared that most of the books used in the university were translations of American textbooks. There were a few introductory texts written by Mexicans, but they primarily reviewed research with subjects who lived in the United States. There were few books written by Mexican authors about research studies with Mexican subjects. Several books attempted to develop an indigenous psychology.

I wondered if one of the factors that would shape an emerging Mexican consciousness would be an awareness of American psychology and its worldview. If Western psychology reflects Western ideals, then it should come as no surprise that Western psychology will assist, for better or for worse, in the process of socializing emerging nations into modernity. In the past century Western missionaries were accused of being the carriers of Western culture.[15] Now it is McDonald's, sitcoms, and Western psychology.

In the fall of 1989 I was given one of those once-in-a-lifetime opportunities: to travel to the then Soviet Union. Mennonite Health Services organized an exchange program and a group of twenty mental

14. Dueck, Alvin. 1987. Pastoral caregivers. In *Deacons and the church, a Brethren / Mennonite project,* ed. Jay Gibble. Elgin; Dueck, Alvin. 1992. Congregational care needs and resources study: A summary. *Direction* 21:26–41; Dueck, Alvin. 1992. The church as a healing community. *Builder,* 1–9.

15. Dueck, Alvin. 1983. Psychology: Native or American? A paper presented at the ethnicity, religion and psychology conference at Fuller school of psychology; Dueck, Alvin. 1985. North American psychology: Gospel of modernity. *Conrad Grebel Review* 3:165–78.

health professionals toured the country and observed firsthand the Soviet mental health programs.

The Soviet Union has played a significant role in my life. My parents were born in the Ukraine. My grandmother told me many stories about life in the "old country." My mother-in-law wrote letters faithfully to relatives in the USSR from the 1930s to the 1990s when she was finally able to visit them in Germany. I could understand the U.S. antipathy for Soviet authoritarianism but I could never endorse its militarism.[16] These people too are made in the image of God. Besides, an all out war might well destroy the Christians and family my mother-in-law prayed for daily. So for me to step on Russian soil was another kind of homecoming.

The first week was spent traveling the Ukraine. I saw the village my forbears had built. But there were no Mennonites left. After the second world war, Stalin had resettled all German-speaking Ukrainians to the interior. A local museum carried a few pieces of Mennonite culture. A hundred years of labor reduced to a dinner plate and some clothing! As I traveled through the villages, I remembered how as a four-year-old my wife's father saw his own father shot in front of him.

It was the Baptist conference that arranged our visit to the mental health agencies in Moscow. The pastor was eager to show off Western mental health professionals who were Christians. The most interesting of experiences was the Kaschenko hospital where the women from the Baptist congregation had been volunteering for the past two years. The Kaschenko hospital in Moscow is one of the oldest (1894) and largest (2600 beds) psychiatric hospitals in the Soviet Union. The hospital boasts 237 doctors, 1,128 psychiatric nurses, 1,035 aides, and 481 other assistants. The catchment area for the hospital was approximately two million people. Patients were placed in wards according to the catchment area from which they came. Interestingly, there were patients who indicated they wished to get into the wards where the Baptist volunteers were working.

Dr. Kozyrev, the clinical director, placed much emphasis on the importance of social rehabilitation of patients. He was concerned that psychiatry had lost its emphasis on the importance of prevention. He also indicated that the most pressing problems for him were financing the hospital, developing new ideas, and that psychiatry is not

16. Dueck, Alvin. 1983. A nuclear blast can ruin your whole day. Forum chaired at CAPS.

changing quickly enough. He indicated that, before, they had political problems; now they have economic problems. With the dissolution of the USSR and its current economic problems, I can only imagine their distress today.

The evidences of *perestroika* were evident at the hospital. First, the openness of our own meeting was evidence. Second, there was a less formal atmosphere at the hospital. Third, wards could decide on a treatment program and initiate new ideas. One ward was organized according to a collective, but patients were promised that the products of their labor (clothing for children) would be sold and the profits would be returned to individual patients. Also, the old concrete walls outside were being removed and wrought iron fences were replacing them. One also sensed that administration was more open to ideas that came up from the various staff.

The question was raised regarding involuntary hospitalization of political dissidents. Kozyrev and his assistant were visibly pained by the question. They indicated that part of the problem was that the press had distorted the situation at least in part. They did admit that in times past there had been involuntary hospitalizations for political reasons. They hoped that we would not judge the services of the hospital on the basis of past history. The day we left, the World Health Organization reinstated the Soviet representatives as full members. Everyone rejoiced.

One of the highlights of our stay at this hospital was the meeting with several hundred staff members. Kozyrev opened the meeting with a moment of silence for victims of the earthquake in California that had occurred the day before. Kozyrev read translated summaries of our vitae and then opened the meeting for questions. The audience was lively. Questions revolved around ethical issues in America, treatment approaches, and so forth. After the meeting, Pastor Zhidkov, the organizer from the Baptist conference, indicated that the meeting was without question historic. This was the first time in the history of the hospital that staff had been invited to a consultation such as this. Also, most of those staff present had probably never before met educated believers who were also professional mental health practitioners. It was quite clear that Zhidkov was proud to show off his American friends who could demonstrate that Christianity and mental health could be integrated.

What has nurtured this international part of me is the fact that the Reign of God is not the property of one ethnic community. Paul saw himself as called to reconcile Jew and Gentile. It is my calling too.

A Matter of Heart, Head, and Hand

Perhaps what has created the most change in me over the past decade is a consequence of listening to the suffering of the persons I see as clients. I have had to take stock of my own heart. Some twenty years of scholarship take their toll. I began wondering what impact there might be on my therapy, not to mention my own spiritual life. Let me share a dream I had that forced me to take more seriously the condition of my own heart.

> I am taking our son Kevin to the hospital. He is around twelve at the time and the event takes place somewhere in Canada. I cannot remember the reason for hospitalization, but I do remember boxes in the aisles I have to avoid. While I am waiting for the examination to end, I hear over the intercom that Kevin is being rushed into emergency surgery. I next remember standing in the surgery room watching as they wheel Kevin in. He is lying on a gurney with doctors hovering over him. The surgeon pours a thick red liquid on him that resembles blood. It gathers on the side. He then takes a knife and begins to cut once lengthwise and once crosswise. I begin to cry uncontrollably, am discovered, and ushered out into the lobby where many relatives have gathered.

I did not sleep well the rest of that night. I took this dream as a warning. It was not my son's heart that needed radical surgery, it was my own. I needed the blood that gives life to my body and so the surgeon had to add it. What I needed was open heart surgery.

Why? Many reasons. The fundamentalist religion I grew up with as a child induced much guilt and fear of the afterlife. It was a harsh religion, and it had a way of silencing the whisperings of a young and sensitive heart. The warm piety I experienced in High School and Bible School was a welcome relief. But by the time I finished graduate school it seemed unconnected from the larger world.

But in all that, I had forgotten the God who is within: the God who has taken on human form and experience. For too many years I had been reading, writing, and teaching, not listening to my heart, not listening to the Spirit of God. I am not sure I trusted a faith that follows a grammar of the heart. Of course, it is not a matter of returning or recovering my adolescent piety; I must encounter God anew given my present stage.

So what is this religion of the heart? Well, first I think that we are so constituted that there is in our hearts a hunger for God's presence. In the words of Augustine, "Our hearts are restless until they find their rest in thee." I think deep within our souls we are invited to recognize a Presence. The God of Sarah and Mary comes to us not only in the gathered community, but also alone, in our hearts.

And what does it mean for me? That I learn to wait for the God who seeks me. If with all my heart I seek God, I discover that I find God's presence in my soul when I create room in my psyche. It comes as I journal: when I am ruthlessly honest with myself about my motives, my hopes, and my fears. It comes when I recognize my injuries and wounds. Our hearts are filled with a mixture of primary metaphors, dreams, stories, images that give meaning to our lives. These I want to be enriched, changed, and affirmed by the presence of God.

Slowly I have begun to understand when I need to separate my inner promptings and God's Spirit, when to say "this is my dream and it is the presence of God; and it is good." Sometimes it has meant for me to be spontaneous and sometimes measured.

In the Christmas season, I am often moved by the example of Mary, the mother of Jesus. Mary is one who saw with her heart. She is silent and reflective. The Angel appears to Joseph, as one would expect in a patriarchal society. But it is Mary's heart that breaks forth in song. It appears there had been some years of preparation of heart. After the shepherds left, "Mary treasured up all these things and pondered them in her heart" (Luke 2:19).

My faith is more than firmly held intellectual convictions. It has also been influenced by the realization that, for many, faith is shaped by the senses: eyes, ears, taste, and touch. Orthodox Christians have reminded me of this simple fact.

The Soviet Orthodox Church, which rose up before me in Kiev one October morning, was an imposing structure. The columns painted white, the walls blue. The golden onion domes glinted in the morning sun. As I entered, the words of a friend familiar with Orthodoxy came back to me: "To enter the church is always to enter worship service already in progress." At this very moment a heavenly host of angels and departed saints praise God. I was told the praise and beauty of the heavenly scene is to be replicated in the church. The beauty of the surroundings are visual reflections of heavenly beauty. They are created to image forth the beauty of truth.

As I entered, the smell of incense, the murmur of prayer, and the smell of human bodies greeted me. A choir nestled somewhere in the many naves of the cathedral responded to the sonorous bass of the priest. The church was lit only by ubiquitous candles; their sputtering and crackling seemed to merge with the litany.

All around me were diminutive elderly women with bowed heads. I stood quietly, hands behind me. I felt a touch on my hands. I turned to hear one of these babushka covered women speaking to me in Russian and pointing to my hands. I used up my entire Russian vocabulary telling her I didn't understand. I thought perhaps my posture was less than reverent and so folded my hands in front of me. The babushka nodded approval.

As in other orthodox cathedrals I had seen, the front was covered with five rows of icons: paintings of God the Father, of Jesus, the Holy Spirit, the patron saint of the cathedral, the disciples, and of the great church fathers. We worshipped under their silent gaze.

I wondered about the superficiality of our national icons. I wondered where were the powerful images in my austere Anabaptist tradition? I think in my tradition I am called to be an icon, a living icon. After all, we are created in the image of God. We are icons that, with care, may show forth the majesty of God. By who we become, we image the beauty of the incarnated Christ. By the sacrifice willingly made, by the conflict resolved, by the voice raised for the voiceless, we become icons.

As I stood there in that cavernous cathedral, from out of the crannies of my mind I heard an old script. "Perhaps word and text are much more important." "No," I said to myself, "Like the Magi of old these Christians bring to worship gold, frankincense and myrrh." Here is a faith that survived Ivan the Terrible and Stalinism. These Eastern Christians understand the connection between incarnation and beauty, theological dyslexia and creativity. Deep down, though, I am still an Anabaptist. The icons that move me most are human: those whose lives reflect the character of their God in kindness, love, courage, and wisdom.

These Orthodox Christians understand the importance of beauty in the spiritual life. I did not grow up in a particularly artistic ethos in the 1950s. There was no Picasso hanging on our walls. I heard neither Beethoven nor Mozart. Rilke and Dostoyevsky were unknowns. And so the journey to Rome at the end of the sabbatical in Germany changed something within me.

Mother cleaned homes, she didn't paint landscapes. But what was absent she made up for by taking us to the Winnipeg music festival, and paying for years of violin and piano lessons. Mother's idea of beauty was a well-cleaned home and a pure heart.

St. Peters was immense, beautiful, awesome. I stood and reflected on the Pieta, the marble sculpture by Michelangelo of the Mother of

Jesus with the dead Jesus draped across her lap. The sense of suffering and impotence in the face of death was overwhelming. I gazed at the ceiling of the Sistine Chapel ablaze with colors with scene after scene of the Biblical story. The Chapel and its incredible churchly art is what the Protestants paid for their separation: a sense of symbol.

And I was not alone. There were hundreds of people around me viewing the same story. And for the past four hundred years or so people have viewed these same images. I did not feel this beauty was the exclusive property of Roman Catholicism. I felt it was ours: it was catholic. What intrigued me was that Michelangelo's work touched the hearts of many people with divergent beliefs, cultures, and lifestyles. He evoked in me the feelings that go with the universal themes of suffering in all of us.

In the midst of the incredible pluralism of modernity there is still clearly some consensus that draws people into religious circles. Again I realized the importance of feeding my soul, of taking the time to soak up the beauty of someone else's spiritual labor. It has a way of relativizing what is trivial.

As a result of my experience in Rome, I have begun to wonder what would happen if I saw my calling as teacher and therapist as one of creating beauty. Not just artists are called to that.

Reflections on My Story

I realized as I wrote this autobiographical essay that I am not one person: I am many. I have described roles and parts of my self. They are not always identical. Parts can remain parts. They can also be embodied in personalities, and these personalities may be recognized by others in particular roles. Students have told me they see different versions of Al. The cast of characters includes the one they see in the office as a program administrator; the scholar/teacher they see in class; the one they see clowning with them at a retreat; and the one they see leading a chapel service. Which is the real Al Dueck? What my students don't know is that I have even more personalities! There is the Al who loves to tinker on the engine of his 1973 VW van or renovate his home. Another is beginning to dabble in working with clay. Occasionally, the Al pops up who loves to learn languages. Then there is Al the father of two children, the lover of one wife, and a devotee of T. S. Eliot. Another dreams of living again in an intentional Christian community. Given the radical pluralism of postmodernity though, I do feel at times fragmented.

I began with the assumption that my identity is composed of many, not simply one coherent self. Object-relations theorists would understand. I am a product of significant introjects. Symbolic interactionists would also share this perspective. I am a product of my interactions with others, and those interactions are carried linguistically. Jungian narratives are helpful. My many selves are personified archetypes. Some of my inner struggles are a conflict between different personalities. The more narrow stories of the behaviorist are of some help. Different situations and persons reinforce and evoke different response patterns.

Another realization as I wrote is that it is narrative that gives coherence to my many selves. There is a central "I" that recognizes a primary story and that coordinates, critiques, and affirms the many selves and their stories. Actually, I have not one story, but many. I am a part of the ethnic Mennonite story with parents who were born in the Ukraine. I am a product of a single parent family, another kind of experience. As a male, I share in the archetypal history that shapes my understanding of my own masculinity. I have been influenced by the saga of African-American Mennonites living in the South. As a psychologist, I share the story of those socialized into the professional narrative. The Anabaptist story is one I have adopted to shape my identity. I can still trace the effects of the year we spent living in an intentional community. Hearing the story of the oppressed, whether in Mexico or the former Soviet Republics or in my office, has changed me. Thus there are many narratives that feed my own. Nevertheless, there is an overarching plot, the story of God's working in history through the ages and cultures and my plot is part of that grander story.

A further awareness emerges that this autobiography is a personal reconstruction. Raw uninterpreted chronology is a myth. I have been shaped by a myriad of relational systems. Each relational subsystem has a narrative. I saw the writing of my story as an attempt to understand which ones shaped me when, which one's are primary, which one's are most helpful. This reconstruction is an attempt to give a coherent account of my selves as a Mennonite, a male, a pastor, a world citizen, a professional psychologist, and as a believer in the light of their individual narratives and a primary narrative.

My story, then, is an attempt to make my life plausible. To be sure, my life is much more than a personally constructed story. I am not that autonomous. However, I do possess assumptions regarding the nature of good plots. I can tell that some stories are better than others. I have heard clients who either seem to have no story, to have a tragic story, to have a meaningless story, to have only one story, or to be denied the right to tell their story. I have been given the freedom to create my story, to incorporate the stories of others, and to enjoy life in the meantime. My story has provided me with a measure of coherence, connectedness with others, concreteness, and uniqueness.

What I have also realized as I reworked drafts of this essay is that I am engaged in a process of pastoring my personal congregation of selves. Writing meant listening, accepting, dialoguing with all of my selves so that a congregational unity would emerge. Writing this piece has reminded me that the very ethic I learned in my Anabaptist community is appropriate to how I treat my many selves. The personality I reject may be the very one that leads me to continued spiritual renewal. After all, the last shall be first. The conflict between the more intellectual and the more emotive personalities needs the same conflict resolution strategies one would use between two feuding parties in the church. My ultimate hope is the formation of an identity that is ethical personally and socially and that is capable of the self-sacrifice necessary for communal existence.

In a pluralistic culture there are many stories, and all stories are considered legitimate. All stories are treated with tolerance—democratized. Civil religion may attempt to create a common story but with little success. One loses the sense of a primary particular story. This autobiography is also an attempt to understand my story as a part of the larger narrative of the Reign of God and of my Mennonite heritage. I see more now than I did when I first experienced what I have written. Even in the writing of my story I would seek first the Reign of God. Its language is my primary language; its plot is to become my primary plot. Its central Character I seek to imitate and assimilate.

10

Adrift in Pain, Anchored by Grace

Hendrika Vande Kemp

All my life I have loved stories, all kinds of stories, whether happy, sad, true, or fantasy. My earliest memories include my mother reading to us from a children's story Bible and stories we heard in Sunday school. The same stories year after year, each year a little different, a little more complicated, with added details and new pictures to unfold the rich depth of God's word. I remember Dad's stories about the war—World War II in the Netherlands, where my family lived through the German occupation—stories about Dad's war work as a communications officer, and Uncle John's work in the resistance movement that aided the Jewish underground. And Mom's stories of defiance to the Nazi soldiers who wanted to take her wedding ring in their quest for plunder. I've always admired that unwavering strength in her, which is also the source of my often irritable stubbornness.

There were the wonderful stories for children by W. G. Vanderhulst, printed in *Moeder,* the weekly magazine. I don't think they were read to us by Mom, but someone—Dad or an older sibling perhaps (there were seven!)—read aloud these wonderful stories that I remember fondly. Stories with realism and humor about children, both naughty and nice. Stories that conveyed to children how much parents, and God, loved them. And one—my favorite!—that was *not* realistic, a story about a little girl who is kind to a caterpillar. In gratitude he shrinks her and gives her a ride on his back up a tree, and later returns as a gorgeous butterfly who takes her flying. I've always known deep in my heart that in the *real* world, like in Narnia, animals can talk. An English translation of the Vanderhulst stories shares space on my bookshelves with later favorites by J. R. R. Tolkien, C. S. Lewis, George MacDonald, and Charles Williams. There were the stories I heard from my brother: stories he heard in school, in classes on church history. These were terrible stories in the way that God's wrath can be terrible, or even God's goodness.[1] Stories about the children's crusades, about catapults and stones, killings on city walls, the horrible face of death. But for me these too were wonderful, because the storyteller was my big brother and we were snuggled close in bed, and I felt secure. It should be no surprise that my storytelling family produced a storytelling daughter, and even during my elementary school years I enjoyed reading stories to smaller children, and learned to read upside-down print so that the pictures could be turned toward the rapt listeners. It is not by chance that I chose to be a psychotherapist, whose task is to collaborate with others in the unraveling and reframing of their stories, or that I teach a course on family psychology in which students explore the "storying" in their own families, and engage in historical research that reconstructs the stories of persons and ideas. So I shall tell a story, a story authored by myself, reflecting only one of the potential images in the kaleidoscope of my memories. A story reflecting only *my* perspective.

Sisterhood

Sisters are an important part of my story. There were seven sisters in the Vande Kemp family, and sisterhood became the model for friendship, peer relationships, and female bonds. I have never understood women who have no women friends. My world is full of such friendships, all of which mirror in some way the relationships with

1. As Charles Williams has Stanhope explain to Pauline in his novel *Descent into Hell* (1937. Grand Rapids: Eerdmans, 1979).

my sisters, many of which venture beyond. I had sisters twelve, eleven, nine, six, and one-and-a-half years older, and one nine years younger. Now I have friendships with women in every decade of life from the twenties through the seventies. I constantly replay in some way the role of younger sister, older sister, and daughter (unfortunately, I had little chance to learn the role of granddaughter).

Sisters talk endlessly, preferably around the kitchen table, long into the night, after the men (wondering what on earth we find to talk about) have all gone to bed. Sisters gossip, an unfortunate habit we have tried to tame. They reminisce about deceased parents and childhood experiences. They talk about love gained and lost; about children; about cooking and needlework and other so-called feminine things; and about ideas, work, and religion. They write letters and send birthday cards and make phone calls when the going gets rough. Sisters can be counted on when every other friend is unavailable.

Sisterhood in itself influenced me positively. *Little* sisterhood much less so, for several reasons. By the time I was old enough to remember, my two oldest sisters were already working away from home, and I seldom saw them (it was quite common in the Netherlands not to attend school beyond sixth grade). I knew of their closeness to each other, but my relationship with them developed only when I was a teenager and they were in their twenties. The next two I observed in their interaction with each other, which had the usual volatile blend of love and hostility. In childhood, the fifth, who was closest to me in age, placed me in the often painful role of "tag-a-long" little sister. We developed a friendship full of love and competition.

But little sisterhood (to sisters *and* brothers) impressed upon me a sense of self that was very much out of touch with reality. I assumed all my life that others were wiser, older, stronger, more competent than I (or is it that they were *supposed* to be?). At home, of course, this was true: there were seven people who were older, wiser, more experienced. I remember no specific incidents of being bossed around or of being made to feel stupid or incompetent. Yet this impression has been with me all my life. The original dynamic must have been one of awe and admiration for my older siblings. Later I encountered people who explicitly said and did things to make me feel inadequate. In junior high and high school I was painfully aware of my hand-me-down clothing; the other girls had matched skirts and sweaters and angora to wrap their boyfriends' class rings. I also felt deficient in social skills, as I was unable to participate in extracurricular activities and a number of social events that were forbidden by the church.

I became senior class valedictorian, but I still felt inferior, small, not good enough. The dynamic at work was the rule that "you must not surpass the performance of your siblings." I had to *make* myself so small as not to be noticed, and in later public situations I have often felt like I should disappear, or worse, that people could render me invisible. During the period of my older sister's mental illness, when we were in the same grade in high school, my straight-A report cards were hidden so she could not see them and be upset. How does "too good" become "not good enough" in the family dance?[2]

In recent years I have been more able to match my self-image to my actual performance. But this took a great deal of struggle and continues to be an area for resolution. I gradually began to understand my "little sister" dynamics in my thirties, when I shared a house for several years with a woman my own age who was the oldest in a family of six. My interactions with her played into the worst of both our "sibling position" characteristics. She pretended to a great deal of competence and knowledgeability that she didn't have, and I bought it. I saw her as more competent, more knowledgeable, wiser, more able to face the world. At the same time (the early 1980s), I was teaching courses on family therapy and family psychology, and beginning to understand in new ways the dynamics of sibling power and control. It was when I recognized "textbook" dynamics in a single pivotal incident that I was able to begin resisting them. This gave me the courage to buy a house on my own: a symbolic act of proving my adulthood and competence. I also began to recognize these dynamics in relationships with faculty colleagues, and attempted new adult-adult relationships with little success, unable to rechoreograph their dances that maintained other systems.

Brotherhood, at least in my family, is not the same as sisterhood. Yet each of my three brothers (eight and four years older, and four years younger) made a strong impression on me. My oldest brother inspired awe, as he was already a man when I was still a girl: I hoped he would teach me what girls need to know about men. There were the cozy incidents of storytelling and games of Monopoly with my middle brother, whom I adored (to his embarrassment): he was my

2. My awareness of this dynamic was aroused by watching an unpublished videotape of Salvador Minuchin conducting family therapy. Minuchin points out to Bill, the identified patient, that "too good" is worse than "good" or "just good." He adds, "Your jail is love, but it is still a jail." Other aspects of this case are discussed in Salvador Minuchin and H. Charles Fishman. 1981. *Family therapy techniques,* 216–27. Cambridge: Harvard University Press.

hero, my protector, my role model, the kind of man I hoped to love. In adulthood, he has become my friend. In adolescence I learned from my little brother about cars. We'd sit on the porch watching the cars go by on I-66 as I learned to recognize and differentiate models and years. That was a sharing of *his* self. All my brothers were a part of teaching me the art of mentoring, modeling detachment, rounding out the many other relational and practical skills I learned from my sisters and parents.

Mom and Dad

I remember very little from my earliest days: in fact, there are more stories told about me that I now remember than actual memories. I remember vaguely my crib and wanting the bars to be up at night to ensure that the (fantasized) animal population under the bed couldn't get in. (I still like to sleep with the covers over my head.) There is also a story about my not sleeping in the crib because I claimed there was a bird in it; with unscreened windows, that story is probably true. I do remember clearly at the age of three or four my middle brother's body brought in on a stretcher before he was brought to the hospital very seriously wounded by a car. And a similar scene at eight, after my younger brother's foot was sliced by a lawn mower. Sisters created no such scenes, except that as a toddler I wandered into the same street and scared everyone. Apparently my search for something different started early.

I look at childhood pictures now and think that Mother especially must have had many moments of joy and happiness: her smile lit the whole picture, and I can still see and touch in my mind the grey fabric of one dress, with its black, velvety design. I often wonder now how she felt as a woman: Did it matter very much to her to feel beautiful? And I know that it did. I remember her joy at making a dress of a beautiful powder blue double-knit fabric, and her frustration at a broken fingernail that seemed unable to repair itself. (I too have "a thing" about my brittle nails, and the bathroom is cluttered with Sally Hansen's virtually ineffective remedies.)

I know one year when I was five or six she stayed up late at night to sew dolls for our St. Nicholas presents. How little sense I had then of her sacrificial nature! She so often stayed up to finish a dress or coat. No wonder she taught us to sew for ourselves by the time we were ten, and I have a pile of blue ribbons earned for 4-H sewing projects! It is tragically ironic that I bought my own sewing machine (a Singer Featherweight 221, now an antique) on the day she died

(April 24, 1971). Along with sewing, Mom taught us well the skills needed for good housekeeping. On Saturdays we cleaned house and scrubbed and organized for Sunday. As an adolescent, I dragged out my dusting and vacuuming and shoe-polishing duties on Saturday afternoons. I didn't particularly dislike these jobs, but they offered good opportunity to be alone and think, and I loved that as much as reading. Finding a place to be alone was a continuous quest in our large household.

I'm not sure what my chores were prior to adolescence, though they included washing dishes and setting the table. We each had our own set of flatware, our own place at the table, and our own unique china cups and silver spoons for Sunday coffee and tea. I can now see these traditions as important contributors to a sense of separateness amidst the welter of belongingness. I remember in the second house I lived in (and maybe even the first) when it was time to wax the floor Mother played a game with us of tying rags to our feet and letting us polish the floor by skating on it. I treasure and cherish that playful part of Mom: that part of *me* is very small, precious, and vulnerable. My sense of humor is hidden at the very inner core of myself, as are many of these pleasant memories; Mom had a difficult time with this child who was so different from herself. We didn't *like* each other very much. I'm not sure how I feel now, twenty years after her death. I do know that I respect her, and I know she did the best she could. How can *anyone* cope with ten children?

When I was eight I had scarlet fever and was out of school for three weeks. That was a lucky time for me because Dad was at home after surgery for a slipped disk. We spent a lot of time together, and he taught me to play checkers. Dad always played checkers with his friends in the Netherlands, where he was in a checkers club. Playing with his kids was an unusual thing, and I knew it. We established a bond that survived through my adolescent and college years, strengthening the bond created when I was named after him. This was also a time when I felt loved and cared for and worried about by Mom. Sure, I picked up harried and scurried kinds of signals from her, but she was really worried when my temperature went up over 104°. She gave me nightly baths in cornstarch to ease the itching, which brings to mind the itching of poison ivy, especially the summer I was sixteen. My face and hands were covered with it, dashing my fantasies of beauty. I was really embarrassed that summer at meeting several handsome young men on a family camping trip in the northern woods of Michigan, and realizing how unattractive I must appear. I've never lost that sensitivity to poison ivy and its relatives (and a host of other things!). These days I visit a dermatologist at the advent of the first blister. Poor Mom and Dad must have been in constant conflict as they wanted to ease the discomfort of poison ivy and my brother's ingrown toenail but lacked the money for a doctor.

Remembering: The Life of the Sense

Memories are linked to our senses, especially the visual and spatial senses that connect us with rooms in houses. I remember the houses we lived in, in terms of what they looked like on the outside and the general atmosphere. I find myself remembering a number of rooms, but only parts of the rooms themselves, not enough to draw a spatial plan of the houses (I've tried and failed on several occasions in my family psychology class). I remember the bedroom shared by the girls in the house on the Portland Road during my latency years. It was a room wonderfully suffused with light. I remember a number of kitchen tables and the conviviality, the comfort, the warmth of being gathered around those tables with my sisters, brothers, parents, neighbors; the smell of coffee and the taste of homemade cookies (often I had baked them myself). I remember lying awake at night and talking—mostly to my sisters, later to roommates in college and graduate school—at church and faculty retreats.

One college Christmas vacation I went to my sister's apartment with my typewriter in order to finish a paper. I just didn't feel I could do it at home. Strange memory, but it represents the increasing alienation I felt as my higher education and exposure to new ideas and friends forced me to inhabit two separate worlds. That's when I first heard the Medical Mission Sisters on record and fell in love with the absolute clarity of the soprano voice I now appreciate so much in my recordings of Bach and Monteverdi. That visit forged a new relationship with my sister, who became a much closer friend in my adult years.

I think of the tastes from my childhood that I crave: double-salted licorice, the numerous Dutch licorices; Dutch chocolate, especially the alphabet letters for Christmas and St. Nicholas Day; "banket," the rich almond pastry; boerekool (kale), a Sunday dinner staple for many years; mashed potatoes with nutmeg, or cauliflower with white sauce and more nutmeg. Even our brussel sprouts were served with nutmeg, to which my cat also is greatly attracted. But even as I edit I must acknowledge passages: she has died, and the new kittens are fond of "people food," period!

Of smells there are not many, but the one most prominent is the shoe repair shop. The smell of leather, glues, and dyes is overwhelmingly comforting. In my moves around the country I've always found the local shoe repair shop as a place where my childhood, if only for a moment, comes back to me. There was the combination smell and taste of the King peppermints Mother always provided for us in church. There was the smell of her Boldoot cologne, a scent I often wear myself (or its nearest equivalent, *4711*).

High School and Early College

As I dictate this I'm supposed to be baking Valentine's cookies. "Supposed to" in the sense that that's what I had planned to do this Saturday morning. It reminds me of the Friday or Saturday baking that was a custom during my adolescence. A number of standard treats were baked regularly: oatmeal cookies, peanut butter cookies (which I hated to make because I couldn't stand the taste or smell of peanut butter—still can't), and in the summer, lemon jelly rolls for which we had a Robin Hood recipe that became a family classic. I still use it on occasion (people are always impressed!). We baked oatmeal cake, a special recipe from Mom's Iowa cousins, and pumpkin bread. I was, and remain, good at these domestic things. I won lots of 4-H blue ribbons cooking and baking, and a few red ones. In high school, as a lark, I competed with all the home economics majors in a homemaking contest and won second place! I was proud of myself for being able to apply measures like gauge and denier to nylon stockings (useless knowledge now), and threads per inch to sheets, for being able to turn a sleeve and hem a skirt and alter a pattern. By that time I was sewing all my own clothes. Although Mom helped us some, she started us on the sewing machine by about age ten so that she wasn't responsible for all the sewing to clothe so many children. I pride myself on being able to do such challenging tasks as relining or altering a jacket or suit or pair of slacks, or sewing my own garments, or making hooded towels for babies (now a classic "Hendrika" gift). But there is seldom time for such domestic luxuries!

I broke the rules even then when I went to a 4-H junior leadership week at Michigan State. I remember very little of it now, except the wonder of meeting so many interesting people, and have used my scrapbook to prod my memory of the high school years. Being picked as special broke the family rule, as did spending the money for a week in a camplike situation. And yet my parents permitted it, not wanting to argue with the outsiders in our lives (and risk being regarded as too "old country," not Americanized). No praise was given for such achievements, and I tried to keep my excitement to myself. Was their lack of enthusiasm due to an effort to be fair? Not to give to their younger children what they couldn't give the older? Or was it due to a deeper envy? I shall never know.

My 4-H leader often gave me the opportunity to baby-sit, which provided the spending money necessary for social life in high school. I was thrilled to be able to attend football games with my best friend and roller skating parties with our church group. Mom and Dad approved of my friend because she was a faithful Christian and active in her church. And they were trusting during our evenings out, not waiting up for me to come home but just leaving on the yard light and knowing we were up to nothing worse than sitting in the car and talking. But I think back now about how much babysitting took the place of the social and dating lives of my friends. In college I babysat fairly frequently for a couple of my professors. In graduate school I did the same, so that my Friday or Saturday evenings were busy, but not with the things my peers were doing. Yet the children were a comfort to me, and much preferred to studying in the dorm. I really don't understand that part of my life, because I've always had lots of friends of both sexes. Later I could understand my pain as a continuation of having my sexual self annihilated at home, for which the healing could not happen with my peers. Now I know that nurturing children is an important part of my life, and Sunday mornings find me caring for toddlers at church, playing a role Mom taught me very well.

I don't remember any decision or moment that led me to the focus on performance that I had in high school. I remember my brother deciding to go to college and being discouraged by the high school guidance counselor who felt his grades weren't good enough. My brother at that time was an underachiever; he didn't care enough about his high school courses to put much energy into them. I didn't want to have either the fight he had with our parents, who felt that college was not for our kind of people, or problems regarding my performance. But that was never a conscious decision. I don't know whom I was trying to please. Perhaps I knew, unconsciously, that it would eventually offer an escape from the present pain. Or a sense that scholarship was the only area in which I could find acceptance. Even though I had gone from an overweight, awkward, clumsy girl who attained all her height by the age of twelve, to a rather thin, attractive high schooler, I didn't feel attractive. In my entire high school career I was only asked out one time, and that one time I was not eager to date the person who asked me. I had so many (at that time unrecognized) fears about sexuality that I turned him down with the excuse that my parents would not let me date, which wasn't true. I yearned to date the boys in my church, who were not interested. It took at least a couple decades—and a revealing dream—for me to see the self-sabotage induced by my interpretation of the family's messages. At my twenty-year high school reunion I realized that the *quality* relationships I had (with a few exceptions) were *not* with people from the church, and that my Christian peers were generally anything *but* friends.

Whatever the motivation, I was able to transform myself from a grade schooler and junior high student who got As and Bs and maybe some Cs on my report cards to a straight-A student and class valedictorian. And I was motivated by more than grades: I was genuinely interested in mathematics, science, English, writing, reading, history. I had some magnificent teachers. Mr. Shanks taught us biology, chemistry, physics, and drivers' training. The greatest wisdom he ever gave was that one out of ten decisions we make will be wrong decisions and that will apply to us and to other drivers. I think of him often as I negotiate Southern California's freeways and daily bear the pain of someone else's bad decision, and the fear generated by my own, on my bad days. Mr. Johnson taught my first algebra class. I can still see his face, hear his voice, recount his rigidities. When he told us to draw "several" of something, he said, he *meant* "more than two." Why does *that* lecture still linger in my mind? I am ashamed to admit that I was one of the skeptics about computers and gave him a hard time. These days I am an experienced and grateful user.

I have written elsewhere of the impact on my life of several of my Hope College professors.[3] I was also touched by William Hillegonds, the chaplain. Bill supported me during a difficult time, when I wondered if I wanted to continue college and felt very much depressed, he encouraged me to sort out psychological from spiritual issues. Even today I'll play a recording of the Hope College Christmas Vespers just to hear Bill pray. The music isn't so great, but the prayers and his voice take me back to a time in my life when every day represented a period of growth. Nancy Taylor challenged us to creative thinking, in a new approach to research (for me, anyhow) that asked for our

3. Vande Kemp, Hendrika. 1987. Influences. *Theology News and Notes,* November, 28–29. Reprinted in *News from Hope College,* August 1988, 3. Persons credited here are Hope professors D. Ivan Dykstra, Jim Reynierse, Elton Bruins, and Bob Palma, as well as Howard Gadlin, my dissertation chair at the University of Massachusetts.

opinions rather than secondary sources. She gave exams with questions that involved not just rote memorization but actually thinking through an application of what we learned in class. These were marvelous challenges, to me and to what I assumed about education. I loved Jim Prins's course on the European novel: the modern, *psychological* novel. In retrospect I see how this enhanced my understanding of historical issues in the nineteenth century, the psychologization, so to speak, of culture. This was an interest of Howard Gadlin, my dissertation chair, and led to my dissertation study of nineteenth-century dream theories.

I had excellent teachers in the mathematics department, with the exception of an unspeakably mediocre instructor in my first calculus class. Statistics came alive through the exquisite teaching of Elliot Tanis. I labored to envision the multidimensional world of linear algebra, the intricacies of which were exposed by Richard Vandervelde. I recognize, two decades later, that my ability to continue visualizing beyond three dimensions lies in a creative use of color (time, the traditional fourth dimension, being of no help). To some, this will sound silly: that's why the debates between the nominalists and the idealists never end. I recall endless hours of battling the computer, writing FORTRAN programs, inserting comment statements that unleashed our feelings of anger and frustration with the all-too-literal computer. This experience serves me well, as I find it is often necessary to "think" like the computer before I can find my way out of a stalemate. But I can never manage to be quite literal or rigid enough. If computers could laugh, mine would be rollicking this morning, as I tried in vain to discover the glitch in my footnoting function and settled for a human solution. And if it could talk, it would be saying, "Why do you care so much, my dear?" I *do* like to write "decently and in order," but it is the almost human refusal to do what can be done that drives me to distraction.

The Joys of Music

As I first dictate this story I am listening to Haydn's "The Seven Last Words of Christ." Classical music, especially religious choral music, has been one of the greatest joys of my adult life. I have vague childhood memories of church music, especially at Christmas, and a favorite recording of the Vienna Boys Choir. But it seems strange to me now that I have little memory of any of the sounds of my childhood akin to the adolescent memories of Sunday morning awakenings to recordings of Pat Boone or the late Ernie Ford. Primarily I remember the music we made ourselves, on the upright piano in the dining room and an electric organ in the living room. My sister Toni and I were both passable pianists by our adolescence, having learned to read music in our junior high music classes and picking up keyboard methods on our own. One of us would play as the rest of the family gathered 'round and sang. One year we provided the organist and choir for worship at a Christian campground, and the Christmas my father was hospitalized with leukemia we formed an a cappella carol choir in his room.

At Hope College I chose to take a music appreciation class and took on the challenge of recognizing instruments and compositions. In the sixth grade (shortly after a change of schools) I'd been expected to identify visually the instruments of the orchestra: the only test I ever flunked! Perhaps this seeded the desire to learn more about orchestral music. I loved the college class and spent solitary morning hours in the music lab listening to the best of the classical repertoire. At home I discovered the Michigan State University radio station with its classical renditions, and Hope's WTAS provided a few hours a week. When I moved to Amherst I quickly discovered the classical music station KFCR and Robert J. Lurtsema, who became a part of my life, a familiar voice connected with music that I loved. Every Sunday morning he played a Bach cantata, which aided my personal worship when I was unable to go to church. My year in Kansas I broadened my appreciation to include the "country countdown" and the deep emotion represented there, but I never resonated with these lyrics as I did with the message of the classics or the popular music of the sixties and seventies: Simon and Garfunkel; Peter, Paul and Mary; Bob Dylan; the Beach Boys—you get the drift!

When I moved to my own house in Monrovia and acquired my own sound system, I could finally listen to KUSC and a new set of voices. I am surprised to discover how important those voices are. When a new announcer comes on or an old one is replaced I experience the processes of bonding or loss. These voices represent home, security, and continuity; they bring the comfort and ecstasy of music, one of God's greatest gifts. I find classical music at all times worshipful, reminding me of the power of the creator and the beauty of creation: the attempt to put into words the sense of God's grace that I feel in the daily gift of music moves me to tears. After my accident in 1989 and my hospitalization in 1990 (discussed below), I found that music I previously enjoyed became an irritation, exacerbating my headaches and distress. I now frequently replace radio selections with my own recordings of Bach, Couperin, Buxtehude, Handel, Pachelbel, and other soothing classical organ works. And I always sleep with my Sleep Mate sound conditioner. While revising my final draft of this chapter, I reached a breaking point in my frustration at losing working time due to the pain and mental fatigue created by the noise of the hydraulic lifts on garbage trucks. Garbage pickup coincides with the one day I can devote to writing at home, and the noise is almost continuous, due to the many rounds required for recycling. I may be the only person in the country wearing a hearing protective antinoise muff in my den! The color even matches my computer decor.

Of Tears and Grace

I need to speak of tears. My tears dried up my sophomore year in high school. In retrospect, I think this happened because so much of my self had been destroyed, buried, or negated. I was frightened by the mental illness of my sister and defended against that by controlling my emotions carefully. I also remember my mother's labeling of me as "melodramatic," being hurt by those comments, and wanting to please her. I didn't realize then, nor for many years, that pleasing her was impossible: she was asking, not for behavioral changes, but for a different kind of "being."

What was going on with me in high school went much deeper than the loss of tears. It had to do with my sister's mental illness, my own vulnerability, and my total confusion in a family that for a time failed to be "good enough." Even now I have little grasp of the family dynamics that required a scapegoat and placed my parents in a position of helplessness (which is, of course, not the same as powerlessness). But perhaps I am talking only about my own reaction. I watched helplessly for several years as my sister developed symptoms of an obsessive-compulsive disorder accompanied by anorexia. She spent endless hours in prayer, developed agonizingly detailed and time-consuming bathing rituals (extremely irritating in a large family with only one bathroom), and dieted constantly. For eighteen months she was in and out of Pine Rest, where she added to her self-destructive productions cigarette burns and cuts on her arms. I was confused, because I had no idea what she was trying to express; the sexuality that caused so much conflict in her, I repressed. The criticisms of my self that dried up my tears I could not then articulate, and I compensated by excelling academically and participating actively in church. I made my Confession of Faith on Palm Sunday of 1966, taught Sunday school and Vacation Bible School, and was active in our youth group. But I did all these things without the sister who had previously been a close part of my life. Only now do I see that her illness and hospitalization created a loss that I never mourned. Those years boldly underlined our differences, and the ties that bind us now are very complex: we share the experience of pain, but not an understanding of its source.

I can distinctly remember when I cried again. It was during my freshman year at Hope College, in the Fall, when we competed with the sophomores in the men's Pull and the women's competition for the Nykerk Cup. When we won the cup my tears were released, and I was able to cry as we gathered around hugging, kissing, and triumphantly congratulating each other. I knew even in that moment that something important was happening to me, but I didn't know what or its ultimate significance. In recent years I have in fact been able to cry a great deal, especially during the years that I was in psychoanalytic psychotherapy. I clearly remember beginning the therapeutic process in late 1979, and the events that triggered it. I had already gone out and bought myself a Pendleton suit (three pieces, *not* on sale!). That was a truly outrageous thing to do by my family's standards. When I bought this suit in a beautiful shade of light bluish-gray, I felt like a million dollars (it was a bargain just the same: I still wear it more than a decade later). The suit was symbolic of a decision to nourish myself, to explore the mysteries of my self with the same dedication I had given to the academic mysteries. I carefully selected a therapist and worked hard during two years of individual psychotherapy (and an additional year in 1985–86). I wanted to get my money's worth, and I felt like I had little to lose by exploring my unconscious to discover sources of pain and by allowing myself to venture into new realms of relatedness. Later, I planned and participated (1983) in an intensive family therapy weekend with Carl Whitaker and David Keith. That experience helped me to let go of most of my agendas for changing my family, and led to an acceptance of our differentness. By that time I was already satisfied with the progress I'd made in pulling out of gossip triangles and was communicating much more directly with each of my siblings. Whitaker wove that into the preparation for the therapy weekend, a process itself filled with pain and growing edges. It exposed some of the deep fear my siblings had of psychotherapy, which included a mistrust of me as a psychotherapist.

I found very deep (inevitable?) pain connected with being the eighth child. These days I put myself into my mother's shoes: I try to imagine what it would be like to be forty-two and to have nine children. I recall an exercise used by Virginia Satir in one of her family therapy cases to demonstrate to the children how hard it was for their widowed mother, with only two arms, to embrace them all. I long ago gained empathy with that mother and the impossibility of her position and cannot watch that videotape without tears. Mother loved each one of us, she was a woman who "fell in love" with her babies. But loving them was not enough to feed them, clothe them, and take care of their needs. What ambivalence she must have felt when she found out that she was pregnant again with her eighth child! How often before my birth she must have wished that it wasn't so, and felt guilty for the wishing. And how much I felt during my childhood and into my adulthood that it would have been better if I had never been born, that I didn't have the right to exist, that people could make me disappear. I am grateful Mother did not make that choice. For her it wasn't even a possibility: she would not exercise the option to make a potential child disappear physically. But it cost me as much as it cost her. That is the existential nature of the fallen universe. I see no justice in the way those childhood messages have translated into an adult reality in which I do not have the opportunity to reproduce myself. I will drop out of existence at my death. There will be no children or grandchildren, no posterity to carry on the reality that is me. I have taught many classes on family therapy and family psychology at Fuller. I've shared my own background with students, gained new insights each time, and acquired understanding of the multiple forces that assign people their family roles. But these forces are many-layered, and our awareness of them comes one piece at a time. Several years ago I shared with a small group of family therapists the pieces of this story. Despite my awareness of the subtle messages of "do not be," I was not prepared for the observation by one of these colleagues that if you have no right to exist, of course you have no right to reproduce yourself. Is our freedom really that constrained?

R. D. Laing, in his essay "Mystification, Confusion, and Conflict,"[4] states that the parental message that produces a neurotic is "you should be different," and the message that produces a psychotic is "you should not be." There was plenty of the first in my upbringing. I was too much the introvert, too subjective, too much a dreamer. I had too much imagination and spent too much time in worlds con-

4. Laing, Ronald D. 1965. Mystification, confusion, and conflict. In *Intensive family therapy: Theoretical and practical aspects,* eds. Ivan Boszormenyi-Nagy and James L. Framo, 343–63. New York: Harper & Row.

structed by creative people, worlds of fantasy and worlds of my own imagination. The psychotic message was much more limited and subtle, of course: no one *wants* to deliver such a message, even to *think* it produces guilt and shame. But I felt it, with the same intuitive, direct knowing that is now so valuable in my clinical practice: it is the "unthought known" that speaks most powerfully.[5]

But ambivalence is the stuff of life. We are, in fact, given lives that are multivalenced. Not only our mothers, but also our fathers are persons with complex emotions and behaviors. My oldest sisters helped Mother take care of me when I was an infant, and I was blessed with seven older siblings who presented me with a rainbow of relational possibilities. My middle brother was very much a nurturing figure, especially in my early childhood and adolescence. I remember the feeling of intimacy when driving with him to the hospital to see my sister during one of the periods she was hospitalized at Pine Rest. My family life has been filled with such nurturing, balancing moments of grace.

Why do the tears flow as I recall my childhood? Recently, when researching a paper on G. Stanley Hall, the pioneer American psychologist, I read his comments on the pity adults have for the child of their own childhood. This sounds much like the currently fashionable literature on the inner child of the past. Therapists encourage their adult clients to love and nurture that child, and consider it one of the goals of psychotherapy to teach them to do that nurturing rather than expect it from others. I have learned to give comfort to the hurting child inside of me, and have discovered my own resources for nurturing. But I cannot prevent the tears. I can only respond to them.

And there remains another problem: there is still the fact that the adult I am is not the adult I might have been. I don't know what kind of woman she would be, what she would be doing, what relationship network she would have. Humanistic psychologists put a great deal of emphasis on choice and responsibility for our own decisions, our own actions, our own lives. But I have seldom felt that I had free choices about the most important things in life: not finding a life partner, not being a parent—these situations have never felt like choices to me. Family therapists would speak about delegation, assignment to specific roles, a process of receiving roles we have not written. The family has us play the parts that it needs. The family has its rules

5. For one discussion of the influence of the preconceptual, see Christopher Bollas. 1987. *The shadow of the object: Psychoanalysis of the unthought known.* New York: Columbia University Press.

that are not to be broken. I've rejected too many of the family's roles, thus breaking their rules, in an effort to be the playwright of my own life. By going to college and graduate school, becoming a professional and utilizing my academic gifts, pursuing my own religious calling, I broke rules that had been in this family for many generations. Choices are made, but we are not in charge of the consequences. Why should the quest for selfhood, when it is the refusal of annihilation and includes the loving and nurturing of others, exact such a price?

I know how I was picked by my father for my rebellious role. My achievements were things that he himself wanted, and he received much satisfaction from my successes. I gave him something to be proud of in a different way than he was proud of his grandchildren. But I sense that no one else in the family was party to this delegation, unless one talks of unconscious collusion, when one is unknowingly forced into a role for which one is later denounced. I suspect that may be so; life is complex, and we may envy even that which we encourage. But that leaves us with only our own unconscious selves to blame, making us traitors to ourselves. I find this conflict between family loyalty and personal psychic survival a cruel reality. But no more cruel than attributing these events to God's will. Providence is indeed a difficult doctrine, but humanistic psychology is no less cruel.

The Interpersonal World

I am grateful that I have in my life a "forever friend." This friendship owes something to the occasional moments of real wisdom with which God has blessed me. We were roommates our sophomore year at Hope in that historic building, Van Vleck Hall. As the end of that year drew near and all of us were making plans for living arrangements for our junior year she was approached by another woman in the dorm who also wanted to be roommates with her. As she was wavering about this decision, seeing it as a 50/50 toss-up—which I perceived as a negation of the quality of our friendship—I received the courage to go to her and challenge her perception. I told her that I felt it was *not* 50/50, that I valued our relationship much more than that. I still marvel at that moment of courage, and very seldom (perhaps never) in later relationships has such an overture been honored: few people have the capacity for true friendship and commitment. I've only recently begun to see our friendship from her perspective, to think of how it might feel to have someone care so much. The letters continue to flow between us regularly.

At my first writing, my friend and I and several other college friends were looking forward to our twentieth reunion. Four of us spent much of that weekend together, sharing memories of friendship and renewing these bonds. It is a precious gift that three people care so much after twenty years, that the gift of friendship can endure. Those three are not the only ones with whom I've maintained contact. Several others who also cherish our friendship would have been there if they could. Recently (September 1991) one of these friends was killed in an auto accident. I was stunned and devastated, but my greatest comfort was that the friend I most wanted to speak to called me even before I could call her, so that we could share our sorrow. Those four years at Hope were a tremendously important time for me. Though there were also moments when I wanted to pack up and go home, ultimately I have no regrets about the time I spent there. I was not prepared—at home or at Hope—for the many persons I've encountered in later years who honor no claims in relationships, who see such claims as possessiveness rather than as an expression of God's plan for our interdependence, and regard confrontation as a warrant for ending a relationship. It is one of the "graces" of my life that such a strong sense of loyalty and commitment was forged in the context of basic trust, in a family that also produced so much pain. I can't imagine an alternative that would have been better. Is pain always a prerequisite to the genuine understanding of grace?

I constantly struggle to understand my relational networks and their influence on my life. Family psychology has done that in its own way and offers a framework much more sensible and accurate to me than the various individually oriented psychologies. I was stimulated by the family therapy seminar at the University of Massachusetts, accompanied by supervised family therapy cases, family sculpting exercises, and guest speakers/workshop leaders such as Carolyn L. Attneave, who expanded the family approach into larger networks. During my internship at Topeka State Hospital (1975–76) I received additional family therapy supervision and experience coleading multifamily groups. Dynamics were made personally relevant when the five group leaders met for discussion and we could see ourselves enacting various family roles. In an extended workshop with H. Peter Laqueur we maintained roles in a simulated family for three days. Family psychology and therapy are integral to my teaching at Fuller, and to my worldview, which embraces also a relational theology that emphasizes God's personhood.

Interpersonal psychology has also offered many perspectives that appear to be "true." I first studied this under Sheldon Cashdan at the University of Massachusetts, whose perspective was rooted in the work of George Herbert Mead and the later theory of Norman Cameron and Ann Magaret.[6] Shelly attempted to integrate this symbolic interactionist perspective with the work of the literary critic Kenneth Burke,[7] planting a seed in my mind that has been germinating for nearly two decades and is reaching fruition in several recent doctoral dissertations completed under my direction.

Later, through the influence of my colleague Clinton McLemore, I was encouraged to read the (prepsychedelic) works of Timothy Leary,[8] Robert Carson,[9] and especially Lorna Benjamin,[10] who has integrated the theoretical work of earlier interpersonalists. Benjamin's work, which I have used in an extensive research program, operationalizes the notion of interpersonal complementary: in any interaction, persons engage in behaviors designed to elicit a specific response in the other. For the other, it is easier to give that desired response (in terms of what is considered socially appropriate), even if it is personally compromising. Our research has examined both the rule and its exception. I am also keenly aware of its function in my own life. I know there are many occasions in which I am not willing to give people what they are pulling for. I am not willing to play the games that are played interpersonally or socially, especially some of the games connected with dating and flirtation. This I attribute to our family's interpretation of Calvinism by my mother's unique application of Christian principles, colored by the fact that she had been conceived out of wedlock. In retrospect, this helps me to identify another very difficult complex message received at home, complex enough, perhaps, to be a double bind. This was the message that it is most important for a woman to be married—this is the greatest thing she can do in life—and at the same time she is not to flirt, be seductive, or present herself as sexual. This might have worked in the old days of matchmakers, when

6. See, for example, Anselm Strauss, ed. 1964. *George Herbert Mead on social psychology.* Rev. ed. Chicago: The University Press; and Norman Cameron and Ann Magaret. 1951. *Behavior pathology.* Boston: Houghton Mifflin.

7. Burke, Kenneth. 1957. *The philosophy of literary form.* New York: Vintage Books; 1945. *A grammar of motives.* New York: Prentice-Hall.

8. Leary, Timothy. 1957. *Interpersonal diagnosis of personality.* New York: Ronald Company.

9. Carson, Robert C. 1969. *Interaction concepts of personality.* Chicago: Aldine.

10. Beginning with Lorna Smith Benjamin. 1974. Structural analysis of social behavior. *Psychological Bulletin* 81:392–425.

marriage was primarily a financial and business arrangement. But it doesn't work very well in a society where romance is key.

How can one really desire marriage when there is a message that men can do terrible things to you? Like the terrible thing done to my grandmother. The marriage between my maternal grandparents was not a happy one, and my mother was often reminded that it was her fault. No wonder Mom was an ambivalent mother to seven daughters! How I wish I could talk to her now about the pain and guilt she bore. She of course was victim of a form of crazymaking: to be told that she was responsible for her own conception. Such messages illuminate the extreme sense of personal responsibility so common in our family, and equally common in much of the church. Only in a worldview that includes predestination along with a very strong sense of personal responsibility can one receive or send such a message. Strange, isn't it, that personal experience and clinical data reveal almost everyone as a Calvinist in this (disturbed) sense? In childhood most of us can have no other view. Such messages of blame also are most powerful in a world where one does not question the teachings of authority, no matter how inconsistent and confusing they are. At the same time, previously described dynamics played their role. I was designated to pursue excellence when the family rule was mediocrity (under the guise of humility). I was allowed to nurture my intellectual gifts when the family rule was sacrifice: the difference in gifts wasn't acknowledged as a factor in the equation. Fairness was defined as equality, not as an equal right to fulfilling one's potential. In my family's subculture, the fulfillment of one's potential is no longer even *conceivable* as a goal once one has married and acquired a family: as if God does not call persons to new vocations. My own Christian living is more attuned to the whispers of the Spirit, not bound by misguided interpretations of the doctrines of predestination and responsibility. God continually surprises us with unexpected callings, as I repeatedly learn from candidates for ministry and events in my own life.

Religious Influences

The Calvinism of my parents taught me to have a deep respect for authority. Life has since shown me that authorities are just people like myself, many of them not even as bright or educated, and I see their vulnerability mirrored in my own. It frightens me. Life was easier when I could believe in human powers higher and wiser than myself, *much* wiser than myself, much more capable of making decisions and running the world and leading me.

As a teenager I was madly in love with a seminary student. My mother's reaction was that "things were going to my head" and I was reaching beyond my status, that these were beyond our kinds of people (never mind that he was a farm boy from our own church). Now I feel the irony of teaching these people who are "not our kinds of people," and serving among them as an equal. Having served as an elder and on the Committee on Preparation for Ministry as a member of Presbytery, I am keenly aware of the fact that the clergy have no more ability to discern or to make decisions, no more wisdom than did people like ourselves. This too is frightening: to discover that spiritual decisions, guidance, and leadership are delivered by those who are also vulnerable, limited, like the people they lead in all their human frailty. It is frightening indeed to think that there are few who are wiser than I am, especially those who do not value my spiritual gifts. I agonize so much over so many decisions; I feel so insufficient so much of the time. I feel so unheard! I know that is also true: The voice I give myself is not sufficient to penetrate the defenses of those around me who want me to be other than I am. It would have saved me a lot of pain to have had more realistic early lessons, to have applied the concept of a normal curve to real life, and my own place on that curve.

Calvinism also taught me to respect books, at least those written by approved Christian leaders and great thinkers. We respected books in the sense that one respected the material object: books themselves were precious, and must not be "damaged." Fortunately, I now know that in a professor's office a tattered and worn book is a loved and respected book, and thus precious indeed. Books were also regarded as the word of those who were wiser. It was a pivotal moment for me when a college professor said that my trouble with understanding Paul Tillich was due not to my lack of intelligence but to Tillich's lack of clarity. This was an unthought possibility in my upbringing, but it has since offered the freedom to refuse to read a book because of the poor writing or inadequate reasoning, despite the kernels of truth hidden in them. I am no more optimistic than Pontius Pilate that we can discover truth, at least in most areas of life. I regard claims for truth in science, philosophy, and the humanities as no more than assertions of a position, attempts at making one's view predominate, and I grow impatient with those who claim more. Truth claims are bound up with bids for power, even when they come from biblical or systematic theologians. I often wonder when Christians will accept that faith is the evidence of things *not* seen, and stop trying to buttress this evidence with reason and science. God is Truth. The gospel is Truth. What else need be said?

Graduate School and Its Impact

Church became an important social event during graduate school. I joined a nondenominational congregation of mostly college students, became involved in Bible studies and the choir, and formed a network of friends. Among them was Nancy Fulton, a true servant who chauffeured a carload of us to church on Sunday nights. We were roommates in Pasadena during the academic year 1976–77, when I joined the Fuller faculty and she was a second-year student. In late 1979 she was diagnosed with a brain tumor. For three years she endured radiation treatments, staph infections, and a transformation of her personality that eventually led most of her friends to abandon her. This time was an opportunity to return God's love to her. I've learned that we need never worry about our indebtedness to others: God will offer opportunities for us to minister in kind, sometimes in the most unlikely circumstances. It is not just that we may be ministering to Christ or to angels unaware, but that in the Kingdom of God the giving and receiving of love and mercy flows constantly, in all directions.

Nancy denied that she was dying until the very end (May 1983), which caused her family (and me) much pain. Hers is a laugh I miss frequently, and my grief binds me closely to her parents, whom I came to know intimately during her hospitalizations and the days after her death. I shared this pain also with Amherst friends Brenda and Dan. With Brenda I laughed, swinging in the park and watching *The Sting,* and had long discussions about Christianity. Now she is a wife and mother, still laughing and still deadly serious. I saw the same combination of laughter and gravity in Dan, who served as the acting parent/custodian of four children orphaned by their mother's death and father's suicide. Dan was a loving, caring parent for these adolescents, and I often had a chance to share their family life. It was many years later that I realized Dan was gay: During those years he was afraid to let any of us know, and he struggled constantly to change. I have grappled at length with the issue of homosexuality. Part of my answer comes from Dan: If this can happen to someone with his devotion, then certainly it is not just blatant sinfulness, but something much more complex, even though it may not be God's will for our lives. The church has forgotten its mission and misaligned its priorities when it turns its back on homosexuals and continues to embrace alcoholics, spouse abusers, tax evaders, and neurotics of all sorts. One might conclude that brokenness comes in hierarchies of acceptability, and that this hierarchy is unconcerned with the harm done to other people. I find this theology intolerable.

There were other significant friendships in Amherst: the Christian men of Amherst College, as well as my friends at the University of Massachusetts. I dated a little, was in love at least once, and brokenhearted. After four years in Amherst I was again primarily in friendships and not in love. An older couple often invited us to have Sunday dinner after church, forcing me to abandon the bad habit of studying on Sunday afternoons.

As memories often do, the Amherst years structure themselves around living quarters. My first year I lived in the dorm and roomed with a social psychology student who had dark hair down to her waist and neurosis from the tips of her toes to the top of her head (she took little blue pills). On Saturday nights we walked the mile into Amherst for dinner at the Gaslight Diner, immortalized in Jane Langton's novel, *Emily Dickinson Is Dead*[11]—Langton's illustrations are wonderful triggers for evocative memory.

There were two years in an apartment with Karel and Maryanne, years in which I watched their old friendship change into a relationship filled with tension, jealousies about men, and competition about grades. I watched them fight, almost like tigers, over the menu and preparation of Thanksgiving dinner. Watching objectively, detached, I wondered how this could be worth fighting about, knowing little then about interpersonal power politics. My third year in the apartment was with Carol and Sally, also old friends, and it was a year marked by tensions. They grew marijuana plants in our living room. I was innocent enough not even to know what the plants were and only to marvel at their ugliness. There was also tension about house cleaning, which seldom met my Dutch standards. I finally realized that this too was an issue of power, rather than a moral one, and relinquished my agenda to change them. Gradually they did become better housekeepers.

Graduate school was not an easy time for me and much of the first year was spent wondering whether I should drop out and go home (does this sound familiar? change is not easy for me). The only thing that stopped me for a long time was the feeling that I didn't have any

11. Langton, Jane. 1984. *Emily Dickinson is dead: A novel of suspense.* New York: St. Martin's Press.

marketable skills: during my college years I worked four summers at the Amway manufacturing plant, spent many hours serving meals in Hope's dining room, and did a little office work in the Psychology Department (Les Beach was a great boss). My anxiety was calmed by Howard Gadlin, who taught history and systems of psychology and loved the papers I wrote. Later I was his research assistant on a project that led to my dissertation on the nineteenth-century psychology of dreams, and a continuing interest in clinical dream interpretation. As a child I was haunted by two repeated nightmares; as an adult I am still occasionally terrorized by dreams, but more frequently glean from them psychological and spiritual insight.

There was no question that I was at the bottom of my class of fourteen in our major clinical courses during the first year. I will never forget the kind individual supervision I received from Norm Watt. He approached me with constructive criticism and remedial help rather than rejection. He was a role model for my own interaction with students at times when confrontation is necessary. I worked hard to live up to Norm's faith in me, but that first year (1971–72) was overwhelming, as I mourned for my mother and adjusted to the new role of graduate student and the East coast ethos.

During the Amherst years I fostered my personal freedom through choice and decision. During the first year I decided to qualify out of Basic Analysis of Variance. (Dave Myers at Hope had tutored several of us over Saturday morning coffee and doughnuts.) I felt the professor could make me hate statistics and end my long love affair with math. I knew I'd be better served by the class Correlation and Regression, which I took a year later. This triggered strange reactions in my classmates: whenever there was a statistics exam, I endured a twenty-four hour "silent treatment." Still, it was a good choice. I enjoyed an elective course in philosophy of science where I made new friends. I remember vividly a Christian couple I met through this class. Once they invited me to their home and paid for a taxi out of their teapot stuffed with dollar bills. I will never forget that act of pure charity.

I also chose not to open my report cards. I wanted to start measuring myself against my own baseline and to avoid the ridiculous comparing and rank ordering that took place every time there was an exam. Later, when I took a seminar on behavioral therapies, I chose not to earn an A because I didn't want to write the kind of paper required for an A. I knew what I wanted to learn, and that wasn't covered by the professor's grading criteria. These decisions were resented and misunderstood by my classmates who found out about them (I kept these decisions to myself, but people always do find out). But I made these choices for myself, not to send a message to anyone else. I wanted to discover *myself,* not myself in comparison to my classmates. Now the whole thing appears a paradox: could I have made these decisions without the self-definition for which I thought I was making them? It was not self-definition itself for which I fought: I wanted to maintain that self-definition in the face of peer pressure.

These years were difficult, but I was able to write a master's thesis, pass comprehensives with honors, and secure an excellent internship. I spent a year in Topeka, Kansas, working hard at Topeka State Hospital, benefitting from an additional class at the Menninger Foundation. I interviewed for a position at Fuller early in that internship year, and in faith devoted my energy to completing my dissertation rather than searching for jobs. That faith often felt like living dangerously, but I also believed that God wasn't asking me for a flurry of activity. And so God provided for the transition from graduate student to a faculty position.

Life Crises and Pain

I mentioned earlier that I thought this story would be difficult to write. This was in part because I thought I should write what I as a historian of psychology regard as an autobiography: a chronological account of my life. But this is impossible. For many months now I have felt like the only thing I could possibly talk about was pain. As I dictate these pieces of my life (January 1991), I have not been without pain for eighteen months. A lifechanging crisis was triggered on July 12, 1989, when my car and I were in a freeway collision with a "big rig." Since then I have been mourning irreparable losses in my scholarly and personal lives. It is an amazing experience to be hit at sixty miles an hour and to take flying trips across three or four lanes of freeway, going to the hospital and being x-rayed and released, with nothing but a tetanus shot, a small bandage, some small bruises, and a state of shock. And then to discover more than a year later that there was injury to your brain: the primary tool of your profession.

On my twentieth birthday (1968) I assessed my life and felt like "all is vanity and vexation of spirit." There have been other pivotal times, events, and losses in my life. Our emigration from the Netherlands in 1957 constitutes a loss that I have never mourned properly. Graduation from college was marred by my mother's death just six weeks earlier, which also distracted me from my early graduate studies. The death of my father in 1977 left me an orphan and more acutely aware of my singleness and the fragility of family ties. I've mourned for friends and students. But none of these events, even at the time, caused me to talk about "before" and "after."

I had been familiar with pain before—lower back pain and sciatic pain caused by spinal misalignment and long-term endometriosis—but those pains I could ultimately ignore if I concentrated hard enough on other things. I'd had sleepless nights and various courses of medication for those and had finally achieved considerable pain relief through chiropractic care. The headaches that resulted from this accident could not be ignored. They were present twenty-four hours a day, seven days a week, constantly interfering with my concentration, leading to incredible fatigue.

In the Spring (1991) I thought about how to sculpt these headaches. How could I depict graphically the pain I was experiencing? I would start with a styrofoam head, a tent peg, several ice picks, and a hammer. I recall the image of Jael driving the tent peg through Sisera's head (Judg. 4 and 5), but that captures only one of many headaches. My head had become a random, chaotic, headache generating machine. There were bilateral cluster headaches that felt like someone driving a handful of nails into my eye, in an inwardly radiating circle, as in the infinitely decreasing spirals of M. C. Escher,[12] one of my favorite Dutch artists. Safety pins of several sizes, ranging from the little gold ones from clothing tags to blanket pins, are fastened in my scalp in various places. A large pair of bear claws holds my brain, skull removed and meninges bared, all the external, pain-sensitive protective tissue exposed. Branding irons burned into the forehead yield searing, pressuring pain. Cat claws or clusters of small staples dig into and wander around my scalp. Alongside a couple deeply wedged razor blades, a hydraulic staple gun strategically places one or two industrial-size staples behind my ears. I once drove one of those staples through a finger when I was stapling boxes at Amway (I was perhaps as startled then as I was when the truck hit my car—some things are inherently unbelievable). A couple extra staples behind the ear might depict the pain there, as might a few razor blades driven in deeply.

My head would be wrapped in a metal band like the one Sears used on the large box that held my bed, the kind of band that springs when it is released or cut. But I wouldn't be sure where to put the band,

12. Ernst, Bruno. 1976. *The magic mirror of M. C. Escher,* trans. John E. Brigham, 102–8. New York: Random House.

whether inside or outside my skull. It should have the inside/outside characteristics of a Moebius strip.[13] Hands would be pulling at bunches of my hair like Indian scalpers, and an intermittent sunburn on my scalp is constantly aggravated by combs and brushes. A hemostat or set of surgical clamps creates just the right sharp, pinching pain: we used to do it with rubber bands on a ponytail. A set of brass knuckles plays haphazardly on my scalp, and vices in several sizes produce agonizing pressure. I actually did fashion this sculpture, and what an exciting trip to the hardware store I had! And what a blessing that pain can only be dimly remembered or even imagined in its absence.

When I was sixteen or seventeen I wrote a paper for Miss McGuckin, my English teacher, that included a summary of C. S. Lewis's, *The Problem of Pain*. I try to recall that innocent adolescent who was so easily satisfied with the standard Christian answer, or afraid to question it. Yet there is nothing "cheap" about Lewis's indirect writings on pain, such as the animal pain depicted in *Perelandra* or the psychic pain in *A Grief Observed,* and perhaps these in part influenced my perspective on pain and suffering, which changed long before this accident in a transformative process, not outwardly discernable, that made my understanding more true to my experience. (Is this simply the reduction of cognitive dissonance? I hope not.) I would never make psychology *the* test of truth, but it must be included in the complex of criteria, and its absence makes many theological/philosophical answers inadequate, indeed false. I have been most satisfied with Gordon Allport's assertion that all religions have addressed the problem of evil, but only Christianity has adequately addressed the problem of good, which dissolves in the Gospel.[14] The truth in that, psychological though it may be, has long been obvious to me, and yet it feels terribly unorthodox, as dangerous as Jung's *Answer to Job.*[15] But such ventures into the unorthodox occur because orthodoxy defends against deep pain with rational and rationalizing defenses. Unfortunately, once such defenses are broken down by experience, it

13. The Moebius strip is an interesting topological phenomenon to mathematicians. It is made of a strip of paper fastened at the edges after making a half turn. The critical feature is that "it can be cut down the middle without falling apart as two rings, and it has only one side and one edge" (Ernst, 99). The result is that the strip has neither inside nor outside, or that paradoxically, the same edge is both inside and outside.

14. Allport, Gordon W. 1944. *The roots of religion.* Advent paper no. 1. Boston: Editorial Board, Advent Papers. Reprinted in 1954. *Pastoral Psychology* 5 (43): 13–24.

15. Jung, Carl G. 1958. *Answer to Job,* trans. R. F. C. Hull. Princeton: Princeton University Press. Bollingen Series 20, vol. 11, in the collected works of C. G. Jung.

is nearly impossible to reconstruct them. What is meaningful to me is the grace of redemption and the knowledge that God can take evil and turn it to good. I look at this time in my life, a time that has required serious alterations in my lifestyle, and wonder where it is taking me, how God's providence will be revealed. And I know a part of the answer lies in God's sparing of my spiritual gifts.

I continue to orient to time in terms of before and after the accident, my personal threshold marking the movement from one world into another. This includes my personal passion and suffering because there was added to my physical pain and all of its psychological ramifications a period of time describable only as pure anguish. This (late May through mid-July 1990) occurred when the neurologist treating me for post-traumatic headaches prescribed a medication to which I had an extreme toxic reaction, resulting in a manic episode that necessitated psychiatric hospitalization. Of these six days I remember very little, except an intense, unwavering sense of the presence of God. The medications used to treat the mania produced equally serious side effects, and for six weeks I was in an altered state of consciousness. I have only sketchy memories of nights when I would awake totally traumatized; of the friends who slept in the guest room so I would not be alone; of restless days when neither sitting still nor walking would bring any peace; of wandering around the house disoriented; of being mystified about what I was to do to emerge from this abyss into which I had been dropped. I wondered how to assure my therapist that these symptoms were not me, to convince him that my observing ego could be believed, to induce him to enter into that void and help me out. I shall never forget the redemptive moment when he apologized, in tears, for his failure to acknowledge that inner core of sanity that screamed "don't let them do this to me any longer!"

Finally I could say, "In order to heal yourself, you must stop taking these medications." That was a difficult assertion to make, because it defied the judgment of two respected physicians who apparently didn't believe that my mania was drug induced (which would have meant admitting to malpractice, or to not understanding the powerful effects of psychotropic drugs in the head injured). It is difficult in the darkness to find the way out. These doctors were oblivious to my symptoms even though I related them repeatedly (they had already decided to discount my perceptions), and repudiated the shattering of my soul, thus exacerbating it. They suspected little of the crucial fear of annihilation, of not being allowed to exist. I was accused by family of scapegoating the doctors, and urged to give them more time. At the core of my being I knew unequivocally that I was being violated. I knew that I couldn't possibly stay in that place any longer and be robbed of my self. The "me" and the "this is happening to me" could not be integrated. Such integration is equally difficult for my current cognitive symptoms, for which I am told I am not responsible. If they are not me, who are they?

I long for these hopelessly tangled threads in the fabric of my life to be transformed into the natural slubs that are part of the beauty of fabric, as they are so often touted on the tags of the silk and linen garments I love to wear. Perhaps it is symbolic that in my most recent purchase of a silk blouse (on sale!) I deviated from my usual monochromatic to a richly colored design in which individual colors can hardly be detected. In my efforts at design, I have *never* been able to attain anything but the abstract, and perhaps my life will continue to require layers of interpretation. It is not only that I lost something of myself (insignificant though it may appear to others), but that all the other parts have taken on new meaning in the kaleidoscopic images of my life. Relationships also changed, transforming interpersonal networks. One long-time friend could not cope with my temporary undefended state (I wasn't finding it easy myself!) and abandoned me. Other peripheral friends moved into central roles, proving true in time of need. A new neurologist has proven himself trustworthy and caring.

Since July 1989 I have learned more than I ever wanted to know about the legal and medical subsystems. It is as if I live in a different world. Phone calls and mail no longer come from the three divisions of APA in which I've been an officer, or the Presbytery of San Fernando, summoning me to meetings, conference calls, the word processor, or to reading national ordination exams. Now communiqués come from attorneys, my neurologist, neuropsychologists, my chiropractor, and psychotherapist. And I must cope with frustrating legal battles, changed appointments that wreak havoc on my schedule, and recordkeeping tasks and billing errors for which my injured brain is ill-equipped, and by which I am totally exhausted. It is a new world entered without choice, calling for new responses in an unfamiliar and frightening context.

This story is filled with the tension of the unknown ending. It leads to courtrooms, support groups of other survivors, perhaps the cessation of pain and freeway anxiety, a decrease in fatigue. Perchance there will be a time when I can walk again some of the paths of the life that lies behind me—colleagues and friends take this for granted;

professionals are much more skeptical, but challenge me to accommodate. Now, I am loath to make any professional commitments. All writing assignments, this one included, become a source of extreme fatigue and pain. My sense of achievement is greater when they are finished, but so is my despair. It feels like I can no longer write my own story, because I don't know the intended course of the revision. I still often think "I don't want this to be true" or "I don't want this to be happening to me." These thoughts come from actual errors and deficits that produce embarrassment and acute awareness of my limitations and the extent of my future abilities. I am forced to face the truth so easily avoided by those who make five-year or ten-year plans for their futures: our plans are always subject to the providence of our maker.

Reflections on This Task

What is it like to try to write autobiographically? For months before starting to dictate this story I was fearful that I couldn't, and even now I am troubled by it. I am known as a meticulous historian, and in that role I think an autobiography should be full of dates, names, places, and events from which the reader can reconstruct my life. But I've been unable, either emotionally or physically, to write that kind of autobiography. I could satisfy that impulse by appending a chronology, but it would ring a false note. Such details of the past seem so irrelevant as I face the struggles of the present. What does all that have to do with my current pilgrimage? Everything, of course. But this conflict about capturing the past versus letting it be reflects the battle I've fought all my life between my Calvinist training and my phenomenological, intuitive inclinations: my therapeutic self.

Why should I tell my story? It isn't the story of every woman, only of one individual, one of God's unique creatures. Is the pain of my story just the pain of fallen humankind, or unique to my own family, or shared with others with a similar background? Do I have the right to tell my story? Will my story lead people to dismiss me even further, to render me more invisible? Or will the telling render me, finally, irreversibly real? The telling has brought more tears, reactivated intolerable pain, forced a sorting and sifting of experiences and memories. I wonder if my readers will be trustworthy and respect my vulnerability. Each time I read the story I have panic attacks about the persons and events I have left out. Will there be a chance for the storying of those?

I do believe that every person's life is worth a story, and is a worthy story.[16] Each of us has an inalienable right to discover a meaningful theme in the often chaotic stories of our lives. That is why my version of this story may startle some who have been a part of it. My fears have included their possible disapproval, and my intense defenselessness. Yet this chapter constitutes one story within the larger story of my life. It is an account of my walk through the valley of suffering and pain and near-death, and my encounter with new limitations. It is also a story about grace, in the larger context of the gospel story, a story about recovery, escape, consolation.[17] Thus, it is not at all merely my story, but my witness to the gospel, testimony that God recognizes us in all our uniqueness, that for each of us there is the story that climaxes in the hope of resurrection.

16. Polster, Erving. 1987. *Every person's life is worth a novel.* New York: Norton.

17. Tolkien, J. R. R. [1947] 1973. On fairy stories. In *Essays presented to Charles Williams,* ed. C. S. Lewis, 38–89. Oxford University Press; Grand Rapids: Eerdmans. Reprinted in J. R. R. Tolkien. 1966. *The Tolkien reader,* 27–84. New York: Ballantine.

Epilogue

D. John Lee

Webster defines an epilogue as a "speech or short poem addressed to the spectators by one of the actors, after the conclusion of a drama." I prefer poetry to a speech but unfortunately I am not a poet. So here is my speech in three parts.

I. Autobiography: Uses, Process, and Effects

Autobiography can be used for a variety of purposes. Historians have used autobiography to outline the history of a discipline.[1] This collection contains some her-stories and his-stories of Christians in psychology, but it was not intended to be a history of Christians in psychology (although some historian may use it this way). Psychologists have made use of autobiography to construct psychological

1. E. G. Boring, who wrote the first history of psychology, collaborated with Lindzey in 1967 to edit a collection of autobiographies of some of the early psychologists.

theory.[2] I have no intent of analyzing the stories here to uncover personality dynamics common to Christian psychologists (although some psychologist may use them this way). My use of autobiography has been to hear the story behind the stories. To learn about the theorist who wrote the theory, the therapist who does the therapy, the administrator who administers. That is, autobiography was my vehicle for uncovering some of the "life history data" necessary to interpret the writings and work of the contributors.[3]

In the opening chapter, I referred to my own research on what and how people remember events from their own lives. This area is referred to as the study of "autobiographical memory." Autobiographical memory researchers will often make a distinction between memory process and memory content. And, although this dichotomy (like most) is problematic, I am going to reflect on the autobiographical process and then consider the content by reviewing the effects of storying ourselves.

The Process of Autobiography

My narrative perspective construes memory as a constructive creative "storying" process. In the case of autobiographical memory, a person's sense of "self," or the "I," can then be conceived as the author constructing a story in which the narrative figure, the "me," is the protagonist. The challenges of writing one's autobiography are thus not unlike the challenges of a nonfiction author.[4] I would like to briefly consider three issues in writing autobiography: audience or perspective, organization, and narrative truth.

Mary Vander Goot described the issue of *audience*. Her first attempt at writing her story was a false start. She initially felt like she was supposed to inform someone else about the important details of her life (Chap. 2, p. 82), but this strategy only frustrated her. When she came back to the task, she "began an inner dialogue" where she became her own audience. This approach worked and led to an insightful definition of a person's story: "my story . . . (is) how I know myself" (p.

2. De Waele and Harre (1979) outline how autobiographical interviews can be used in social and personality research.

3. Bennett Berger (1990) had twenty American sociologists write their intellectual autobiographies to provide the "life history data" necessary to read sociological theory. Berger wanted his students "to get a sense of the *presence* of the theorist in the text, learn to read between the lines, and hence more fully appreciate the meanings projected in them," (p. xiv).

4. James Olney and Paul John Eakin have explored autobiography as a literary art form (cf. Olney, 1988).

83). Although Mary's approach should not be considered as normative, it does reveal how important the author's perspective can be in writing (and interpreting) a narrative.

Kirk Farnsworth used the distinction between "chronicity" and "narrative unity" (Chap. 6, p. 155) to describe the issue of *organization* within the task of autobiography. Sometimes ordering events in a chronological fashion works for the author, as it did for Siang-Yang Tan (Chap. 5). For others, however, using chronicity to present one's life acts as a barrier, since sequence is sometimes not as important as content. Such was the case for Kirk, Mary, and Hendrika Vande Kemp (Chap. 10), who framed their autobiographies around themes rather than time. And, while Tan used a calendar to organize his story, each period of time represented a different "place" or a new challenge within his life. The process of remembering is not random; it begins from a theme (or what memory researchers have called a "schema") and moves through time, but not necessarily in chronological time!

A third issue within the process of autobiography is similar to what Donald Spence described as *narrative truth* and *historical truth* within psychoanalysis.[5] A therapist's or client's interpretation of the past is really a narrative that may or may not be linked to actual historical truth. To Spence, the truth of a narrative should be evaluated on the basis of its therapeutic value and not its historical accuracy. For the autobiographical process, this distinction was captured nicely by Vivian Nix-Early: "I'm not sure if the events and quotes I have related happened just exactly as I stated them, but they are true to the message being conveyed and true to the way I experienced them then" (Chap. 1, p. 55). That is, Vivian admitted her uncertainty about the exact accuracy of her story, but she did attribute narrative truth to her autobiography. Of course, it is impossible to discern what exactly happened and who said exactly what in Vivian's life, but if she had been seeking historical truth she would have used a different set of criteria to evaluate her narrative (for example, institutional records, archeological data, other people's testimony).

The Effects of Autobiography

At my request, each of the contributors reflected on the effects of writing their autobiography. In my review of the contributors'

5. Donald Spence's *Narrative Truth and Historical Truth* (1982) has become a classic for narrative theorists.

responses, I have discerned at least five things that can occur as a result of storying oneself:

1. Discovery. Almost all of the contributors said that this storying exercise was a learning experience. However, this discovery process was not like finding something new, but rather transforming something old. Mary Vander Goot explains, "It was not that I did not know what I intended to say, but I was surprised once an image or memory that was mine but never before formed for words was now transformed by words" (Chap. 2, p. 83). Similarly, Bonnidell Clouse (Chap. 3, p. 109) commented that she did not uncover anything new about herself, but there was a "slightly different twist" in writing them down. Not unlike all creative writing, the act of autobiography can be a dialogue between the author's experience and imagination. This dynamic was described nicely by David Benner: "Writing has always been a form of discovery for me. I do not write because of what I know or think. I write to discover what I know or what I think" (Chap. 8, p. 235).

2. Relatedness. At some point in their stories, several of the authors made mention of their spouses, parents, or other significant people who influenced them a great deal. I think this reveals the connectedness of our lives. Telling our stories emphasizes that they are not our own. We are intimately related and connected to others and their stories. To remember is the opposite of dismember. When we remember, we put ourselves together by honoring those relationships that define us. Al Dueck said, "I am a product of my interactions with others" (Chap. 9, p. 259). We are not "authors of our own lives," but "coauthors" living in relationship with other people and with God.

The metaphor of "coauthoring" life presents the dynamic tension between partners and their products. It is not uncommon for me to refer to Kristen as "my" daughter or Brandon as "my" son. But obviously my children are not "mine"; they are "ours." Our children are the products of our love relationship. It is easy to take ownership of something that you have participated in creating and forget that there were others involved in the process. Or conversely, as David Benner commented, it is "easy to live my life feeling myself to be reacting to events and influences around me, not always (or even often) in control of these events" (Chap. 8, p. 236). Through autobiography, David confirmed that he has the responsibility or "ability to respond" in shaping his story. Like all cooperative projects however, this coauthoring does not necessarily proceed smoothly. Both Siang-Yang Tan (Chap. 5, p. 153) and Kirk Farnsworth (Chap. 6, p. 186) mentioned the importance of "balancing" their responsibilities between work and family. Applying a different metaphor, they sensed the need for members of their "choir" to sing in harmony. That is, a dominant voice can have the effect of disrupting our songs.

3. Thankfulness. Without exception, the participants were thankful for the opportunity to story themselves. This thankfulness seemed to have two sides. On one side was a gratitude directed toward God and significant others for what happened in their lives; on the other side was an appreciation for God's presence throughout their pilgrimages. Stephen Evans referred to his journey as "a *privileged* calling in the sense that the vocation I have been assigned is one that corresponds to my most cherished desires" (Chap. 7, p. 208). From a different slant, Mary Vander Goot sensed "great joy and relief" as she affirmed her destiny or "starting points" from which her life has emerged (Chap. 2, p. 83). I suspect, as Stephen and Mary declare, that their stories, or any of the others, should not be taken as normative. These stories are witnesses to the mysterious paradoxical nature of God, which is both creative *and* providential.

4. Healing. Psychotherapists have recognized for quite some time the therapeutic value of doing an autobiography. Talking about our problems within the framework of a story will often reveal where those difficulties originated and how they persist. Writing about one's life involves evaluating it, and thus autobiography presents an opportunity for change. Doing autobiography can be a conscious and deliberate way to keep one's story moving. That is, storying ourselves can actually redirect our stories. Al Dueck's analogy of his autobiography as a process of "pastoring his personal congregation of selves" (Chap. 9, p. 260) reveals this healing quality of storying oneself. Storying ourselves can be an opportunity for the "author and finisher of our faith" to assist us in reauthoring our lives.

5. Hope. Paul Vitz's autobiography left him facing the future. The title of his essay, "The Story of My Life . . . Up to Now" clearly indicates his awareness that his story is far from over. Paul's reflection on his *past* in the *present* prepared him to move into the *future*. His last sentence repeats this idea about how recalling the past can propel someone into the future: "This Christian Odyssey is still far from over, and who knows what lies ahead—for in spite of retrospectives, such as this report, the prize lies ahead, and I pray, with St. Paul, to be able to finish the race" (Chap. 4, p. 129). It is not uncommon for elderly people to write their "memoirs" or even attempt to do an autobiography. I suspect that part of the reason for this compulsion is that these exercises can be helpful in preparing a person for death.

Vivian Nix-Early's fear of a premature death was dissolved by a friend's words, and then in her own words she said, "My life has been rich and full, and I often feel content and ready to die, assured that whenever I am called, it will be the absolute right time" (Chap. 1, p. 56).

Sometimes God is silent. Sometimes nothing we do or say can alleviate the suffering of our present experience. In the midst of our pain, autobiography can be an invitation to God to be present with us, to remind us of the Resurrection and the Hope. For example, Hendrika's chapter is "adrift in pain," but her disclosure brings with it the "anchor of grace." Or, as she stated so beautifully, ". . . for each of us there is the story that climaxes in the hope of the resurrection" (Chap. 10, p. 291).

A nice way to summarize the effects of autobiography is to use the Apostle Paul's distinction between faith, hope, and love. Autobiography can review our *faith* in the past to offer us *hope* for the future in order that we can continue to *love* in the present. In this light, St. Paul's prioritizing can be seen as a call to stay with the challenges of the present rather than dwelling on the past or waiting for tomorrow: "And now these three remain: faith, hope, and love. But the greatest of these is love" (1 Cor. 13:13 NIV).

II. Psychology and Christianity

One of the reasons I had for putting this anthology together was to comment on the topic of the "integration of psychology and Christianity." Several people have described what they believe to be the nature of the relationship between the science and practice of psychology in twentieth-century North America and the Christian faith.[6] One person has used autobiography as a method to explore this topic. In 1978, Newton Malony published a book, *Psychology and Faith: The Christian Experience of Eighteen Psychologists*. As the title indicates, this book contained eighteen short autobiographies of psychologists who were also Christians. In the Foreword, Malony described the purpose of his collection:

6. Stanton Jones (1986) has done an excellent job of summarizing the "integration" literature and Hendrika Vande Kemp's (1984) annotated bibliography provides the background for how this topic developed up to 1965. Also, there are two periodicals in this area, the *Journal of Psychology and Theology* and the *Journal of Psychology and Christianity*. My own perspective resonates what Al Dueck (1989) and Kirk Farnsworth (1985) have published. Al's sensitivity to culture and ethnicity and Kirk's emphasis on harmonizing psychology through *word and deed* fit with my approach.

> I went to eighteen of them and asked the question, "Tell me about yourself," I inquired. "How did you decide to be a psychologist? Share your Christian experience. Describe what you do in your daily life. How do you relate your faith with your work? What difference does being Christian make to you?" (p. i).

How these psychologists related their faith to their vocation varied from person to person. For some of the contributors, becoming a psychologist and doing psychology was a natural expression of their Christian faith. Others, however, experienced some conflicts or described points of tension between doing psychology and professing Christ. Interestingly, Malony used autobiography to explore how different people integrate, and autobiography turned out to be his answer to integration as well. Here are some quotes from his concluding chapter:

> . . . being a psychologist-Christian is autobiographical. It is a confessional stance one takes. Each expression of this inner faith is more than likely an original personal creation.
>
> . . . It is the contention of this volume that the experience of being a psychologist-Christian is a reality in spite of the fact that it does not refer to behavior that discriminates between those who do and do not claim the label. As suggested earlier, the expressions of the Christian faith in the profession of psychology are many and varied. As can be seen in the foregoing essays, this self-conscious expression can be within the interpersonal, professional, experimental, conceptual, or interprofessional aspects of one's life. And within a given area of integration, there will be individual interpretations. But in all cases, psychologist-Christians are self-conscious and intentional about their faith. They know and state that they are Christians.
>
> . . . Psychologist-Christians are those who say they are. Psychologist-Christians have made explicit for themselves the ground on which they stand. They are unashamedly Christian by their own confession. The task then is not *whether,* but *how* this faith will be expressed. So it is and must be with Christians who are psychologists (pp. 245–47).

To Malony, the integration of psychology and Christianity is a personal task. Autobiography thus becomes important since integrating one's faith and vocation is an autobiographical task: people integrate as they live out their lives. When I share Malony's conclusion with my students, most of them respond with ambivalence. They like the idea that working out one's faith is a unique pilgrimage with God, but they are uncomfortable with the lack of road signs. Malony's only guide is that integration is "confessional," or that the only commonality between people trying to relate their Christianity to their vocation is that they are "self-conscious and intentional about their faith."

I too feel ambivalent about Malony's conclusion. I believe that each person is a unique creation of God, uniquely working out her or his relationship with the Creator. But I also believe that the story of Jesus and his disciples provides some guideposts or directives in our journey with God. Malony's understanding of the relationship between the Christian faith and psychology appears to be a narrative one. That is, he conceives of the integration task as an autobiographical process, a pilgrimage, or a story. However, I do not think that Malony took this metaphor far enough.

The story of relating the Christian faith and psychology is a special kind of story. It is a story that honors the story of Jesus, what Dueck referred to as the Reign of God. Jews and Christians share a tradition up to the point of Jesus Christ's resurrection. The Christian story continues with Jesus' command, "Love each other as I have loved you" (John 15:12 NIV), and the arrival of the Holy Spirit. Accepting Jesus as the "author and finisher of our faith" implies that we are willing to hear God's voice as we set our priorities and make our life decisions. The Jesus story is given authority over the myriad of other stories that define our lives. That is, the story of Jesus Christ is normative. The Jesus story provides the way or acts as a guide for our own stories. But how do we recognize the voice of authority? How do we acknowledge and respect the authority of Jesus? How can we be intentional and deliberate about having our own stories resonate with "The Story"?[7]

I believe that "storying ourselves" is one way we can invite Christ's authority into our lives. As I argued in my introduction, telling our stories to one another can be an opportunity for God's incarnation. Speaking honestly and truthfully with one another about our pilgrimage is one way to "gather together in Christ's name" (Matt. 18:20 KJV). But, storying ourselves is much more than sharing our "testimonies" or the story of how we met Jesus Christ. It is stepping out of our comfort zones and being transparent with one another with our current struggles and challenges of living a life in relationship

7. Robert McAfee Brown (1975) discussed how "The Story" might once again be told in such a way that we could respond "That's my story, too." He recommended that Christians listen to the faith stories of others with a willingness to be changed by them. And he encouraged us to actually participate in "The Story" through liturgy and an identification with the poor and oppressed.

with Christ. Storying ourselves means we hold each other accountable to the authority of Jesus Christ. Christ *authors* us as we author one another. And as the Holy Spirit chooses to participate in this process we are empowered to give and receive God's love. Storying ourselves can involve healing the past, providing hope or direction for the future, and learning to love one another in the present. I am convinced that "speaking the truth in love, we will in all things grow up into him who is the Head, that is, Christ" (Eph. 4:15 NIV).

III. Thank You

I would like to take this opportunity to thank the contributors for sharing their lives with me. To allow your stories to be published and widely distributed is both an honor and a risk. My invitation to participate in this book was my way of honoring your work as Christian psychologists and expressing my gratitude for what you have meant in my life. However, I know that there can be a dark side to this public self-disclosure. There is always that possibility that someone will take what you have shared and distort it or use it against you in some way. I pray that this does not happen to any one of you.

Finally, thanks to Maria Den Boer for your editorial assistance. Thanks also to Jim Weaver and Baker Book House for being willing to publish this book. I know anthologies rarely top the best seller list. Storying ourselves has been a challenging, exciting, and rewarding exercise.

Shalom,
D. John Lee
August 23, 1992

References

Berger, B. M. 1990. *Authors of their own lives: Intellectual autobiographies by twenty American sociologists.* Berkeley: University of California Press.

Boring, E. G., and G. Lindzey. 1967. *A history of psychology in autobiography.* New York: Appleton-Century-Crofts.

Brown, R. M. 1975. My story and "The Story." *Theology Today* 32 (2): 166–73.

De Waele, J. P., and R. Harre. 1979. Autobiography as a psychological method. In *Emerging strategies in social psychological research,* ed. G. Ginsburg, pp. 177–224. New York: John Wiley & Sons.

Dueck, A. 1989. On living in Athens: Models of relating psychology, church, and culture. *Journal of Psychology and Christianity* 8:5–18.

Farnsworth, K. E. 1985. *Whole-hearted integration: Harmonizing psychology and Christianity through word and deed.* Grand Rapids: Baker Book House.

Jones, S. L. 1986. Relating the Christian faith to psychology. In *Psychology and the Christian faith: An introductory reader,* ed. S. L. Jones, pp. 15–33. Grand Rapids: Baker Book House.

Malony, H. N. 1978. *Psychology and faith: The Christian experience of eighteen psychologists.* Washington, D. C.: University Press of America.

Olney, J. 1988. *Studies in autobiography.* New York: Oxford University Press.

Spence, D. P. 1982. *Narrative truth and historical truth: Meaning and interpretation in psychoanalysis.* New York: Norton.

Vande Kemp, H. 1984. *Psychology and theology in western thought: 1672–1965: A historical and annotated bibliography.* Millwood, N.Y.: Kraus International.

About the Authors

D. John Lee

D. John Lee is an associate professor of psychology at Calvin College. He is a graduate of Trinity Western College (A.A.), the University of British Columbia (B.A.), Western Washington University (M.S.), and Kansas State University (Ph.D.). He taught psychology and social work at Tabor College in Hillsboro, Kansas, for five years before moving to Grand Rapids, Michigan, to assume a position at Calvin. He co-edited (with Alvaro L. Nieves and Henry L. Allen) *Ethnic-Minorities and Evangelical Christian Colleges* (1991) and is currently editing two other books, *Life and Story: Autobiographies for a Narrative Psychology* and *Assessment in Christian Higher Education: Theory and Practice* (both forthcoming). He has written several chapters in books and articles for a variety of journals, including the *Journal of Psychology and Christianity, Personnel and Guidance Journal, Discourse Processes,* and *Memory and Cognition.* In addition to his teaching and research, he is a part-time clinical intern at Mental Health and Psychological Services in Grand Rapids.

Vivian Nix-Early

Vivian Nix-Early is the assistant vice-president for academic affairs at West Chester University of Pennsylvania. She is a graduate of the University of Pennsylvania (B.A.) and New York University (Ph.D.). Following seven years as a clinical psychologist and music therapist in both the public and private sectors of New York's mental health system, she entered higher education as an assistant, and then associate professor in the Department of Counseling and Psychological

Services at West Chester University. She counseled students and taught undergraduate and graduate psychology courses for five years before moving into administration. In addition to her current position, she serves as a consultant to other colleges and universities in the areas of program review and evaluation, faculty development, leadership for women, and management of diversity. She has delivered numerous papers and presentations on these topics as well as on issues of faith, race, and psychotherapy. She also continues a small private psychotherapy practice. She is the successful author of two articles, several federal and state grants, and a tutor-training videotape. She is a member of the American Psychological Association and the National Association for Women in Education, and worships at the Star of Hope Baptist Church in Northeast Philadelphia, where she serves as director of youth activities, Sunday school teacher, and member of the board of Christian education.

Mary Vander Goot

Mary Vander Goot is a licensed psychologist in private practice. She is a licensed marriage and family therapist, a certified addictions counselor, a member of the American Society of Clinical Hypnosis, a diplomate of the American Board of Psychotherapy, and a diplomate of the American Board of Medical Psychotherapists. A graduate of Calvin College and Princeton University, she was a professor in the Department of Psychology at Calvin College for eleven years. In addition to many articles, she is the author of four books: *A Life Planning Guide for Women* (1982), *Piaget as a Visionary Thinker* (1989), *Narrating Psychology* (1987), and *Healthy Emotions* (1987).

Bonnidell Clouse

Bonnidell Clouse is professor of educational and school psychology at Indiana State University. She is a graduate of Wheaton College (B.A.), Boston University (M.A.), and Indiana University (Ph.D.). She taught at Bryan College in Dayton, Tennessee, for two years and was an elementary teacher in Marion, Iowa, for five years. She has written *Moral Development: Perspectives in Psychology and Christian Belief* (1985), *Teaching for Moral Growth: A Guide for the Christian Community* (1993), and numerous articles. She has co-edited (with Robert Clouse) *Women in Ministry: Four Views* (1989). She is a contributing editor of *Journal of Psychology and Theology* and a member of the Christian Association for Psychological Studies (CAPS), the American Psychological Association, and the American Heart Foundation.

Paul C. Vitz

Paul C. Vitz is professor of psychology at New York University, where he has taught since 1965. He is a graduate of the University of Michigan (B.A.) and Stanford University (Ph.D.). He is the author of *Psychology as Religion: The Cult of Self-Worship* (1977), *Modern Art and Modern Science* (1984), *Censorship: Evidence of Bias in Our Children's Textbooks* (1986), *Sigmund Freud's Christian Unconscious* (1988), and many articles. He is presently working on a narrative model of Christian counseling, a Christian model of personality, and a revision of his first book. He is a member of the Fellowship of Catholic Scholars, an adjunct professor at the John Paul II Institute for Marriage and Family, in Washington, D.C., and a resource scholar for the Christianity Today Institute.

Siang-Yang Tan

Siang-Yang Tan is director of the Doctor of Psychology Program in Clinical Psychology and associate professor of psychology in the Graduate School of Psychology at Fuller Theological Seminary in Pasadena, California. He is a licensed psychologist with a Ph.D. in clinical psychology from McGill University. He has published articles on lay counseling and lay counselor training, intrapersonal integration and spirituality, cognitive-behavior therapy, epilepsy, pain, and psychopathology and culture in the Asian-American context, as well as two books, *Lay Counseling: Equipping Christians for a Helping Ministry* (1991) and (with Joan Sturkie) *Peer Counseling in Youth Groups* (1992). He is associate editor of the *Journal of Psychology and Christianity* and serves or has served on the editorial boards of the *Journal of Consulting and Clinical Psychology, Journal of Psychology and Theology,* and *Journal of Pastoral Counseling.* He was also pastor of the Malaysian-Singaporean Bible Church in Toronto and has served as director of the Campus Life Division of Montreal Youth for Christ. He also serves as assistant minister to the English congregation at First Evangelical Church in Glendale, California. He is originally from Singapore.

Kirk E. Farnsworth

Kirk E. Farnsworth is the executive director of CRISTA Counseling Service and vice-president of CRISTA Ministries, a nonprofit Christian conglomerate in Seattle, Washington. He is a graduate of Iowa State University (B.S., M.S., Ph.D.). He has been a naval officer, college professor, psychotherapist in private practice, and corporate executive. His prior positions include associate professor of psychology at the University of New Hampshire and professor of psychology at Trinity College (Illinois) and Wheaton College (Illinois). He has written *Integrating Psychology and Theology: Elbows Together but Hearts Apart* (1981) and *Wholehearted Integration: Harmonizing Psychology and Christianity Through Word and Deed* (1985). He has also co-authored (with Wendell Lawhead) *Life Planning: A Christian Approach to Careers* (1981) and written individual chapters in five books and thirty-five articles in professional journals and Christian magazines. He is presently working on a book on the wounded worker in dysfunctional Christian organizations. He is a contributing editor for the *Journal of Psychology and Theology,* a member of the American Psychological Association and Christian Association for Psychological Studies, and a fellow in the American Scientific Affiliation.

C. Stephen Evans

C. Stephen Evans is professor of philosophy and curator of the Howard and Adna Hong Kierkegaard Library at St. Olaf College. He has long-time interests in the philosophy of psychology, and while teaching philosophy at Wheaton College also taught in the psychology program at the Wheaton College Graduate School. Evans received his Ph.D. in philosophy from Yale University, and his B.A. from Wheaton College. Although perhaps best known for his publications about Kierkegaard, three of Evans's nine books deal with psychology: *Preserving the Person* (1977), *Wisdom and Humanness in Psychology* (1989), and *Søren Kierkegaard's Christian Psychology* (1990). He is the editor of the *Contours of Christian Philosophy* series and the *Søren Kierkegaard Newsletter.* Evans is a member of the American Philosophical Association, the American Academy of Religion, the Søren Kierkegaard Society, and the executive committee of the Society of Christian Philosophers.

David G. Benner

David G. Benner is a licensed psychologist with degrees from McMaster University (Honours B.A.) and York University (M.A., Ph.D.) and postdoctoral training from the Chicago Institute of Psychoanalysis. His current academic appointments include serving as professor and chair of the Department of Psychology at Redeemer College (Ancaster, Ontario) and adjunct professor of psychology and Christianity at the University of Toronto (St. Michael's College). Prior to these positions he spent ten years as professor of psychology and founding chair of the Graduate Department of Psychological Studies at Wheaton College (Wheaton, Illinois). He has also held numerous clinical appointments in Canada and the United States, including supervising psychologist for outpatient services at Thistletown Regional Centre for Children and Adolescents (Toronto), senior psychologist for child and adolescent services at Queen Street Mental Health Centre (Toronto), and clinical director for the Institute for Eating Disorders (Chicago). He has authored three books: *Psychotherapy and the Spiritual Quest* (1988), *Healing Emotional Wounds* (1990), and *Strategic Pastoral Counseling* (1992). In addition he has edited or co-edited six other books, most notably the *Baker Encyclopedia of Psychology,* which was the recipient of a 1986 Gold Medallion Book Award from the Evangelical Christian Publishers Association.

Al Dueck

Al Dueck is professor of pastoral counseling and psychology and director of supervision for the Marriage and Family Counseling Program at the Mennonite Brethren Biblical Seminary in Fresno, California. He is a graduate of Stanford University in psychology and completed postdoctoral work in social theory (University of Notre Dame), theology (Associated Mennonite Biblical Seminaries), psychology of religion (Yale University), and family therapy (Heidelberg University). He taught undergraduate psychology at Tabor College and Fresno Pacific College for eleven years. He presented the Integration Seminar lectures on the integration of Christianity and therapy at Fuller Theological Seminary in 1986, which have since been published in *Christianity Today*'s volume, *The Best in Evangelical Theology* (1988). He has a forthcoming book to be published by Baker Book House on the subject of the dialogue between psychology and theology. He is a member of the American Family Therapy Association and the American Psychological Association.

Hendrika Vande Kemp

Hendrika Vande Kemp is professor of psychology at Fuller Theological Seminary, where she has been on the faculty of the Graduate School of Psychology since 1976. She is a graduate of Hope College (B.A.) and the University of Massachusetts at Amherst (M.S., Ph.D.), and completed a clinical internship at Topeka State Hospital. She is the editor of *Family Therapy: Christian Perspectives* (1992) and author of *Psychology and Theology in Western Thought, 1672–1965: A Historical and Annotated Bibliography* (1984) and numerous journal articles. She is a fellow of the American Psychological Association and a member of the American Family Therapy Academy, the American Association for Marriage and Family Therapy, the American Academy of Religion, the Society for the Scientific Study of Religion, the Association for Case Teaching, CHEIRON: the International Society for the History of the Behavioral and Social Sciences, and the Southern California C. S. Lewis Society.

Index